The American Way of Sex

The American Way of Sex

by Peter Whittaker

Published by
Berkley Publishing Corporation
Distributed by G.P. Putnam's Sons
New York

COPYRIGHT © BY PETER WHITTAKER

All rights reserved. This book, or parts thereof, may not be reproduced in any form without permission. Published simultaneously in Canada by Longman Canada Limited, Toronto

SBN: 399-11313-4

Library of Congress Catalog
Card Number: 73-94105

PRINTED IN THE UNITED STATES OF AMERICA

The research and interviews upon which *The American Way of Sex* is based were conducted by me throughout 1973. I am grateful for the extraordinary candor and cooperation of my very numerous collaborators. This is one book for which the acknowledgment "without them this book could not have been written" is altogether and literally true.

—PETER WHITTAKER

CONTENTS

Introduction

THE much-touted and highly publicized "sexual revolution" of the past decade has, for all that some may wish to deny its very existence, caused a genuine series of drastic changes in the most basic elements of the way we live. The importance of these innovations in life-style has by no means suffered exaggeration by the mass media; if anything, their significance and their extent have been understated. Contrary to one popular minority opinion, the recent alterations in the sexual standards of our society are *not* simply a matter of "everybody behaving the same as always, but just talking about it more." Great segments of the American population have begun to taste true liberation from their own worst, Puritanically ingrained fears, and nothing will ever be the same again.

In this book I have chosen to focus on one aspect of the new sexual mores, but one which is an enlightening microcosm of the entire spectrum of changes that have taken place: sex as practiced in the euphemistically named "massage parlors" of New York and other cities across the country, a new institution whose staff (and clientele) may be said to represent the cutting edge, the wave of the future, the prototype of the upcoming generation's sexual practices.

During the 1960's, as society experienced an unprecedented myriad of convulsive mutations (including dozens in the sexual sphere), prostitution remained only a minor concern, its style an anachronistic hangover from earlier times: street hookers and their pimps, call girls and their furs, Cadillacs and heroin, Iceberg Slim and Butterfield Eight. It was only in the closing weeks of the decade that the harbinger of yet another counterculture made its appearance: an amateurish tabloid weekly called *Screw: A Sex Review*, whose very final half-inch of type contained a tiny ad for *Private "Body-Painting" Sessions*. Of such stuff are empires built and revolutions made.

By 1972 the "body-painting" or "nude modeling" cover had long since given way to the universal term "massage parlor." These establishments had spread from coast to coast, located primarily in large cities or in college towns. In New York alone, *Screw* (along with a half dozen imitative publications) was advertising some thirty-five massage parlors and had introduced a consumer's rating guide of from one to four stylized penises for each place. A basic East Side/West Side differentiation in quality had been established, ranging from filthy Eighth Avenue rip-off joints to the Miami Beach-type velvet plushness of Caesar's Retreat. The latter category of "studios" (as they are generically referred to by everyone connected with the business) routinely featured free liquor and champagne, heated water beds, sauna baths, and a large selection of exceptionally attractive young women. The motivations and perceptions of these women (and some men) are the pivotal aspects of what can only be categorized as a "revolution" in the sex business.

Thousands of girls, maturing in a new climate of sexual honesty and freedom, began to realize that the life-long sexual repression of their elders could be exploited for material gain. This was the origin of the pornography explosion, as college-age women throughout the country capitalized on their almost total lack of irrational taboos against nudity, and posed for countless new sexually oriented magazines and films (many of which were directed and produced by those girls' male counterparts, who found therein a profitable alternative to film school). Then, a steeply increasing number of middle-class young women began to further recognize that prostitution, in a new guise and setting, offered an even more lucrative temporary career, one which could be adopted not through coercion or desperation, but simply because it was easy, interesting, adventurous, and extremely profitable. The intense moral outrage with which the profession had been unanimously beheld by their parents' generation was slackening almost daily, leaving little more than an intriguing tinge of "naughtiness." Prostitution was one of the few remaining forbidden fruits of the 1970's, almost the only sexual activity which could still be considered even mildly shocking.

The current public image of prostitution is one of wicked glamor instead of degradation; to be called a "party girl" these days isn't an insult, it's a mark of social success for nine-tenths of the readers of *Cosmopolitan*. Prostitutes and their men have also been fashion pacesetters since the introduction of textured stockings, and a glance at the crowd in any popular discotheque of today will show that the intervening years have only served to solidify that channel of innovation in clothing styles.

Legal maneuvers aimed at the elimination of massage parlors have been as unsuccessful as the efforts to reverse the moral climate. Even after the passage of New York's most recent law requiring licenses for all persons or establishments using the word "massage," most of the places have either renamed themselves "rap studios" or "Yoga centers," while others have obtained licenses with no change in their operating procedure. Genuine support for enforcement of the sexist-oriented prostitution laws is almost nonexistent, since it is clear that, *at this level,* the occupation is a classic example of victimless crime. Even policemen and judges are increasingly reluctant to attach serious culpability to the women themselves, and sociologists and legal organizations continue to demand a rehabilitative, not criminal, approach to prostitution.

Rehabilitation is, no doubt, an excellent solution for the plight of the Times Square hookers, the grade-school dropouts supporting their pimps and their habits in a rat-infested Harlem "crib." But what are we to make of women like Gladys, Angela, Cassandra, and the others interviewed here? They are intelligent, attractive, well-educated people who could easily pursue successful careers in any of several legitimate fields. It is extremely difficult to imagine them being helped by free typing lessons or by weekly meetings with some middle-aged, establishmentarian psychiatrist or minister. Almost all of the subjects in this book already display a high degree of critical self-awareness, and an unusual familiarity with the concepts and methods of psychoanalysis and therapy, from Freud to Jung to Reich

Nor could Gloria Steinem or Betty Friedan convince these very independent individuals that they are exploited tools of the ruling class, naïve "oppressees" of the male chauvinist pigs. On the contrary, the people in this book firmly and distinctly feel that it is *they* who are exploiting the system, they who are controlling, profiting from, manipulating, "ripping off" the supposedly powerful arch-villains. It's a power trip, with a thousand dollars a week thrown in.

The girls who are drawn to massage parlor work are very different from the traditional image of the prostitute: students, housewives, and college graduates are no longer a rarity in the business, but the coming norm. In the course of a year's research in such diverse locales as New York, Louisville, Madison, Wisconsin, Boston, and Raleigh, North Carolina, I have come to know dozens of employees in other massage parlors. They have included two stewardesses, a teacher and author of children's books, several happy wives and mothers, many college and postgraduate students, a librarian, numerous executive secretaries, three registered nurses, and an ex-lieutenant of the Israeli Army. Only three of the girls I spoke to had previous arrest records, all for possession of marijuana, and of the two heroin addicts I encountered, one has now been off drugs for nine months straight.

The stereotype of the vicious black pimp and his regularly beaten "stable" of girls is ludicrously inapplicable. Several of the women I met are living with a husband or lover, but in only one case did the situation resemble the standard pimp/ hooker definition. The women themselves are in complete control of their earnings and their choice of work, while the men hold jobs of their own. The structure is that of any other economically cooperative marriage or relationship, except that the woman happens to be making eight to ten times as much as either party could, in most cases, earn at a "straight" job. And her income i~ effectively tax-free.

This book is not intended as a definitive, statistically precise sociological study, but I did conduct a small, informal random survey, the results of which proved rather interesting. In all 37 girls completed the questionnaire: 22 in New York City, 9 in Madison, Wisconsin, and 6 in Boston. All of the percentages quoted are rounded off to the nearest percentage point.

The median age of the women who responded was 23.3, with a range of 19 to 31. Thirty-two of the women who responded, or 86 percent, were between the ages of 20 and 25.

Twenty-two percent of the women were black, 73 percent were white, and 5 percent were oriental. Almost half of them had been raised as Protestants, with a nearly equal split among the others between Catholicism and Judaism. Only four of the girls, or 11 percent, had attended any religious service in the past year.

All of the people who answered had had at least some high school; 92 percent were high school graduates, and 81 percent had attended college, with 35 percent having graduated and a sizable proportion of those going on for some postgraduate study, extraordinarily comparable to average middle-class urban/suburban people, in short, not in the least disadvantaged or exotic. Of those who had not completed college, over a third were still students or had plans to return.

The largest group of the respondents, 46 percent, had spent their childhoods in a suburban area, while most of the others had been raised in large or medium-sized cities.

The majority were from a middle-class background; 54 percent came from families having an income between ten and twenty-five thousand dollars a year, and 22 percent were from families with incomes in excess of that figure. More than half have traveled to Europe at least once, and 62 percent have made trips outside the United States during the past year.

One hundred percent of the women have tried marijuana, a large majority have also sampled cocaine, and nearly half have experimented with LSD, mescaline, or similar psychedelics; but only 19 percent have ever even tried heroin once, in any fashion, and, of those, only two girls have actually injected it into their veins more than four times. This calls into serious question again the conventional belief that almost all prostitutes are addicts, as well as the attitude that "soft" drug experimentation naturally leads to opiate use. The wide split between the regular heroin users and those who have merely tried it, usually through inhalation, also seems to place some doubt on the assumptions concerning that drug's supposedly irresistible powers over the will of even a onetime user.

Most of the women found their jobs through ads in *Screw* or similar "underground" publications in other cities; 41 percent heard about the massage parlor work possibilities through friends; 59 percent were aware of the existence of the studios through general word-of-mouth; and nearly a third were also aided by ads in ordinary newspapers or the yellow pages of the telephone directory (these percentages overlap, as many were alerted by more than one source).

Most of them seem to have been no more than usually promiscuous before beginning this work, given the temper of the times; less than a third had previously had more than ten full-fledged sexual encounters, with different partners, and an even larger number had slept with fewer than five individuals.

Most of the girls, but fewer than might be expected, are naturally reticent about their work with their immediate families. Only 27 percent discussed it with their parents, whereas close to half of them had told one or more former friends about their jobs.

The highly significant temporary nature of massage parlor work, as opposed to ordinary prostitution, is indicated by the fact that fully 78 percent of the women have been working for less than a year, and only seven of them plan to continue in their current occupation for another year or more. Judging from the untaxed profits that they are accumulating, longer periods of work would certainly seem unnecessary: the median weekly income of the 37 girls is $770, with the overall range extending from $400 to $1,800 per week.

The various acts for which these princessly sums are performed have fairly standard individual prices: all of the women offer at least masturbation to their clients, at a median price of $15 (at some studios in smaller cities, and one or two in New York, "hand-jobs" are supposedly the only extra service available, and are automatically included in the price of admission; strict adherence to this rule is relatively rare, and varies from girl to girl). Of those surveyed 95 percent had performed at least one or more acts of fellatio, for a median price of $35; 84 percent sometimes engaged in straight intercourse—the median price for that being $60. Just under half had also dealt with masochistic customers, charging them in the vicinity of $50; for the same median price, five of the girls had also had transvestite customers, but only two had ever consented to anal intercourse, a service for which they charged $100 and up.

Bisexual leanings are extremely common among the women in the massage parlors, with 65 percent having had at least one homosexual experience and another 24 percent saying they would consider it. This seems more likely due to the general openness of the women's life-styles and sexual attitudes than to any direct correlation between prostitution and outright lesbianism, however: only three of the respondents, or 7 percent, have *exclusively* homosexual relations outside their work.

Slightly more than half of the women who replied have been married, and almost a third of them still are, a divorce rate not notably dissimilar to the population as a whole. Twenty-four percent are unmarried but have been living with the same man for one year or more; the combined total of those involved in ongoing relationships with a man thus comes to 20 girls, or 54 percent of the overall sample.

Of all the girls 62 percent have had some form of group sex experience (with two or more people simultaneously) outside their work; and of those 20 women involved in semipermanent or permanent relationships with a man, 70 percent have joined with their mates in group sex activities, while another 25 percent would consider doing so.

Of that same group of married or quasi-married girls, 65 percent of their husbands or lovers add to the family income; only two of those who do not could be even vaguely considered professional pimps though, as 25 percent of the men are currently college or postgraduate students. The next-largest group is involved in some creative occupation (acting, photography, etc.), closely followed by general businessmen (advertising, sales), teachers, and other professional occupations. Only one of the women's husbands is a blue-collar worker and one a drug dealer. The mates' educational levels are very similar to those of the women.

With regard to attitudes, only 11 percent of the girls said they felt generally guilty about the work they are doing. By far the largest group, 65 percent, declared themselves basically indifferent to their jobs except for the money, and 24 percent said they actually enjoyed their work, a much higher percentage than might be expected, judging from the usual image of the frigid and emotionally detached prostitute. Thirty-two percent said they did feel guilty or ashamed at least some of the time; but 89 percent said that they enjoyed their work at least occasionally. Only one girl expressed regret at having become involved; all the rest said they were glad they had discovered the job.

In short, these people are young, bright, and talented;

they are fully aware of what they are doing, and they have entered into the profession, in most cases very temporarily, through a freely made personal decision. *They are generally quite comfortable with their own sexuality, and are pleased and amused to have parlayed their already liberated life-styles into absurdly high-paying jobs.* They are part and parcel of the younger generation that constitutes the dominating sector of our society. Their personal life-styles, if not their professions, are soon to be, if not already, the American way of sex.

The people you will meet in the following pages are not criminals, and they have grown up learning to ignore stupid and unenforceable commandments that supposedly tell them and their peers what they can smoke, what they can say, what they can read or see, where they can travel, and who, how, and why they can screw.

These people also have a high level of social consciousness, and many of them feel that what they are doing is genuinely useful work. Masters and Johnson have, of course, used professional and amateur prostitutes as an integral part of their sexual therapy programs. One highly respected British psychiatrist offers counseling in which his own wife plays an active sexual role with some of the patients. *Newsweek* magazine recently published a photograph of and interview with Sandi Enders, of the Berkeley Group for Sexual Development, a therapy organization directed by clinical psychologist Dr. Bernard Apfelbaum. Ms. Enders was described as a "sexual therapist," working her way through San José State University by conducting $50 sessions for Dr. Apfelbaum's patients in her water-bed-equipped apartment. She was quoted as saying, "What I'm doing is technically prostitution, but I'm convinced that helping men out of their hang-ups is valid, important work."

What makes Ms. Enders' sessions so different from those offered at, say, Caesar's Retreat? The sanction of a psychologist? Her stated ideals? Her picture in *Newsweek?* Sexual frustration and ignorance are rampant in our society, and men (and women!) who have no other real need for psychiatric treatment should be able to find release and understanding in a safe, comfortable setting.

In her celebrated work *Lovers, Friends, Slaves . . . The Nine Male Sexual Types*, a four-year study of call girls' clients, social worker Martha Stein compellingly documents the constructive, often essential therapeutic role that call girls play. She calls attention vividly to the personal crises epidemic among middle-aged American men, and she explores with bold insights the kinds of sexual therapy implied by the practices of the call girls she researched.

The massage parlors and the men and women who work in them have made it clear that all our previous opinions with respect to prostitution, as with any other form of sexual behavior, must be redefined. I do not pretend or imply that the older, exploitative forms of the profession will disappear overnight, or that everyone who works in a massage parlor has the understanding or the relaxed self-confidence of most of the subjects in this book. But that is unquestionably the direction in which the business is heading, and I see no indications that this is about to change.

At any rate, the people whose interviews you are about to read offer a candid and insightful view of American sexuality from an unusual variety of vantage points. This *is* the way it is. I believe that their widespread experience with almost every form of sexual experience constitutes a valuable document of our rapidly changing patterns of behavior and attitude, and I hope that you, as I did, find their comments enlightening.

1. Gladys

GLADYS *is twenty-two years old, black, with a childhood back-ground of poverty in the ghettos of an industrial northern city. She has worked as a prostitute in a New York massage parlor for the past seven months, with one arrest on prostitution charges during that time. Gladys also has a BA in sociology, was previously employed as a planner in a state-funded criminal rehabilitation program, and is now studying architectural design in her off hours.*

The massage parlor in which Gladys works is Caesar's Retreat. Located on East Forty-sixth Street, Caesar's is the plushest and most expensive of them all. SCREW *magazine, in its rating guide to the Manhattan sex scene, gives Caesar's the only "four-star" award. Caesar's is decorated in acres of red velveteen and plaster Roman statuary, and its ads promise that "toga-clad goddesses will pamper you breathless . . ."; they will also leave you moneyless, if Gladys' expertise at eliciting the customers' "generosity" is any indication.*

Gladys' upturned nose is perfectly complemented by her wide, bright eyes and delightful mouth, and she has a tinklingly infectious stoned giggle. At each of our several meetings she was always immaculately groomed and fashionably dressed. She is fond of floppy, colorful hats and tailored pants suits and dresses which display her shapely body to maximum advantage, without the slightest hint of vulgarity. She is girlishly flirtatious but always alert and highly articulate.

There are no simple explanations for Gladys' involvement in, and continuing fascination with, prostitution: though she obviously enjoys dressing and living well, money per se does not seem to be among her major concerns. Furthermore, she is eminently qualified,

19

through education, intelligence, experience, and personality, to hold a variety of well-paying positions of responsibility. Having escaped the ghetto and achieved the traditional liberal formula for success, Gladys entered the world of prostitution from the precise opposite end of the spectrum from that which might be expected.

Perhaps the most striking feature of Gladys' situation is her position as a living refutation of the universal validity of the often-touted "rehabilitation programs" for prostitutes, black or white; her background would, in fact, qualify her to originate and direct such a program, but she has instead chosen to become a prostitute herself.

* * *

QUESTION: How did you first get into the massage parlor scene?

GLADYS: I had just come to New York, and my employer told me that he had a friend who owned a massage parlor, and the girls there made five, six hundred dollars a week. Now, I had come to New York because I was broke, and I needed to find a way to make a lot of bread; so when that situation presented itself, I really got into it.

I started talking to him about having his friend get me a job there; and he says, "All right, I'll get you a job there, but I don't want you to quit here, because you're a good secretary." I'm good, right, but I was only making a hundred and twenty-five dollars a week. So like an idiot, for about a month and a half I worked two jobs. I went to my secretarial job out of loyalty to my boss and out of sheer stupidity. I got up at seven o'clock and went to that job; at six o'clock I went into Caesar's, and I got home about four; then I got up again at seven o'clock and started the whole thing all over. For a month and a half.

QUESTION: How did the idea of working in a massage parlor strike you to begin with—emotionally?

GLADYS: Well, I felt a little strange about it; but when somebody's throwing the prospect of five hundred dollars a week in your face you get over the strangeness real easily.

QUESTION: What happened when you went to apply for the job?

GLADYS: I went in with my boss, Sam; he was goin' to introduce me to the manager. I was pretty nervous; in fact, I had to go to the bar across the street and have a couple of drinks first, and Sam had to give me some pep talk. Finally I got my courage up, and I walked in. Then it was really no big thing; I was impressed by the kind of place that Caesar's is: it's very elegantly decorated, and the girls there, man, really flipped me out. They wore these nice little costumes, and . . . I had never known any prostitutes, or "masseuses," or any kind of people like that before; I mean, I had grown up around that, I came from a poverty, ghetto situation where life is supposedly so earthy and very close to reality, but I always dissociated myself from that, and my mores and values were very much white middle class. So it was just very strange.

QUESTION: You mean the girls there didn't fit your preconceptions about prostitutes?

GLADYS: No, because they all seemed to be girls who were pretty much like myself, girls who would probably not be into that kind of thing if it weren't for Caesar's Retreat and five hundred dollars a week, you know?

There was quite a little social stratum there. Some girls were sort of like "The" girls, and others were generally resented in a way, because the rest of the girls didn't feel that they deserved to be working at Caesar's, either because their physical attributes weren't up to par or because of their cultural background or whatever.

QUESTION: Did you start working the same day you applied?

GLADYS: No. I was told that the manager really liked me, and thought I could do really well there, but he couldn't put me on right away. Some of the girls I had seen were really pretty, and some of them were . . . you know, not my idea of what a "masseuse" should be. So I told Sam, "Tell him to get rid of some of the dogs."

Evidently he got rid of some of the dogs within a couple

of days. I started working about June first. The first night
I worked there was really strange because I was very self-
conscious—first of all, about walking around half-nude in
front of all these people.

QUESTION: What sort of costumes do you wear?

GLADYS: These toga-like kind of things—they're all white
and really cute . . . on some girls. They're very miniskirted,
A-line type of things; the top is just a backless kind of strap
that covers *some* of your breasts, and you wear a gold chain
belt, white shoes, and whatever jewelry you want. Some girls
look really nice in them.

QUESTION: What happened when you first went to work
there?

GLADYS: Well, first you have a sort of brief training period.
They show you where everything is, how to keep the bar
straight; everybody has little chores they have to do, like
keeping the linen supplied and keeping the shower areas
or the session rooms clean; so they showed me how to do
all that stuff right.

Then they put you in a massage session with another girl,
and you watch and listen to everything that she does. The
first thing you have to do is get the customer all settled in
the room and take him to the showers; then you take him
back to the room and the massage session starts. You're
trained to be very personable and charming and sort of make
the nervous guy, who's never been around a young, nice-
looking girl before, feel not so nervous; or at least not so
bad about being in a massage parlor [*laughs*].

QUESTION: What was your training session like?

GLADYS: Well, the guy said that he wanted a French; there
was a price negotiation, and finally the girl that I was training with told him, in a very discreet manner, how much it
would be.

The customer is supposed to ask you for "extras," if he
wants any; he'll say, "Can I get a *complete* massage?" or "Can
I get some kind of satisfaction?" You have to be kind of
modest and coy. He'll pursue the issue and you say, "Well,

that's really not part of the program, you know; you just get a massage, there's nothing sexual included." So he says, "Well, what can I do to have something included?" and you kind of hint around to him that it really depends upon his generosity.

QUESTION: You aren't allowed to mention specific prices?

GLADYS: No, you aren't; but after you get to know the ropes you find it expedient to hint around, and see if he's cool, and then if you really feel he's cool . . . it's a psychic thing, you have to *know* if a person's cool, like you can read minds or something, you know. And if you feel he's cool, then you say, "Well, it's twenty dollars for a hand massage, thirty dollars for a French. . . . "

I don't get into selling the ultimate that much, I don't know why. I never liked fucking, anyway; I've never had a real orgasm, even with people who were especially endowed or especially talented. It's just a psychological hang-up, I guess. So I don't really like screwing, and there's also a racial thing—I don't like all these bigoted mother-fuckers to think that they can screw any black chick, just because she's a black chick and they're white. So I often sort of put my nose up in the air when they talk about screwing.

QUESTION: Have you ever encountered any open racial bigotry?

GLADYS: Oh, yeah, yeah, a lot of times. But I don't care if they're bigoted; if they're bigoted, I charge them more. So if they're that way, I like them, 'cause that means that before they get one single smile from me, I'm gonna get as much money from them as they have; because, obviously, dealing with a bigoted person is a pain in the ass, and I deserve to be highly compensated. They're usually very subtle things, but as long as I can capitalize on them I don't really care.

There was one situation with this really strange young guy, and we all hate young guys; he was sort of crazy. He was sitting in the lounge with a paper, and I was whizzing through the lounge on my way to do something. So he stopped me, and he said, "Would you baby-sit me?" and I said, "I don't know, I have something to do right now. I'll see about it." So I left, and I went back and finished doing my other customer. Then finally I got chosen for this guy's massage; sometimes the customers would have a chance to select the girl they wanted, and sometimes we'd just be assigned to a customer on a revolving basis.

This guy was really crazy; I kept trying to explain to him that he had to wrap the towel around him before he could go out into the shower area, and after I'd left him for a few minutes to do that, I came back and he was standing there completely nude. So I said, "Well, you have to put the towel around you," and he put the towel up to his chin like a bib. I said, "No, you have to put it around your waist, like this," and I wrapped it around his waist; and then he wrapped the towel around his knees, and then he wrapped it around his neck . . . real fun and games. He was really farting around, wasting my time.

So finally I got him to wrap the towel around him; and then he's a problem in the sauna room, he's a problem in the showers. . . . He gave me a long bullshit line about why he didn't want to take a shower; he insisted upon taking his newspaper into the shower. He asked me if it was all right to wash his penis in the shower; he asked me if I'd wash his penis for him. Finally he took a shower, and then he wouldn't get *out* of the shower; he'd been in there for about ten minutes.

So I decided the only way to handle him was to be just as crazy as he was. I opened the shower curtain, placed my hand around his jugular vein and squeezed it real tight, and said, "Look, bastard, get out of the shower." He got scared and uptight and turned fifty million shades of red, but he came out of the shower. By then he was uptight; I don't know whether he was afraid of me or just a lunatic, but he started insulting me when we got to the room. He said, "You know, I've had a lot of black women before, and I really think it's a drag." So I said, "Why is that?" and he said, "Well, they're really ugly; the only things they have are big tits and big asses." So I said, "That's why you picked me, huh? Well, I have some really nice ones, but you know what? You're not even gonna get a chance to see them."

I just kept coming back at him. I said, "I bet you'd really like me if I was light blue, or if I was purple. Oh, no, you wouldn't like me if I was purple, because purple is too close to black. But yellow—what if I was a bright, sunshiney yellow, or a really groovy orange? Then you'd like me." And I'm really flipping out! But I was determined not to let this guy get me mad or hurt my feelings; I decided that as sick and neurotic and insane as he was, I was gonna be that way, too. Plus, in my whole life, I had never had a real gut-level racial confrontation. No one had ever done that to me, ever. Just about everything that I wanted in life, I got; and if people had any things about my being black, I usually took that situation and turned it into an advantage, you know.

But this guy just kept going on and on, telling me how superior he was to me, first of all because he was a male, and, secondly and most importantly, because he was white, so he was intellectually my superior, and all this shit. I made a lot of sarcastic remarks back to him, like, "Yeah, you're right; that's why I worship and admire you so much," but nothing would shut him up. So I reached around behind me and lowered the little bottle of massage oil right down directly into the candle flame that was keeping it warm; and then just as he's in the middle of one of his bullshit raps about how "All black chicks are whores, anyway," I suddenly pour this burning hot oil all over his prick. It was a pretty sick thing to do, but it shut him right up [*laughs*].

QUESTION: Have you ever had a masochist as a customer?

GLADYS: Oh yeah, oh yeah; I sorta got a little reputation around there for giving Englishes. And I'm not really violent, you know. I'm really like a very peaceful, beautiful, wouldn't-hurt-anybody kind of person. But you get into these sexual situations, and these money situations, and they tend to distort your mind a little bit. I have about five regular English customers; one of them is a slave.

QUESTION: What was it like the first time this happened to you?

GLADYS: The way it all got started, I was giving a guy a massage, and he kept asking me questions like, "Have you ever heard of an 'English' massage?" And I said, "Yeah, but you wouldn't want one; that's a pain thing, you know. In those 'English' massage studios people come in and ask to be beaten." And he says, "Oh, yeah? What do they beat you with?" So I told him, "Well, some people like to be beaten with whips, some get beaten with leather straps, and pieces of wood, and coat-hangers—you know, all kinds of things." I learned about that kind of stuff from reading some dirty books, but I'd never had an English or given one.

So he said, "Well, do you mind giving them?" And I said, "That all depends upon your generosity." Then he told me that the only way he had an orgasm was if he got spanked, and he's talking about seventy-five dollars. Seventy-five dollars, just like that [snap], in half an hour! Of course, you're not gonna turn it down; some people work a week or more for seventy-five dollars. So I went back into the lounge, and I talked to some girls about it and got a little advice on how I should do it, and got a hairbrush. So he was bending over, and I was smacking him away with the hairbrush; and I got into it, I was really enjoying it, you know? Just smacking this guy—first of all, because he was a male, and males have fucked me over all my life, it's about time, and he was really digging it, just "oohing" and "aahing" away.

QUESTION: Was he masturbating while you were doing this?

GLADYS: No, he wasn't masturbating; he was just standing there bending over. But I started really getting into it, and I hit him with the bristle side of the brush, which really turned him on, of course; that was really painful. I mean, a million bristles smacking you in the behind . . . and he'd get these little dots, and there would be blood squirting from these teeny little pockmarks, and there would be blood getting on the sheets, not a lot, just little dots of it, you know; tiny splashes, kind of. And at that point he usually comes, whenever I start to hit him with the bristles and he gets a little marked up. He just spontaneously comes, from being beaten and nothing else.

He started being one of my regulars; he comes in all the time. Once I called him a "bastard," and he really got mad; he was really crushed that I'd called him a bastard. But it was only in play, it was only to sort of like set the scene. I was gonna, you know, make him feel a little pleasantly debased. But he really got his feelings hurt, and he said, "Well, I can't come here anymore; I can't face you anymore if you really think of me that way." I had to take the time to apologize and explain to him that I was only trying to make it more enjoyable for him.

So he comes back to me quite often, still; and I notice occasionally that he has little bruises on him, and scars, from previous beatings which weren't mine. He lives in Connecticut, and I think every time he comes in from Connecticut he makes the rounds; he just goes to different massage parlors, or different girls, and gets Englishes . . . and this is his big Fun City business trip [*laughs*]. He must have a good bit of money, because just with me, he pays thirty-five dollars for an hour massage session, and then he always gives me at least seventy-five dollars, sometimes a little more, but never less.

Then I had this other guy for a while, he was the slave; Richard was my slave. Richard was an old guy, short and kinda fat; he looked like he would have a heart attack if you beat him or worked him too hard. He always called me "Miss Gladys"; he would say, "Miss Gladys, I'll do anything you want. I'll do anything you say, Miss Gladys." So I wouldn't beat him all the time; I'd put him to work. I'd say, "Richard, I want *you* to give *me* a massage. Undress me, Richard." So he would undress me, and if he did anything like touch me, touch my pussy or touch my breasts or anything, sort of like slyly while he was undressing me, that was a no-no. I'd hit him across the head, or kick him, or step on his foot or something, and he would just put his hands up as if to try and protect his face, and act like a turtle in a shell, you know; but all the while, he loved it. He absolutely loved it; he would beg for it, beg for me to hit him.

I had never had any power trips like that before in real life, so I decided that every time Richard came, for the money I was gonna get my cookies off. Because Richard didn't have a lot of money; he gave me this poor story about how he used to be an alcoholic, and this elderly black lady named Hannah took him off the streets and nursed him back to health. He lived there, and he didn't have to pay her any rent, but he would have to protect her, because she was old and only had one leg; he would have to do all the chores around the house, he'd have to cook and things like that. But sometimes she would get mad at him, and she would beat him. Can you imagine this old black lady with one leg and a cane, beating on this chubby little white guy, and him screaming for more? I mean, it was really sick, it was incredible. And he had to give his money to her, so he didn't have too much. He fixed jukeboxes, that was his occupation.

Most of the guys who come to Caesar's are successful businessmen, but Richard only had one suit that looked all right, and when he came in he would only have fifteen or twenty dollars on him. For an English, that was nothing; so I would do it mainly out of the charitableness of my heart —and to get my cookies off [laughs]. Yeah, Richard would only give me fifteen or twenty dollars; once he gave me ten dollars and I beat the shit out of him. He loved every minute of it.

Once I made him play like he was a dog, and I made him take my shoe in his mouth and crawl around the table, while I hit him and said, "Faster, Richard, faster!" I would try and take the shoe away from him, and if he didn't give it to me I would slap him in the face. I'm not a cruel person, but this was fun, this was really fun.

QUESTION: And you had never been into this kind of thing before?

GLADYS: No, no, never; never dreamed about it. I mean, it wasn't even one of my fantasies, and I have sick fantasies; but this wasn't one of them. Somehow, for some reason, I just got off on it in these situations; it really became enjoyable, in a weird kind of way. I'd slap Richard in the face and I would make him beg to touch me, or I would make him beg to eat my pussy, which was a thing he just loved to do. He really loved to do that, so I would make him beg. He would beg me to French him, but I would never touch him; I never touched Richard sexually. I would say, "Richard, if you can make me come by eating my pussy, I'll give you a French;" but that was an unusual challenge, see, because nobody ever made me come, and I knew it. I still enjoyed it, though, so I would just lie there for twenty minutes and let him eat my pussy.

Sometimes I wouldn't even beat him; sometimes I would say, "Well, Richard, just get down on your knees and undress me; you can do that for the next twenty minutes, and then you'll have to leave." And he would be thankful, he really would be thankful; he would say, "Thank you, Miss Gladys . . . God bless you, Miss Gladys" as he left. He was really sick . . . I was, too, but it was fun [laughs]. And he never gave me more than twenty dollars; that's why I abused him so much, because he couldn't pay me correctly. It was on charity, and he realized it.

QUESTION: What do you usually charge for someone to perform oral sex on you?

GLADYS: If you want to eat me, it's fifty dollars. A lot of girls get fifty dollars fucking, but I'm not gonna do that; fifty dollars buys a nice big bite of my pussy, and that's it. Some guys think that if they do something nice for you then you won't charge them for it; they'll say, "I'm really good at Frenching girls," and I just say, "What do you think I am, a nymphomaniac or something?"

I'm telling all the bad sides about it; there are good sides.

I really am sweet—that's my whole image, very charming and sweet, almost sicky-sweet. But the way I'm telling it is the things that I think, how I subconsciously feel about everything.

QUESTION: Have you ever had any sadists as customers, or anyone who asked for anything else out of the ordinary?

GLADYS: Never any sadists, no; but it seems like I have *all* the pussy eaters; you'd think it was flavored like whipped cream and strawberries the way they lap it up. I don't know whether the other girls have much of that or not, but . . . you know, we just don't talk about that.

QUESTION: How open is the conversation among the girls about what goes on?

GLADYS: It's fairly open, but not very intimate; like, everybody has set things that they do or don't do, and you sorta know. Some people have a reputation for being fifty-dollar fucks, seventy-five-dollar fucks, others aren't fucks. I wasn't, at first; but after a while I decided that if they could produce a yard—that's a hundred dollars—I guess I could. Before that, if they wanted to screw I would just put them off and suggest a "hand massage" or a French; or with some guys I might even say it was a racial thing, and I just didn't want them putting their hands on me.

It's really strange what we do to guys; we're half-naked, anyway, and we really act like teases. I've always felt that sex and femininity are an art, even though I sometimes resented being a woman. It's still an art, and I wanted to develop that to the fullest; so we really do a number on these guys. Just body movements, you know—not anything vulgar. I never really like to consider myself vulgar; that is, before we get into the sex. When we get into the sex, that's different [laughs]. But while we're playing this scene, the scene is like very cool, very classy: an intelligently charming, very together chick doing an extremely erotic number, but in a very subtle way.

Everybody always asks what I'm doing in a massage parlor, and I always reply, "Making more money than you are." I have to laugh at them because they're losers. They really

are losers; they come in and give me thirty dollars or more
for giving them a blow job, not getting to touch me or anything, just having to lie there. And the minute they have
an orgasm, I never let it go in my mouth; that's it, that's
the end. As soon as I feel something throbbing there, that's
the end. I do a damn good job with what I do, up until
that point; but some guys, they always want you to swallow
it. I say, "What do you think I am, a receptacle for waste?
Have you ever tasted any of that stuff? Do you like it? Well,
I don't either."

I'm really not nasty though; I always smile, and I'm very
charming with them. A lot of times the guys really don't
get what they came in there for, and would normally complain; but I've just developed such a cool way of like making
them laugh, and at least momentarily forget that they've been
sexually disappointed in some way. One time I got two
hundred dollars from a guy for doing nothing: he wanted
to screw, and he was a peckerwood from down south, so
I was really gonna, you know . . . anyway, he could *not* get
a hard-on, and I would laugh and say, "You know what?
I'm just gonna take all that money from you, and you're
not even gonna be able to get a hard-on; you'd be complainin',
you'd be mad at me, and it wouldn't be my fault, 'cause
I warned you." I went on and on, and he couldn't stand
it; it was driving him crazy. He'd name a price, and I'd say,
"Nooo . . . I'm not gonna make you waste all that money,
I'm not gonna let you make a fool of yourself"; and the
more I said no, the higher his price got. Finally he offered
me two hundred dollars; and I said, "OK, but I'm getting
my money up front, and if the thing isn't consummated it's
really not my fault." So we get up there on the table, and
the guy cannot get a hard-on, which I knew would be the
case; and he says, "You were right, you were right, damn
you; you put a curse on me, didn't you? I bet you did."
We were just laughing and joking, and the guy went out
of the place in hysterics; meanwhile, I had two hundred
dollars for nothing, for absolutely nothing.

QUESTION: You've said that you came from a background

of poverty; what were some of your early experiences, including sexual ones?

GLADYS: Well, my mother's very poor, and my father's been in and out of mental institutions. He was a junkie for the first few years of my life. When I was six years old, he got arrested for dealing dope and being a junkie. He was in several mental institutions, and he finally got over it to the point that he was no longer addicted, but he was still . . . well, he was highly intelligent and very nervous, and the doctors said he was a paranoid schizophrenic. I love my father, but he really has been sick. He would beat my mother; sometimes they would get into fights; he would hear things, you know; and he also sexually molested his children. I can remember that happening when I was very young, and I would feel horrible about it; it would cause terrible guilt feelings. When I was a little kid I didn't feel anything; all I remember is him doing something to me, and him being my father, and very stern; of course, what could I say? So I just lay there . . . I sorta had the feeling it was a no-no, but as to why or anything . . . I was very young. And then I remember it happening later on in my life, when I was about thirteen or fourteen. This is when I remember it happening the most, because this was a sexually awakening period of my life, I guess. I was going to a Catholic high school, and I had been thoroughly ingrained with a lot of deep religious beliefs; I even wanted to be a nun [*laughs*]. The incestuously violated daughter of a junkie becomes a nun. I don't know how I thought I could escape this life.

Anyway, I remember my father coming into my bedroom at night, and he would put his hands under the covers, and he would start to play with my pussy with his fingers. I would pretend like I was asleep, because it was so horrible, I didn't want to . . . I would think to myself, "No, this is not happening." I would make myself pretend that I was asleep and didn't know what was happening; that was the only way I could do it without going crazy. If I yelled or woke up my mother, he would beat my mother; he would beat her up, and he would do horrible things to us . . . and my father isn't an unkind person, he's just sick. He was; he's not like this right now. He's harmless and lovable right now, and I forgive him; but he did do sexual things like that to me when I was a kid, and as a result of the guilt feelings, and trying to blot it out, I was never able to appreciate or enjoy sex normally as I grew up.

I know that I had deep sexual desires when I was a teen-ager, desires that were never fulfilled because of these experiences, and because of being brought up as a Catholic, to think that any kind of sex was wrong. So I imagine that I must have enjoyed my early regular sexual experiences, but subconsciously I would try and control my mind, and really block out the awareness of what was happening. I believe that I have had orgasms, but would just not be cogniz-ant of the fact; this has carried over into my adult life. I don't have orgasms still. I experience pleasure, but if it's intense pleasure it becomes almost as if it were intense pain, and I freak out; I really freak out, and I shut it off. So I never have orgasms. People have told me that I have, because they've felt me contracting, and reacting as if I had an orgasm, but I've never felt it. I know that I'm frustrated because of that, and I try and deal with it. There was a period in my life when I tried actively to have an orgasm, both through promiscuous relationships, and then later in a relationship with a person that I loved, who was perfectly adequate in every way to do the job; but it just never hap-pened. I know it's a mental thing, but I don't know what I can do about it.

QUESTION: Have you ever become at all sexually excited at Caesar's?

GLADYS: Yeah . . . yeah, I basically enjoy oral things being done to me, and I guess I must enjoy doing oral things to other people. I must enjoy sheer carnality . . . I mean, I *bathe* in it [*laughs*]. And I pride myself on giving the most exquisite

French massages in the whole place; so, naturally, I must enjoy it—well, at least I take pride in the way I do it; I am a highly skilled worker [*laughs*].

QUESTION: Have you ever had any lesbian experiences, either at Caesar's or in your personal life?

GLADYS: When I was in college. I had a few normal girl-friends; I never had a lot of friends, but once in a while I would have a close girlfriend, and I always liked them a lot. But I wasn't aware of the fact that I had any lesbian tendencies—until I found myself surrounded by faggots [*laughs*].

I was working in a record store while I was going to school, and I had all these "groovy" male friends; mostly platonic relationships, but an intense amount of mutual respect and admiration and closeness, you know; people who helped me to grow and develop as a person. But it finally began to dawn on me that they were all a little strange. A couple of the guys were married, but they were having affairs with other guys that worked at the same place where we all worked. I didn't know it for a long time, and it didn't bother me when I found out, because I loved them. I really did love them; they were really beautiful people and I just loved them, so it didn't matter. So at that time I began checking out the relationships that I had with girls; you know, "Where am I? What is this? Am I that way, too?" And I decided that I did have some curiosities in that direction.

So I had close girlfriends at that time, too, one of whom I became roommates with for a short while. We liked each other and saw each other as sort of mirror images of ourselves: like, if I was white, I would have been her, I would have been Barbara. I would have been doing the things that she was doing and would have been into the things that she was into. And if she had been black, she would have been just the way that I was. We were as much like each other as society and genetic situations permitted us to be. We would talk about things with guys; she was always horny, and I was seldom horny; when I did get horny I would go stalking a guy, but I never got horny the way girls usually do, and they sit around wishing their boyfriends would call or something like that. I never felt that way unless I met a person who was really groovy and he turned me on; then I'd let him know exactly what was happening, you know? "You can come home with me. . . ." I never liked to get "conquered" by a guy; I never liked a guy to have the ego trip of being able to say that he turned me on, or he convinced me or persuaded me; I consider myself an independent, thinking, liberated woman, and if I want to fuck, you'll know it [*laughs*]. And then it's "I got you, you didn't get me."

So Barbara and I would talk about things like that, and we were both lonely, in the sense that we really didn't have any guys around us that we could really identify with. One time we almost got into a scene together . . . but then our "hero" came over—Bob Epstein. Bob was this political hero in our town and nationally, in a small way. He was an antiwar demonstrator and a defector, one of the first ones; it was a big issue at the time. This was back in the sixties, and like "hippie," "radical" . . . you know [*laughs*]. So he was our big hero; he was really taking a lot of shit, and we were always demonstrating for him. He'd been in jail, and . . . he wasn't going with either of us, but every girl liked Bob Epstein, you know? After all, he was a hero [*laughs*]. I mean, if he was gonna spend all those months in jail for us and our country and the things we believed in, the least we could do was give him a good lay [*laughs*].

So just as Barbara and I were obviously about to get a lovemaking sort of thing, Bob came over, and then he and Barbara started getting into something, and I really felt intensely cheated. I didn't know exactly of what, but I definitely felt cheated: I wanted Bob, and I also wanted Barbara; but none of us had ever been into any kind of share situation or threesome before, so I just went home, and I really felt disappointed.

My first real lesbian relationship happened with a girl named Janet, who's in Honolulu now. We were both sort of married; I was living with a guy, and she was living with her husband. I met her through her husband, who was a faggot that I was in love with before I met her, and then I loved the both of them, because they were both so beautiful. It was a platonic thing, and I did my first acid trip with them, at their house; it was really beautiful, nothing sexual, but just beautiful and close, good vibes. We saw each other off and on, and later we got to be really close. Then when we discovered that we had so many mutual friends who were homosexuals I guess it caused us to check each other out. We had always dug each other, you know. I always thought she was very beautiful, and she always thought that I was.

So, finally, one afternoon when we were spending the day together, getting high and drinking wine and talking about our feelings about a lot of things . . . we just got very close . . . and naked and warm with each other . . . and had a very beautiful experience. We were stupid enough to think we could share it with the guys, and her husband got pissed off about it. He didn't want her being into the same thing he was into, I guess; I don't know. And my old man was mad because he really dug Janet and he wanted to get her, but it wasn't that kind of thing, you know? So they tried to like get in our way, and she moved to Hawaii shortly after that . . . so that was all there was to that.

After that, I knew that I kind of enjoyed having relationships with women, but it's not the kind of thing where you just see a girl and get the hots for her, or something like that; it's a thing that's more sensitive and has to grow and develop from a friendship and a mutual admiration. More so than with a man, because it's more tender and groovy.

QUESTION: Do you think that women are better lovers than men?

GLADYS: Yeah, because a woman knows how she herself would like to be made love to, so when you make love with another woman, you do it just as you'd most like it yourself, and I think all women like to be made love to in similar ways. I've never had an orgasm with a woman either; but

I have found it extremely and intensely pleasurable.

QUESTION: Have you ever had any homosexual attraction to the other girls at Caesar's?

GLADYS: I've grown to have close ties with some of them . . . first of all, the stimuli around there are really fantastic. All these girls are walking around half-nude, and you sometimes have double programs, a session together where a guy will pick two girls. Here you are in a room together with this girl who you don't know, really; all you know is that you both want as much money as you can get. So because of that, you're willing to ignore or accept the fact that she's there. Whenever I had a program with other girls I would watch them because I found it aesthetically pleasing. I would ignore the fact that the man was there, I would just watch the girl; that was pleasurable. For instance, like one girl would be Frenching the guy, and the other girl would be kissing him, or letting him suck her breasts, and you'd sort of take turns; or sometimes the guy may want a more elaborate kind of thing, like a 69 kind of thing with the both of you. Some girls aren't into that, so I act like I'm not, either; and with other girls you can sort of feel it out that that's acceptable. I've had a session like that with a couple of girls; and I don't know if the thought of doing each other ever crossed either of their minds, but there was one girl in particular that I really wouldn't mind a situation like that occurring with.

QUESTION: Have any of the customers ever requested the two girls to do something with each other?

GLADYS: No; I'm always waiting for that to happen. I'm curious to see just how much money it would take to make that kind of thing happen, and I sometimes fantasize about it. Yeah, I think about how nice it would be if I had a session with a certain person and the guy gave us a lot of bread to do each other—'cause I figure that would be about the only way it would happen. But it would be nice.

QUESTION: Getting back to your early life; what sort of schooling did you have?

GLADYS: Well, I was raised as a Catholic, and I went to

a very ritzy kind of all-girl private Catholic high school in Philadelphia, noted for its good, good training [*laughs*]—instilling the fear of God, making pillars of society, good Catholics and eventually neurotics; that's the syndrome. It cost me more money in tuition to go there than it cost me to go to college 'cause I went to a state school.

We were really poor, and we couldn't actually afford it: I never had lunch money, I had to walk to school, I didn't have nice clothes like everybody else . . . but I was there because I didn't want to go to a public school. I didn't want to come into contact with the harsh realities of life [*laughs*]. I lived in the middle of enough of them, what with our money problems and my father being a junkie and everything else. I just didn't want to associate myself with any more pain.

It was really weird, going to a Catholic school, and hearing all this bullshit about sex and life; all these high, idealistic things that don't exist in reality. And I know that because I live in the reality that most people don't even know about. Yet I'm still stupidly trying, at least subconsciously, to aspire to these "ideal" standards and codes of behavior and wants and desires . . . I'm really fucked up [*laughs*], really fucked up.

QUESTION: What was your college training?

GLADYS: I went to a very big, but very good, urban university in my hometown; I have a BA in sociology. I could do any number of things, and I will; I mean, I'm gonna get my shit off, you know? I've got a lotta stuff to do, and I'm gonna do it; but none of the stuff I can do pays off like Caesar's does. I know that I can amass wealth; it's my desire in life to be wealthy and successful and happy, not at the expense of other people, but with other people, like helping other people get to be the same way that I hope to make myself. It's just a matter of developing your potential. I can do that with myself, and I can help other people do that; and I know that in doing it I will become wealthy in much more than just a material sense, but in a material sense as well. I know that I'm gonna have a lot of money, I know I'm gonna be happy, I'm gonna find something to do that I really groove on; it's all gonna be cool.

QUESTION: What previous jobs had you held before you went to work at Caesar's?

GLADYS: One of my first jobs was as a salesclerk in a record store during college; then later during college I got a really good job in an urban planning office. It was a federal job, and the purpose of it was to get black people to participate in the planning process of the city; they did it with students, and they paid us very well. I worked on housing studies and became quite interested in that. I'd like to become an architect, and right now I'm taking postgraduate courses in illustration, drafting, and design, so I can at least draw what I might want to get into. I find it a fascinating field and would definitely like to continue in that direction.

I've also worked as a research analyst for a state crime control agency; we collected and analyzed mountains of data, coming up with studies that were utterly irrelevant, mostly helping pad people's pockets, getting jobs and money. We would create a supposed need for a program, then create the program itself as a "solution" for whatever problem we had developed or imagined or pretended to have found. Naturally, it always related to crime and law enforcement, more money for police cars or something, or money for a drug addiction program that might hire six or eight people, with a twenty-two-thousand-dollar salary for the director, and of course if it was your proposal and if the thing got funded, you'd be the director [laughs]. Fun things like that. We'd just create little things trying to get money, you know. So I was doing this, and I was very unhappy 'cause I knew I was not doing the right thing by me, and I also wasn't making any bread. If you're gonna be wrong, you might as well get some money for it, right? So I was getting fed up with that; and that was the last job I had before I went to work at Caesar's Retreat.

QUESTION: What are your feelings about Women's Lib—and how it relates to what you're doing?

GLADYS: Oh, wow . . . I definitely feel that women should

be liberated, but I believe that for me it's like a personal kind of liberation: choosing what I want in life and going after it, getting it in spite of barriers that people may put in my way because I'm a woman or because I'm black or because I'm poor. You know, *everybody* needs to be liberated. I'm pretty certain that the organized Women's Libbers would definitely put their thumbs down on me [*laughs*], but I've loved every minute of being exploited. You see, you can exploit me, go ahead, exploit me for a hundred dollars a day or more. Many nights I walk out of that place with two or three hundred dollars, without even screwing anybody. That's fantastic as far as I'm concerned because I hate screwing; and I always related to prostitution in terms of screwing, you had to screw all the time, you know? And here I am making all that money and hardly ever screwing; it's fantastic. As for the Women's Lib movement, I don't follow it too much; I just don't think about it very often. I've managed to liberate myself, in my own way, and that's what counts.

QUESTION: Do you feel, then, that you are more in a position of exploiting the men who come to you, rather than being exploited by them?

GLADYS: Of course—that's what makes the situation so much fun and makes it doubly worthwhile. You're exploited in that you consciously lead the men to believe that you are; you seem to be terribly exploited, they can do anything. You know, you just put yourself in that situation, and all the typical things that a male wants a woman to be, you can of course be . . . depending upon his generosity [*laughs*]. So it's all cool, even though there are things that you personally don't believe in, just bullshit little things: like, I've always considered myself a really earthy person, and all of a sudden I'm putting on airs and acting much more feminine than I had ever before felt necessary or comfortable with, just to, you know, get my message across.

The whole thing is like a play: Caesar's Retreat is this amazing fantasy land . . . it's an odyssey of the mind every time you walk in the door, because you're walking into a world of absolute nonreality. Nothing is real, which is basically a good attitude to take, because if you let it in your head for one moment that it's real you'd have to say, "What the fuck am I doing here?" and you'd have to leave; and of course you can't leave because you can make two or three hundred dollars that night, what the fuck are you gonna leave for?

QUESTION: Have you known of any drug use at Caesar's?

GLADYS: It's fairly common, I'd say. Not real common, but not rare either. A lot of the younger guys come in high; they just get high and go get a massage, which can be a very groovy experience when you're high. And sometimes they bring things with them, and they turn you on: mostly grass, and a couple of times I've had some mescaline there. One guy wanted to get laid and all he had to bargain with was some mescaline, so I told him I wasn't a junkie, no deal [laughs]. But a lot of guys will give me bread for doing something, plus turn me on to whatever they have, usually grass. Sometimes I don't smoke it there, because it might be too obvious, and I don't want to get busted for it, so I'll take it home with me. Or sometimes they'll turn you on to cocaine or THC. One time I left there really flying on some THC, and I had to walk out the door with a bunch of other girls, sort of like hiding in the middle of the group, so the manager couldn't tell how high I was. I don't know how I made it home, with the taxicab driver or anything. I was really bouncing. It was really fine stuff; the guy gave me a whole bunch of it, and it lasted about a week; but after I did it that once I knew to do it in smaller amounts.

I always keep a little something around; whenever it gets to be around 12 o'clock, and my energy level starts to drain, I just go into the bathroom. I have a little aspirin box with a little spoon in it, and I keep whatever my latest snorting drug is in there. So around midnight I go in and do a little coke, or THC, or whatever I happen to have. Several of the other girls dig it, too, and we kind of all turn each other on; big cocaine parties in the bathroom [laughs]. But it's all done very coolly; because you don't want the "Gestapo Girls," the ones that are in alliance with the manager, to know what's happening. They say that females are catty and petty, and I guess I've come to experience that. I never had that many girlfriends; I never really did have like a whole group of girls that I hung around with; so I really wasn't too experienced in my dealings with that sort of thing.

QUESTION: What are some of the other girls at Caesar's like?

GLADYS: Oh, a lot of the girls around there are really nice; some girls who've been fairly successful fashion models, and done commercials, that type of thing. Most of them you really wouldn't expect to find in a massage parlor; some of them look more like they belong on a tennis court in Acapulco or something—really classy girls. Almost all of them have never done anything like this before and, after Caesar's, probably won't again. Then there's this ex-Playboy bunny from Vienna, who's in her thirties and getting a little on the chubby side; an extremely beautiful face, but she is starting to deteriorate. Still, she does all right at Caesar's; she has a very sophisticated way with the men, and a lot of them seem to dig that.

There are a lot of girls there from other countries: girls from Scotland, Germany; and one girl who claims she's Swedish, but I know she's Russian 'cause she gets on the phone with her mother and they speak Russian. I've studied Russian a little; I can't speak it well, but I know it when I hear it . . . and she tells everybody she's from Sweden. The spy in the massage parlor.

QUESTION: How does the customer go about choosing the girl he wants for his massage?

GLADYS: Well, first of all, he goes to the front desk and selects the "program" he wants; the programs, or massage sessions, vary according to the amount of time or the number of girls involved. They cost anywhere from twenty to a hundred dollars. For twenty dollars, you get a half-hour massage with one girl, and for a hundred you get a champagne bubble bath and a 90-minute massage on a huge water bed, with three girls. All of these include a sauna and a shower, of course, but no "extras"; that's all up to you and the girl.

Then, after the customer's decided which program he wants, he goes into the lounge, which is comfortably furnished with big chairs and leather couches; there's also a color television and a bar where we serve free wine and soft drinks. Some of the men are just immediately very aggressive when they walk in, and they make themselves feel at ease; others are kind of shy and unsure of what to do, so ideally the girls are supposed to create an atmosphere of congeniality; but that's not always the case, especially if a person doesn't look as if his pockets are very well padded; everyone kind of gives him the snub then because they don't want to take the chance of wasting their time if he doesn't have any money on him.

QUESTION: How do you make that snap judgment on how much money the customer has?

GLADYS: Well, you can tell a sixty-dollar suit from a two-hundred-dollar suit—or by their shoes, or just the general quality of their clothes, their taste. Then a lot of freaks, or "hippies," come in, but you just don't apply the same standards to them because, even though they're wearing old jeans, they may have a lot of money, but, with straight people, the preference is always toward the older guys. Younger guys come in and they think maybe they're a little handsome or appealing or something, and they want to get everything for nothing or pay you twenty dollars for a screw; whereas you figure an older man doesn't have the opportunity to be with a young, attractive woman that often, so you take advantage of his desires. It's much easier to manipulate an older man because they usually aren't off on such heavy ego trips.

QUESTION: Are most of the girls just sitting in the lounge when the customer comes in?

GLADYS: Yeah, the girls that aren't involved in a session at the time are usually sitting out in the lounge watching television, or behind the bar serving drinks, or passing through now and then. Some customers will just walk in and go from girl to girl like they were in the zoo, looking at animals in a cage, and pick the one with the biggest tits, or whatever; or they may narrow it down to two girls and sit there doing a comparative analysis until they make up their minds. A lot of them seem to like to play God with the situation; and sometimes they just fart around like that until somebody else picks you, and your name is called, and that's it; they missed out. That can be a drag for the girls, too, of course; there may be a prime customer, one who looks like he has quite a bit of money on him, and suddenly you're called to go with some guy that you'll be lucky to get ten dollars out of. You can't refuse to take any customer; but you don't have to do anything except give them a massage, of course, and there are ways of cheating on the time: with a really lousy customer I may lie and tell him the time he spent in the sauna was included in this massage time, and only have to spend 15 minutes with him.

QUESTION: Do the girls in the lounge try to act provocatively, to attract customers?

GLADYS: Some girls do, and some don't. The other girls don't like it if you hustle the customers too much, and neither does the management. We used to have this one girl, a little girl with very large breasts, who would sort of pull her toga to the side to expose herself even more, and she'd make eyes at the customers, and wiggle her shoulders; and people didn't like that at all, not even the customers.

Some of the girls act very snobbish and aloof, and that appeals to some men; some of the others act sort of sicky-sweet and smile a lot; and some girls don't do anything to make themselves or their personalities attractive in any way, and still get customers; so it really doesn't seem to make that much difference.

QUESTION: Just how much of a real "massage" does a customer get?

GLADYS: About 30 seconds, usually [laughs]. No, really, we give them a fairly nice massage; not what you'd get at the

"Y," but then that's not the point, is it? After you've shown them to the sauna and the showers you bring them back to the room, and then you start by giving them a facial, with hot towels, and then a hot oil rub on their back; and then you turn them over and do their front. And as you're doing the lower part of their body, in the general area of their genitals, you sort of make the motions there a little more erotic than your back massage, you know? You don't even have to do that to some of the customers; a lot of them just have a hard-on from the minute they walk into the door, and it never goes away, through the shower and all; but with some of the customers it takes them a little while to get an awareness of what's happening.

QUESTION: Have you had any customers who only wanted a straight massage?

GLADYS: Yeah, a few. I've had customers say, "Could you please not do it around there; it'll excite me too much," but these are very, very rare [laughs]. I've gone for as long as two months without having a single straight massage, unless it was through my own choice—someone who was just a hassle and hard to get along with, or someone without the right amount of money. Then there are some customers that you can just tell would have a very difficult time managing to come, and they're not worth the trouble; particularly the ones that are drunk. Them you wouldn't touch with a ten-foot pole because you know you could be there for four hours and they'd never get an erection.

Some of the customers who have some trouble getting it up will pay to stay an extra half hour and try some more; and sometimes somebody is super-stupid and doesn't get around to bringing up the idea of sex until like 25 minutes are gone, and I have 5 minutes to get something going and completed. That isn't really hard in most cases though; the sexual act usually doesn't even last 3 minutes, and that's what I like.

QUESTION: Do many of your customers tend to have premature ejaculations?

GLADYS: Oh, yeah, a lot—quite a few. A lot of them are embarrassed about it and apologize to me. Can you imagine apologizing to a prostitute for coming in 2 seconds? [*laughs*]. You feel like just saying, "Hey, that's great; you made my work that much easier." But what I actually do is sort of straighten myself up and look very somber, and say, "Oh, that's too bad; I really wanted to keep going"; and they'll give you five or ten dollars extra.

I don't like to do things like "wham-bam, thank you ma'am"; I prefer to do things sort of artistically erotic and fairly imaginative; and some people can't handle it. They just come before you think you've even got them aroused.

QUESTION: Do many of the customers seem concerned about the size of their penises?

GLADYS: Yeah, a lot of them say things like, "I bet you've seen a lot of big ones in here; how's mine?" I really feel sorry for guys with small penises; but some of them will come in there with two and a half inches, erect, and say, "Go to it, baby, get it *all*!" [*laughs*]. If they really seem concerned about it, I'll try and comfort them without lying to them; I'll say something like, "It all depends on how you use it," or "I don't really like them too big," and change the subject. Unless the guy's a really pissy, obnoxious person who's been a hassle in some way—then I may make some nasty comments and *that* sort of comment usually has a pretty immediate effect of shutting them up and getting them out of there.

QUESTION: You've said you don't have intercourse with the customers very often . . . .

GLADYS: No; if I'm in a situation where I can get a hundred dollars from a customer, I will; but anything under that, I wouldn't consider it. When they want to screw and they can't afford that, I sell them on a "deluxe" French [*laughs*]. For the regular French I just take my top down, and they can caress and kiss my breasts, but they can't touch my legs or my underpanties, or anything like that; they just have to lie there and I give them a French. But for the deluxe French I'll take off all my clothes and we can "intimately explore each other," which can include 69 if that's what they want. I insist on at least a fifty-dollar tip for that, but a lot of times I get more, often seventy or eighty dollars, for what is basically just a French.

QUESTION: When you do have intercourse with a customer, what sort of contraceptive do you use?

GLADYS: Oh, I always use Trojan "Naturalambs" [*laughs*]. After I got over my squeamish feelings about having intercourse, and made the decision that I would if I could get a hundred dollars for it, I went to a drugstore and bought some. Well, actually I had a guy buy them for me. I didn't have the guts to do that; I can't lie [*laughs*].

QUESTION: Do you worry about contracting V.D.?

GLADYS: I am afraid of V.D. of the mouth; I don't know whether that's possible, but I suppose I should go to the doctor. I'm really rather embarrassed about saying, "I'd like a V.D. test, please; would you look at my throat?" [*laughs*] I have reservations about saying that to someone, but maybe if I could find a cool doctor.... Sometimes I get panicky when I get a sore throat, and I think, "Oh, no! I'm gonna lose my vocal cords!" I'll tell you, we keep the Listerine company in business, we really do [*laughs*]; the familiar sound of gargling in the girls' lounge.

QUESTION: Have you ever made an outside appointment with any of your customers from Caesar's?

GLADYS: I've taken some business cards, but most of them I just threw away because I don't have time for these fuckers. Which is stupid; I should've made the time for them because there's a lot of bread that I could have made outside of Caesar's. But I just have so little time that's actually mine, I don't want to spend it with them; and I'm making so much money I don't feel I need to.

QUESTION: Do you have a husband or a steady boyfriend?

GLADYS: Yeah, there's a guy that I've been living with for about three years now.

QUESTION: How has your working at Caesar's affected your relationship?

GLADYS: We used to be closer before than we have been since I started doing this. I left him in Philadelphia and came to New York on my own—not breaking up with him, but just to get away for a while, and to do some things on my own. Then I got the job at Caesar's, and I started making a lot of bread, and he came up to visit me for a weekend, and we just got back together. He's got a job with a new company, as a salesman, working on a commission basis. So he's been working with that, but that hasn't been occupying much of his time, and hasn't been bringing bread in, though I'm sure it'll work out in the future; right now they're just doing a lot of legal things, policy things, getting that together.

QUESTION: How did he react to the idea of you working at Caesar's?

GLADYS: Poor thing . . . kinda strangely. 'Cause we have values and things, you know; but for seven hundred dollars a week anybody's values can be bought [laughs]. So even though he may not like me doing what I'm doing, he doesn't mind it. He misses me, and I know he must know that it isn't doing my head that much good; but he's in a situation where he really can't make any bread at the moment, so there's really nothing we can do about it. A lot of times he's told me to quit, and I say, "What, you fucker, quit for what? So we can be broke? You're crazy. I'm not gonna quit."

QUESTION: Has he ever seemed jealous of your activities with the customers?

GLADYS: Well, as a result of it our own sexual activities have been reduced drastically; because I come home at 3 o'clock in the morning, I'm tired, I want to go to sleep, and I certainly don't feel like Frenching him [laughs]. Not that I mind Frenching so much, I could get into it, but he takes such a long time; it's like a 45-minute French with him, and I'm used to doing it in . . . well, three minutes is the longest time it's ever taken me to do anybody at Caesar's. So 45 minutes, and I'm not even getting paid for it . . . [laughs]. When he first came to New York we did a lot more, because I'd missed him; we'd been separated for a month. But once the newness had worn off, I just really didn't get into it that much; so I know he's suffered [*laughs*].

QUESTION: Have your feelings about sex changed at all as a result of doing this?

GLADYS: Well, I'm definitely very open-minded about sex. I've had my horizons broadened, and I've gained some expertise and talent in certain fields [*laughs*]; but my feelings about it are really hard to define.

I no longer have any reservations about prostitution; I mean, you'll never find me out on Eighth Avenue and Forty-second Street, or anything like that . . . but "discreet relationships" with nice businessmen, I don't think I'll ever turn my nose up at. Even if I decide to go straight and just be with Bill, unless he gets to the point where he's really wealthy and I don't have to want for anything; but as long as I want something and I see a way to get it [*laughs*] . . . I'm just morally corrupt at this point, I believe.

QUESTION: How have your experiences at Caesar's affected your own sexual desires in your personal life?

GLADYS: Well, I never have the desire to go picking up a guy, and I rarely have the desire for sex at all. I really rarely do, unless there's money in it [*laughs*]. If somebody says "money," then Bingo, let's go. Of course it's not very emotionally satisfying, and most of the time it's not sexually satisfying; but that situation . . . I seem to be drawn to it [*laughs*].

QUESTION: How do you feel about having to deal sexually with people you might find physically repulsive?

GLADYS: You just *don't* deal with it, actually—not on any meaningful or conscious level. You just blank it right out of your mind. That's hard to do, sometimes. Of course the act is done with a basically unavoidable displeasure, and you'll complain to the girls; you'll say, "Oh, did you see that guy I have? Look at him in the shower . . . did you see all those big knots on his head?" [*laughs*], or "Did you see his belly?" or "Did you see all those little warts around his prick?" So you complain about it, superficially, to the other girls, but you just overlook it yourself; you just take a deep breath, concentrate on something else, and . . . it's all over, he's gone.

To tell you the truth, though, I hate handsome guys, or guys who *think* they're handsome, even more. Their egos can be more disgusting than any physical abnormality I've ever run across.

QUESTION: Have you ever been arrested for prostitution?

GLADYS: Yeah, I was arrested once last October—not for prostitution directly, not for "soliciting"; I was charged with "loitering for the purposes of prostitution." This was part of a large bust at Caesar's; they arrested the manager and thirteen of the girls.

QUESTION: Had any of you thought or discussed in advance that a raid like this might happen, and what you might do if it did?

GLADYS: Yes, of course; that's a running topic of conversation around massage parlors all the time, and for the two weeks beforehand there had been a tremendous amount of publicity about massage parlors and about Caesar's in particular, so it was obvious that the heat was on, so to speak. We'd been more or less expecting it to happen, though of course we hoped it wouldn't, and we sort of felt that maybe Caesar's was too big, too "influential" to get busted. Several of the sleazier Eighth Avenue joints had been busted, but we thought we might escape the crackdown. The New York *Post* had done a story saying that one of our girls, Joan, had propositioned their reporter for a topless hand-job at twenty-five dollars, so that freaked us out a bit and got us all pissed at Joan; but then the New York *Times* did a story on Caesar's that sounded like a fucking p.r. release for the place and made us sound sexy but legit; so then we relaxed again, somewhat.

In the middle of all this the people who owned the place called a meeting of all the girls, or rapped to some of us individually, and told us to be extra careful about solicitation, especially with new customers. They also told us there was nothing to worry about, anyway, since if we *were* busted they'd provide us with a lawyer, they'd see to it that we weren't fingerprinted or given a permanent police record, that we'd only be held for an hour or so, and that they would pay all our expenses and fines. About 40 percent of that turned out to be true.

None of us wanted to quit at that point because, in spite of the increased danger, all the publicity had given us a fantastic amount of new business. Lots of guys who hadn't known much about massage parlors, or who hadn't really been sure that any sex was available in them, started coming in droves. We were all extra careful, of course, but we were making a hell of a lot of money at this time—up to three or four hundred a day or more.

QUESTION: How did the bust actually come about?

GLADYS: Well, there were three plainclothes cops who came into the place one at a time early that evening; they'd go to the desk and look at the list of available programs, or walk in and look around the lounge, and then walk out as if they'd changed their minds about getting a massage. Later that night, they all gradually came back in and signed up for programs. There was one guy in particular, the cop who ended up making the actual bust, who really stood out. He had on some strange plaid pants that looked like they came from the mod department of Korvette's, some Thom McAn shoes with white socks, a cheap trench coat, and a funny little 1950's hat with a feather sticking out of the band. He looked like a lousy customer to get stuck with, if nothing else.

I wasn't busy when it happened; I was in the lounge, standing at the bar and checking out the customers. I remember saying to Ina, one of the Scandinavian girls who worked there, 'that there sure are an awful lot of creeps in here tonight. No shit. Something was obviously a little odd, but I wasn't sure exactly what.

The cop with the feather in his hat had a little discussion with the manager about which girl he should ask for and finally picked Sundae, a very soft-spoken blond girl from down South. Now, I wasn't there, of course, but according to what she told me later, she took him back to the room and told him to undress and put his things away, like we always did; then when she went back to take him to the sauna, he was standing there in a towel, with his shorts on underneath, and he immediately flashed a badge and told her she was under arrest. This was before *anything* had happened between them at all, before she'd even started to give him a back rub. I know damn well she didn't just proposition him the minute he walked in the door; Sundae wouldn't have solicited the guy anyway, she knew better than that. So I definitely believe her story that it was just a purely unwarranted bust. Not even entrapment, just a totally illegal arrest with no basis whatsoever.

QUESTION: The policeman never undressed himself entirely?

GLADYS: No, he kept his shorts on and never even let the session get started. Then, as soon as he'd told Sundae she was under arrest and to keep quiet, he came bursting out into the lounge area, pulling up his pants. His shirt was unbuttoned and his hair was sticking out all over the place, and he yelled, "Nobody move, this is an arrest!" Then he pulled a gun on Ramos, the manager, searched him, told Ramos not to touch any alarms or any of the money at the desk, and called the station house to send more officers and a paddy wagon.

QUESTION: Did you actually see all of this, including the policeman pulling the gun?

GLADYS: Yes, I had a clear view of all this from the lounge. The rest of the girls were herded into the lounge, and another cop came in with a gun to guard us. All of a sudden there were cops, in and out of uniform, all over the place [*laughs*]. Well, by "out of uniform" I mean in plainclothes; they were all apparently scared to get naked, at any point.

QUESTION: Were any of the customers searched, asked to produce identification, or arrested?

GLADYS: None of them were arrested; they were all allowed to leave, and the police let some of them get their money back. The cops asked one guy, who looked pretty young, to show his driver's license; but that was all. The customers weren't hassled at all. Meanwhile, the cops are all laughing and joking, pointing at the girls and making comments about us.

After a while they let us go back and get dressed, a few at a time, while they waited outside the dressing room door. We're all confused and panicky, and while we're in the dressing room we're all madly trying to get rid of any nonprescription drugs, or even liquor, that we might have around. I had some brandy in a Listerine bottle, but I decided I needed it too much at that point to pour it down the drain; so I carried it to jail with me, and while we were in the "bullpen" at the Seventeenth Precinct, waiting for the arrest records to be filled out, I was sitting there sipping cognac [*laughs*].

QUESTION: Were there any reporters or photographers on the street when they took you outside to the paddy wagon?

GLADYS: No; we'd all been afraid of that 'cause that's not the best way to become a TV star; but there weren't any around, fortunately. While we were at the Seventeenth Precinct, though, the arresting officer called the New York *Post* and told them about the bust; I heard him say, "Ahhh . . . the girl propositioned me for a B.J. You know what I mean, a 'B.J.'" He couldn't bring himself to say "blow job." After that was taken care of, we were led out of our cage, one by one, to fill out our arrest sheets.

QUESTION: Did you give them your real name and address?

GLADYS: No, I didn't want my real name in the papers, so I gave them a fake name; but by the time we got to court, they'd found it out and had my real name on the court records.

QUESTION: How did they determine your real name?

GLADYS: I'd been fingerprinted once for that federal job I held and they compared the records.

QUESTION: You were fingerprinted at the police station?

GLADYS: Yeah, we all were—fingerprinted and photographed. I don't believe they're supposed to do that on a misdemeanor charge like loitering, but they did it anyway.

QUESTION: How were you treated at the police station?

GLADYS: We were treated as objects of contempt and ridicule; there was a steady stream of guys coming in, just milling around and checking us out. Every cop in that precinct seemed to be hanging around the station that night, and most of them were making obscene comments to us or about us, picking out the ones they liked, pointing at us and saying, "I'd like to put it to that one," and so forth.

Then, around five A.M., they took us down to the Fourteenth Precinct, where we were searched, and I do mean *searched.* "Take off your wigs, pull down your pants, bend over . . . " This was done by some policewomen. If anything, they were nastier than the male cops, but I think they enjoyed their jobs.

All during the rest of that day we kept getting shuffled around from one cell to another, one jail to another; we finally ended up at the Tombs, but once we were there we were moved around four or five more times. I think they were afraid we might get some rest or something if they didn't keep us busy. This went on from one A.M., when we were first arrested, until nine thirty the next night, when we eventually got to court. They didn't give us anything to eat until two P.M., when we got a breakfast of stale bologna sandwiches.

All this time we had no idea what was going on, when we would go to court—nothing. Some of the girls started to freak out after a while because it was getting pretty Kafkaesque; but the rest of us would always manage to talk them down again. We kept ourselves amused by playing little games—like at one point we made up a club, "The Pussy-Pushers of America," and held joke elections for president and treasurer and so on. That kept us laughing for a while and helped us to forget our situation a little.

We were lucky that we'd all been arrested at once because we were kept together most of the time; if we'd been alone I'm sure there would have been some trouble, some violent trouble, with a few of the other girls in the large cells they stuck us in. There were some very tough street hookers in there, some really heavy chicks who weren't too pleased with us fancy little "masseuses" from Caesar's Retreat. The place was really filthy, very cold and very dirty, and we were constantly subjected to verbal abuse by the other girls who were in the cells and by the male and female police officers. At one point, while we were being booked, I started to get a drink from a water fountain, and some beefy cop yelled, "Hey, that fountain's not for prisoners. You want us to get some kind of a disease?" A lot of the girls got very scared by some of the shit that went on.

QUESTION: What happened when you finally got to court?

GLADYS: Well, like I said, we weren't taken to court until nine thirty the next night; then we were all led out together, and that's when we saw our lawyer for the first time. He came around to each of us and said, "Plead guilty," which really freaked us out because the management at Caesar's had told us to plead "not guilty" if we were ever busted. It was very confusing, and I was totally unnerved and exhausted by this time; but we went ahead and pleaded guilty, like the lawyer said. We were all lined up in front of the judge together, and the courtroom was packed; I guess we were the main attraction that night.

Most of us, including me, were released and told that the charges would be dropped in six months if we weren't arrested again during that time; but Sundae had to return to court at a later date. She was the only one who was hit with a direct prostitution charge. She, the manager, and another girl who'd had a couple of previous arrests were released on bail and told to return to court the following week.

QUESTION: Who paid their bail?

GLADYS: The attorney for Caesar's.

QUESTION: What happened when they went back to court?

GLADYS: They were all fined; Sundae got a $250 fine, which I believe was also paid by Caesar's.

QUESTION: But the charges against you were completely dropped?

GLADYS: On the condition that I keep my record clean for six months, yes. I don't know if that means they'll also destroy the fingerprints and mug shots, though.

The whole thing was a very funny feeling for me; I'd spent a good deal of time in and around courtrooms before, involved in SDS and Black Student Union and other kinds of protest things, and also doing research for classes or for my previous jobs; but I'd never been arrested, never appeared in court as a defendant. It was an enlightening experience [*laughs*].

QUESTION: Does anyone in your family know about what you've been doing?

GLADYS: No, of course not. They would be heartbroken, even the more liberal members of my family; but I don't think they'll find out. If they do find out about it . . . it's just reality, they'll just have to live with it. I mean, they've done some things in their lives that I wasn't too proud of, but there's nothing I could say about it; a person is a person, and he or she has a right to live his own life however he chooses. *I* don't feel like I've done anything wrong, and that's what really counts.

QUESTION: Do any of your former friends know about your job at Caesar's?

GLADYS: No, and that's been one of the biggest hassles in my mind: I've had to live a lie, just because of other people's limited attitudes, and I've never done that before. Whatever I was, I always flaunted it. There was a period when I considered myself a libertine, and I flaunted that. I fucked whoever I wanted to fuck and didn't care who knew about it. That was just the kind of person I was—if you dig me, you dig me; if you don't, it's cool. Among my friends I was always extremely open about everything, about things I felt, things I did—everything. If I felt like crying, I'd cry; if I felt like fucking, I'd fuck. I was just very open about myself. But I know that this is something different, that it's just too much for my friends to understand. There are some people here in New York from my hometown, from my school, and I've had to lie to them about what kind of job I had, and hide things, important and often meaningful things, from them. That's what has hurt me the most.

2. Angela

ANGELA is exceptionally pretty and well-spoken, a reserved but lively young woman of twenty-two with a slender body and long, soft, auburn hair. Her manner is deceptively demure, and she is exceedingly polite. She seems to be the prototypical "girl next door," hipper and more intelligent than the usual interpretation of that image, but decidedly clean, neat, and middle-class American. Her personality and appearance are those of the supposedly ideal niece or young housewife, and it is easy to imagine her amiably chatting with husband and friends over a perfectly prepared candlelight dinner in some spotless but comfortably homey alcove. Some of the things she had to say seemed absurdly incongruous coming from her lips, and I could not escape the sensation that she was a slightly shy young mother auditioning for a little theater role in which she would be hopelessly miscast. Angela could be the archetypal "nice girl gone wrong" but for the unusually high level of insightful and realistic self-analysis which she brings to her situation.

Angela's account of her entry into the massage parlor world is an excellent illustration of the gradual defusing of prostitution as a serious moral issue in our times. An easy familiarity with sex is the universal birthright of this generation; and when these young women are confronted with a need or desire for extra income, prostitution seems to be increasingly seen as a logical part-time or temporary occupation.

It must be apparent by now that this is a recurrent theme: the application of pure rationality and calculated decision making to a subject which has traditionally been smothered in hysterical, often nonsensical, emotion. Sex is the only human activity which may be performed with relative impunity if done for simple pleasure or when the payment is indirect (dinners, houses, cars, etc.), but it is suddenly classified as "criminal" when the profit motive is honestly stated. Angela and her peers have an inherent understanding of the sheer hypocrisy of this position, an understanding that is reflected and expanded in the calmly casual approach to sex in their private lives, but let her tell you about it. . . .

* * *

QUESTION: Let's start off with your childhood. What was your father's occupation?

ANGELA: He was, and still is, a criminal defense attorney in Cleveland. More in the William Kunstler mold than F. Lee Bailey; he was slightly radical for his time, and he liked to take on cases that involved some issue like civil rights or freedom of the press, whether the client could pay full fees or not; he also gave a lot of his time to the ACLU and the OCLU [Ohio Civil Liberties Union]. Because of that, we never really got rich or anything; we always had enough money around, but not as much as we might have if he'd run after big lawsuits or whatever.

QUESTION: Was your family very religious?

ANGELA: In a way, yeah; my father was a deacon of the neighborhood Episcopal church, and my mother was always heading charity fund drives and things like that. But they were pretty open, liberal-minded people; my parents were more concerned with raising Cleveland's consciousness than with hammering a lot of dogma into my head. We went to church every Sunday, but the sermons there were always pretty low-key, and my parents never handed me any morality and sin stuff. They were more concerned with broader social issues, and they just assumed that individuals were generally capable of managing their own personal affairs.

QUESTION: What sort of sex education did you receive?

ANGELA: Very little, in the formal sense; most of my information about sex, and a lot of misinformation, I got through books or conversations with friends. There was no sex education in school, or none to speak of; and although my parents weren't wildly moralistic on the subject, they weren't terribly open or relaxed about it, either. Sex just wasn't mentioned much, one way or the other, in my house. Not that it was some ultra-taboo subject; it just seldom came up, and when it did it was usually in a very reserved, abstracted sort of way. My father would occasionally crack some mild *double entendre*, but for the most part their attitude toward sex was rather humorless and slightly nervous. Repressed, but in a very "civilized" kind of way, you know.

One weird thing, though; there was always a heavy undercurrent of unspoken, and even unrecognized incestuous feeling in my family. I had one brother, three years older than me, and there was a lot of physical contact among all the members of my family—rubbing each other's backs, hugging a lot, combing and brushing each other's hair, that kind of thing. It never developed into anything remotely explicit, and I never even thought about it in that way until I'd been away from home for a year or so, when I was about nineteen. Then my brother confessed to me that when I was twelve and he was fifteen he'd actually had an ejaculation during one of those innocent little back-rubbing sessions on the floor in front of the TV. See, I started my "masseuse" career early, but my brother never gave me a dime for it, the cheapskate [*laughs*].

QUESTION: Did you have any strict curfews or other "dating rules" as an adolescent?

ANGELA: No; if anything, my parents were a little too lenient and never even helped me make necessary decisions about dating or sex, things that I would have appreciated getting some honest advice or reasonable guidelines about now and then. They were always too trusting, too giving. Like I said, they weren't super-religious, but I think they did kind of go overboard on the "other cheek" syndrome, and their general faith in human nature. My father was a very committed neo-Rousseauvian, both in his work and at home; all the violence and brutality in the world was supposed to be caused by the problems of the society or by people who weren't able to recognize the natural nobility of the "savages." They taught me to assume that you can trust just about anyone you meet, that it's up to you to make friendly overtures, and everything will work out fine. They just didn't teach me to be very discerning about people. When I grew up and started spending more time away from home, I ran into lots of situations where it was *impossible* to trust the people involved; and my first reaction to that was to become overly cynical, even half-paranoid. I'm just now learning to balance out those extremes and hit some middle ground of . . . selfish humanitarianism, I guess.

So in terms of dating, their policy was more or less "Let's just see what happens if we don't say much of anything"; and what happened was, I'd always introduce my boyfriends to my family, and I'd always come in at a decent hour, and I got pregnant in my senior year of high school. I mean, they told me to make friendly overtures, right? [*laughs*].

QUESTION: How old were you when you got pregnant?

ANGELA: About a month before my seventeenth birthday. It was a ridiculous thing to happen; but somehow the idea of going in the drugstore and buying a contraceptive was too much for me and my natural guilt feelings to handle. The whole idea of planning it in advance, of admitting to myself that next Saturday night I would have sexual intercourse, *again*; it's very difficult to think in those terms when you're sixteen.

QUESTION: What was the outcome of your pregnancy?

ANGELA: An illegal abortion. My parents accepted the whole thing very well; they even felt kind of good about it in a strange way, since they could be responsible for me again, like I was eight years old with a bruised knee.

The abortion itself was a bummer, of course. I'm not into any big motherhood thing, but I suddenly had all these hormones making me weepy and telling me to start buying diapers. Then I had to go through a whole surgery trip, since I'd gotten past the three-month limit for a simple D & C, and aside from all the pains and infections and everything, I was just generally very down for quite a while. I don't have any objections to the idea of abortion, I don't think it's like murder or anything; but it does kind of play hell with the biological influences on your mind, especially when it's done that late into a pregnancy.

QUESTION: Did you have to leave school for the abortion?

ANGELA: No, it happened in the first part of the summer, just after I'd graduated. I had a couple of months to rest up, and then I left for college.

QUESTION: Where did you go?

ANGELA: Antioch—I was a psych major. Antioch's a kind of freaky school and it put me through a lot of changes. I got into drugs there, mainly grass and hash and mescaline, and I stopped wearing my bra, and I slept with four or five people, and I got briefly but firmly politicized, and I discovered Blake and Goethe and Proust and Baudelaire, and I ran a lot of rats through a lot of mazes, and I worked backstage at the theater . . . just the regular college trip, you know.

QUESTION: Did you graduate?

ANGELA: No, I still have about twenty hours to go; I'm taking a couple of courses at NYU this spring. I fell madly in love with this guy named Blair during my junior year at Antioch; he was in the art school, doing a photography number. He talked me into modeling for him, and then we moved in together, and then right after he graduated we moved to New York and got married.

QUESTION: What was your marriage like?

ANGELA: Excellent; we're very much in love with each other. There were a few outside difficulties at first, of course, mainly involved with Blair's having to do enough crappy commercial photography to keep us going; and neither of us really wants to live in New York, although we know it's necessary for a while. So there were some financial tensions, and at the same time a lot of the gauzily romantic feelings started to dissipate, which is natural.

By the end of our first year together it was obvious that we both wanted to stay married but that we were also interested in some kind of sexual variety.

Of course, coming to that decision is one thing, and then finding the experiences for yourself is another. At first we decided to see how it would go with people who were just friends of ours, couples that we had known previous to this; which didn't work out, unfortunately, because they weren't quite ready to involve themselves in something that open.

Then we finally got courageous enough, or stupid enough, to contact some people through the mail; we came across a swinger's magazine and found one ad out of about two thousand that looked all right. We answered the ad, and it worked out very well; but since then we've found out that that isn't usually the case—going through those ads can be a very unpleasant experience, or even dangerous. We were just lucky.

These people were a little bit older than we had expected, both in their early thirties; but it was actually nice, as a first time, to be with some people who were slightly older, and who had some experience with this. They knew that this was our first time and that we would be a little uncomfortable, so we had a lobster dinner with them and just spent the afternoon talking. Then they asked over some other, younger, couples that they knew, and we felt happy with everyone who was there; everyone was getting along very well, and there were no feelings of jealousy or uptightness. It was a nice apartment, with plenty of good music and grass and wine; everybody eventually got undressed, and it all happened very smoothly. I was surprised to find that I *enjoyed* having sex in front of other people; it was really stimulating. It was also exciting to see my husband involved with somebody else in front of me; the whole thing was kind of like a game, and it brought out feelings in me that I hadn't felt before, and other feelings that I hadn't had for a long time: sort of like first-date flirtation thrills, only more strongly sexual, and without any kind of commitment hang-ups. Definitely a turn-on.

QUESTION: Did you go on to meet and have sex with other couples after that first experience?

ANGELA: No [*laughs*], we liked it so much we quit and never did it again. I'm sorry, but that really was kind of a silly question.

QUESTION: All right . . . what are some of the other situations you've been into since that first party?

ANGELA: Well, we went to two or three more parties at Paul and Karen's, and then we got curious about what kind of people we might meet someplace else; so first we tried going to a couple of the established clubs here in the city, where couples congregate on a certain night every week. That was a *real* drag, just like the East Side singles bars, only worse. Very, very straight, very, very pushy scene. We only went like twice and never found anybody we liked.

At one of these clubs, though, we saw a brochure for this whole weekend thing, where an entire resort hotel in upstate New York was being rented out just for "swingers." Now, regardless of who we might or might not meet, we figured that was just too fascinating a scene to miss seeing; even if everybody there was ugly and totally obnoxious, it was bound to be an interesting and unusual experience, right?

QUESTION: I can't argue with that. Where did you say this hotel was?

ANGELA: In the Catskills someplace. Anyway, we went, and there were about six hundred people there, all ages and all types. It was just amazing to watch how all these people related to each other, all in the context of this massive group-sex situation; there were some really classic scenes going on up there, fantastically entertaining. Six hundred horny people roaming around this big resort, all trying to get nonchalant at first while they check out each other's wives and husbands. Then one night there was a costume party in the nightclub, with a couple of dozen Caesars and Cleopatras; the winners were a couple dressed up like thermometers, and when they introduced themselves for the judging on stage they said "I'm oral," "I'm rectal." By that time everybody was popping amys and stripping off by the pool, and on Saturday there was a "contest" where all the men were given a bunch of Monopoly money, and the women competed to see who could collect the biggest bankroll by the end of the day. I find that one particularly interesting [laughs]. Anyway, believe it or not, we did manage to meet a few nice, attractive young people, and when we got back to the city we started to go to various parties that they and their friends were having. We've gone to two or three in the Village where this guy has completely renovated a whole brownstone, with a heated swimming pool, saunas, a fireplace, and a huge bar; it's been very nice, very comfortable, with some good people around.

QUESTION: How much homosexuality, male or female, is involved in swinging as you've seen it?

ANGELA: A fair amount, generally among the women; that seems to be something that most people can accept a little more easily than male homosexuality. Women have a lot of physical contact with each other just in "normal" behavior, kissing when they meet and so on, so seeing two girls making it at a party is just not that strange. Two guys together is a different matter, even to people who are into open scenes; but I don't think it should be, and I think that'll change eventually.

I think it's been pretty well established that everybody's bisexual to some extent or another; I mean, it's all flesh, and it's all warm, right? You don't have to have some sort of compulsion toward homosexuality just to know that you might conceivably enjoy it; I've never had any strong homosexual leanings at all. When I was a child, of course, I had the usual mild encounters with friends, and I was aware of it; but it was never anything that I felt really drawn to. I've always been a very heterosexually oriented person.

But getting into a bisexual thing was no great shock to me; it just happened, and I suppose if I'd thought about it I could have at least half-expected it. There was just this one party where I suddenly found myself in a three-way situation with me and another couple, and I started getting involved with the girl as well as the guy. It was a very natural thing to do, and we both enjoyed it, even though neither of us had done anything like that before. Since then, I've gotten into "lesbian" things at a number of parties and also in other situations. It's a minor part of myself, but it is something that I want to continue to enjoy.

QUESTION: How did you get involved with the massage parlors?

ANGELA: Well, like I told you, during the first year that we were living in New York we were having some mild financial difficulties; nothing serious, we were far from starving. But this is a very expensive city, and a little extra money never hurts. Then at one point we were planning a weekend trip to Montreal, and there just wasn't as much money in the bank as we'd thought, so we had to cancel it, which was a big disappointment; we really needed to get away for a few days.

We occasionally picked up a copy of *Screw*, and I noticed all the massage parlor ads, and it occurred to me that it might not be such a bad idea if I just did that for a week, made the money for the trip, and then forgot about it. So I went over to one of the places that seemed to be fairly nice, a place called Elizabethan Studios, and I applied for a job.

QUESTION: Were you aware in advance that any sexual activity was expected at this place?

ANGELA: After finding it through an ad in *Screw*? Of course, I knew exactly what was going on, but the idea of having sex with strangers was nothing odd to me, after being into swinging; and that also eased my husband's reaction to it. We'd both already seen each other making it with fifteen or twenty other people, so the idea of me being employed for that purpose wasn't anything he couldn't deal with. I think it even turned him on a little. So I applied for the job and started working right away.

QUESTION: What happened when you went to apply for the job?

ANGELA: I was given a general sort of interview; they wanted to know what kind of experience I had had [*laughs*], whether I knew what was going on there, and whether I would be able to deal with it successfully. I told them that I would be, and everything was set.

Once I'd been hired, the manager took me back to show me the session rooms and so forth, and then we went into one room where he had me undress so he could take a couple of Polaroid pictures. From what I understand, this isn't usually the case at most massage parlors, but at Elizabethan the customer selects the girl out of a photo album with nude or seminude pictures of all the girls available. That also lets him see all of the girls who work there, so if one that he might like is off that day, he still knows she's there, and maybe he'll come back later.

Having the picture made was sort of strange; I wasn't really too interested in having any photographs of me made in connection with this kind of thing, but it was just a Polaroid, and what with my husband's business and all the parties we've been to, it wasn't as if I'd never been photographed naked before. There was nothing to connect the picture with a massage parlor, so they could hardly blackmail me with one

QUESTION: What was the work routine at Elizabethan?

ANGELA: There *wasn't* a hell of a lot of work, in any sense; I was sent in with one other girl for a "training" session, to find out what to do with the massage oils and so on; and she told me about the regular procedure. The place really *was* Victorian—you were only allowed to give hand jobs, and that was strictly it. Masturbation city. It was a topless massage, we just took off our blouses or lowered our tops; we couldn't remove any more of our clothes and the customer wasn't supposed to touch us anywhere except our backs. There was also a precise limit to the definition of the word "back." We weren't even supposed to negotiate prices; the hand job was automatically included in what the man had paid out front, and we were expected to just go ahead and do it to him, and then hope for the best when it came tip time.

QUESTION: What did you do if someone expressed interest in something beyond a hand job?

ANGELA: That depended on the girl; most of them were afraid of being fired, and the management was very uptight about any other activities going on. They figured that they couldn't get busted on prostitution charges if that's all that was happening, and maybe they were right; that would make an interesting test case, to see if masturbation is officially considered prostitution. Most of the girls stuck to the rules; but there was no way that I was just going to wait and see what somebody would give me, particularly since I was only going to be there for a week. So I'd always negotiate a little, nothing blatant, but just kind of tease them and give them the idea that they'd get a much better hand job if they met my price, which was usually twenty or twenty-five dollars. You'd generally get ten dollars or less if you didn't say anything.

QUESTION: So the amount of money you could make must have been fairly limited?

ANGELA: Yes, of course; I still made more money than I would have at any straight job, enough to more than pay for our weekend in Canada, but it wasn't any incredible amount. I figured I could make a lot more at some other place, and I'd found out that it just wasn't that difficult or disgusting a thing to do; so I talked to my husband and told him that I didn't see any reason why I shouldn't continue to do this in another massage parlor where I could make even more money. He finally agreed, because after my having worked at Elizabethan for a week he could see that it was no more than a job to me; there were no worries that he could have, no real jealousies; and an awful lot of very useful money could be made in a short time.

QUESTION: How long did you work at Elizabethan?

ANGELA: About ten days, like I'd originally planned; then I went to another place called Mademoiselle's, that I had heard about through a friend at Elizabethan. Again, it was very simple: I walked in and applied for the job—and was working the next day.

QUESTION: How do the rules and customs at Mademoiselle's differ from those at Elizabethan?

ANGELA: At Mademoiselle's we're allowed to do anything that we want to in the massage session; the management just doesn't give any orders or ask any questions, which is nice. You can get a hand job for about twenty dollars, thirty or thirty-five for a blow job, and fifty or sixty dollars for a screw.

QUESTION: What is the process of selection like; were you also photographed at Mademoiselle's?

ANGELA: No—the customer just walks in and makes his choice from the girls there, sitting around on the couches in the lounge.

QUESTION: How are you dressed?

ANGELA: We can dress any way we want to; most of us usually wear something kind of brief because we want to be both comfortable and attractive. Some of the girls wear long dresses, but the most common thing is some sort of bodysuit, or leotardlike thing, with stockings. Everybody looks different, which is nice; at some massage parlors I've heard about, they have to wear uniforms or costumes, so everybody looks pretty much the same. I wouldn't like that, and I don't imagine most of the customers would either. It just seems to make more sense for there to be some variety and individuality. And it's very nice as far as we're concerned, because a girl with nice legs, say, can wear a leotard or a miniskirt, while a girl who has thin legs but really nice breasts can wear a long, low-cut dress.

QUESTION: What happens in the average massage session at Mademoiselle's?

ANGELA: Well, after the man has selected one of the girls, we take him back to the room and have him undress; then we take off all our clothes. That's the only sort of rule about what you have to do or not do there: whether the customer tips you or not, he does get a totally nude massage, but no sex is included unless he pays extra for it. That's another element to be considered in deciding what to wear there: how quickly and easily you can get your clothes off and on again, sometimes a dozen times a night. I wore a pair of very tight purple hot pants one night, and I must've wasted an hour in all just tugging back and forth at the damn zipper.

So I get the customer all settled, and then I strip down; sometimes in a perfunctory kind of way, and sometimes in a slower, more teasing kind of way, depending on how much money I figure the guy has. Then I pour a little oil on his body, and while I'm massaging him, I start in with a very friendly, but noncommital, sort of rap: what he does, where he's from, that kind of thing. After a few minutes of that, I just ask him, "What kind of massage did you have in mind?" They know what they're coming in there for, and they're usually very open about what they want, so you negotiate for a price, and then you just do the number, whatever's been decided on.

QUESTION: How do you get along with the other girls at Mademoiselle's?

ANGELA: Initially, I didn't communicate with them very well; there are two shifts of girls, and the night girls, for whatever reasons, are generally a little better-looking and a little hipper than those who work during the day, so encountering the day girls in particular was not always too pleasant. There were some immediate jealousies and ill feelings involved there when we'd run into each other at six o'clock, and even the other night girls were a little slow to make friends. After a while, though, they get used to the fact that you're going to be around, and if someone is more attractive than you are, you simply have to accept that and deal with it. *Everyone* is making more bread than they would at a straight job, so all in all it doesn't really matter. If you do get a lot of sessions, or if a lot of people sign up for an hour with you, that's just that much less time that you'll be out front as "competition" for the other customers who are coming in. If I do have more customers than average, or if I get more money from the customers I have, I don't try to make that obvious or brag about it. If anything, in recounting my customer experiences to the other girls, I'll bring up negative ones: you know, I come out and say, "Wow, I just had this really obnoxious guy," or "That last guy stiffed me, the prick"; and in that way, things gradually get a little more comfortable.

QUESTION: What was your first reaction to working at Mademoiselle's, now that you were involved in full-scale prostitution rather than just massage and masturbation?

ANGELA: It was weird, of course; I hadn't had any experience like this before, and no associations with it. A few of the other girls have; they come from environments where this doesn't really sound so strange to them, and they may have had friends who were involved in this sort of thing. But I really didn't think that much about what I was doing; I looked on it as a job from the start, and as far as the sexual contact I was having, it was simply an even exchange for the money I wanted to make. I do make a *lot* of money, and in order to have that sort of income you'd expect to do something that might not be your first choice of activity.

QUESTION: You didn't have any heavy emotional reaction or feelings of moral guilt?

ANGELA: No; in the first place, I think prostitution is a basically good thing, and I think it should be both legalized and also seen in a more rational, less hypocritical way. Nobody's being hurt particularly in this form of prostitution; both the customer and I get exactly what we want from the situation, and everybody goes away happy or content. There are a lot of frustrated individuals around who really need something like this, and with a lot of people I'm very happy to see that I can have a positive effect on them.

QUESTION: Do many of the girls at Mademoiselle's fit the typical "street hooker" stereotype?

ANGELA: God, no; even though some of them have had experience in the street. There's quite a range of girls. A few of them are from kind of depressing backgrounds, and they've really *had* to do this for some length of time; to them, working in a massage parlor is just a cleaner way of doing their job. So you do have that type; but you also have girls who are well educated, pretty, very normal middle-class. I've met several girls who have BA's or MA's, very knowledgeable people, who have traveled a lot and have had well-rounded, healthy home lives. They're doing this simply because it's a very logical way to make money, and the old social stigmas about prostitution just don't apply any more than the idea of being faithfully monogamous and having as many children as possible. I guess at first I thought of myself as some kind of unusual "freethinker" to have done this, because I was really surprised myself at the number of other "nice," intelligent girls getting into it. It's just easy money, that's all.

QUESTION: How much money do you make?

ANGELA: At Mademoiselle's, I average around a thousand a week—tax-free, of course, but don't tell anybody [*laughs*].

QUESTION: Do you ever enjoy yourself sexually at the massage parlor?

ANGELA: Yeah, I have enjoyed myself sometimes, certainly not all the time: for the most part, it's a rather grueling experience sexually. But there are times when I've gotten into it, and I've even discovered a lot about myself sexually through those experiences. I was never frigid, but I have had occasional difficulties in feeling really free sexually; and in this situation, where you're not having to commit yourself to it on a personal basis, or really impress anybody that you care about, it can get to be a very loose, pure gut-level sex trip. That's a lot rarer than you might think, even in group-sex scenes.

I sometimes get into the fantasy aspects of the situation, a "Belle de Jour" kind of thing; that's a universal female fantasy, usually well-hidden. Every woman secretly wants to be a prostitute at some time in her life, and it can be extremely stimulating when you periodically realize that you're actually living out one of those masturbatory "biggies," in a reasonably safe way and without being committed to it for any length of time. So I use ideas like that now and then when I do want to become aroused; after you've spent six hours dealing with some people who've caused you a lot of aggravation, then if someone comes in who's a bit younger, and is nice, and you think you might be able to have at least something of a pleasant time, you can use those fantasies for the purpose of enjoying yourself, and it often works.

Some of the pleasure that I've gotten through doing this came as a complete surprise to me, though; I started having orgasms with paunchy, very nondescript middle-aged men. This just floored me when it first started happening because they'd be people that I would *never* have considered going to bed with, or even looking at, in my personal life. But when I go to work, I become an entirely different person, with some drastically different reaction patterns; it's a kind of controlled schizophrenia, which helps you to abstract yourself the necessary amount in order to deal with the job. And separating yourself from the situation in that way, sometimes you can begin to appreciate, in a generalized and sort of diffused way, the things that a customer may do to try and get you aroused, in spite of how he might look or act otherwise.

QUESTION: Do most of the customers make an attempt to get you aroused?

ANGELA: Most of them want to, because they may feel a little odd about having a sexual experience with someone who isn't at all interested in what's going on; and if you just come on with a heavy-breathing act right away, they usually know you're faking it, and it may be difficult for them to get excited. They don't want to feel like you're anxious to get through with them and get them out, no matter how true that may be, so they almost always ask if they can "give you some satisfaction." I usually just politely decline because I'm seldom interested in the people and a lot of the time I can hardly bear to have them touch me; but there are some men who are sort of middle-range, and even though you might not specifically want them to be touching you, you don't mind, and if it helps them to have their orgasm sooner that just makes it easier for me. So sometimes I'll be performing a hand-job or a blow-job on somebody, and they'll be playing around with me at the same time, and without my even realizing it, I find myself getting aroused.

It's kind of a paradoxical situation in certain ways. In spite of my conscious desire for sexual freedom and openness, I do still retain some guilt feelings—from my background, in particular, and from the whole cultural framework that we've all been raised in. So in a lot of the sex I have in my personal life, I find myself subconsciously trying to ignore what I'm feeling or even trying to turn myself off because of those guilt feelings that keep insisting that I "shouldn't" get excited. But in working at a massage parlor, a lot of those mechanisms are shut off, simply because I don't feel that I have to put them to use. It isn't as though I was attracted to someone, a date or whoever, and could feel some sort of basic responsibility for my sexual excitement with them. That's the source of most female guilt, I think, that sensation that you've expected and planned to feel all these "dirty" things in your mind and body, out of some preexisting desire. Same reason I couldn't bring myself to buy contraceptives as a kid. But instead, when I'm dealing with a customer, I work from the prior assumption that I *won't* get turned on by them, that there's nothing I have to fight against; and once I've set that aside, then I'm able to get turned on before I even really know what's happening. I don't need to make an effort to relax and accept what I'm feeling; I'm simply at work, doing my job, and I can just let the occasional orgasms catch me by surprise.

QUESTION: Then you're saying that, contrary to traditional assumptions, a prostitute's general detachment from sexual involvement with a customer may, in some circumstances, not only not "deaden" her potential response, but even increase its frequency or potency—not in spite of her detachment, but as a direct result of it. Is that right?

ANGELA: Yes— being detached like that lets you get into a pure sex trip, with no commitment whatsoever, not even the commitment to try for a good orgasm for yourself or to show the man you're with that you even like him. It's based on irresponsibility in a good sense of the word.

That's not to say that I'm against commitment or sexual pleasure along with emotional involvement, not at all. That's obviously the epitome of the sexual experience, but there's just no way for it to be a very common occurrence. A lot of people just seem to assume that *every* sex act has to be founded on, and surrounded by, this whole complicated structure of love or something close to it; I think that's sad because it pushes so many people into a whole set of false actions and reactions, and it causes an incredible amount of unnecessary guilt. I mean, we all get just plain horny sometimes; and I think people should be able to accept that for what it is and enjoy it.

I've had some better times, sexually, at the massage parlor than I have at a lot of swinging parties; a lot of pretense goes on among those people. Much more than many of them seem to realize. Organized swinging is certainly a step in the right direction; it's a hell of a lot better than straight monogamy or secret affairs. But there's still a lot more honesty needed, both about emotions and about nice, ordinary, raunchy sex. A good mix of the two is rare, and in the absence of that I really prefer a cup of hot tea and some gentle, nonsexual cuddling with my husband or an unexpected crazy orgasm in some semisleazy massage parlor. Blair understands that, and he also understands the subtle balance of those things that make for the best of all possible fucks. When our sex at home is good, it's very, very good; but we both want to be able to at least partially extend that to other people, which is more difficult than it might seem. The people you want to go wildly to bed with keep giving you all these stupid "soulful" looks of adoration, and the people you just want to hug and curl up with only want to screw; or the people that you might be able to experience *both* with never seem to catch on to your emotional and sexual rhythms, so everything is always off by an hour or so.

The same relaxation that I often feel at the massage parlor also applies to the customers, of course; this isn't his wife, or his girlfriend, or even a casual date: It's "just" a prostitute, no matter how attractive or intelligent or exciting she may be, and he doesn't feel such a heavy pressure to perform or to commit himself some way or another. They often end up doing that anyway, though, maybe slightly out of guilt. I couldn't begin to count the number of customers who profess their undying love for me or offer to "take me away from 'all this.'" Which is really just an annoying waste of both our time because that's not what either one of us is there for; and no matter how good-looking or wealthy they might be, I've got a fantastic permanent relationship with my husband, and it's not about to be changed by an orgasm or a ticket to Paris. I've already been to Paris, and the orgasms I have with Blair aren't replaceable.

QUESTION: Do you ever tell your customers that you're married?

ANGELA: Sometimes; always, if they start getting "romantic" [*laughs*]. Their reaction ranges from titillation to being really disturbed. I don't particularly care whether they know or not, unless it might affect the amount of money I can make. Sometimes I take off my ring to go to work, sometimes not; it just isn't that relevant a thing, one way or the other. Almost half the girls I've met in this are married; some of them are married to very well-off men, and they commute in from Scarsdale, just like their husbands. They do it for kicks, and also to have some money around that's really their own. Three or four thousand a month fills up a lot of cookie jars, and it buys a lot of hats.

QUESTION: Do you feel oppressed or exploited by your job—in a Women's Lib sense?

ANGELA: No, I don't; I certainly agree with a lot of the opinions that the women in the movement have, but I haven't felt exploited by being in this occupation. It's something that I have chosen to do, and any time I want to stop I can walk out the door. If anybody's getting ripped off in any way, it's the customer; he's the one paying these absurd prices for something that I really don't mind doing that much.

I have felt very exploited at other times in my life. A lot of people have seen me as nothing but an attractive sex object or whatever, in situations where that was an inappropriate or unwanted response. I enjoy knowing that I can be sexually appealing, but it would have made some things in my life less difficult if I could've just blended with the wallpaper a little more easily.

Of course, you can carry that out to a ridiculous, clichéd point: "Men only want you for your body, never your mind." The sad thing is, most of the women saying that the loudest are really begging to be lusted after because they've seldom had their bodies really appreciated—and I mean *really* appreciated, lavished over with equal amounts of tenderness and passion and friendship; those times make all the "sex-object" crap worth putting up with.

At a massage parlor, though, you know what you're offering and they know what they're coming for; nobody's playing any games and the customers aren't trying to exploit me in any way. They're not in a position to do so. If anyone ought to feel put down, it's them, for having come there. I don't think that mutually agreed-upon rental of skilled time at a fair price is "exploitation"; and sex is very definitely a skill. I only feel exploited when somebody tries to use me without my knowledge or entirely to my own detriment; and prostitution isn't any of those things, as long as it's a freely made individual choice. Girls who are junkies, or who are paying a tenth of the upkeep on their pimp's El Dorado, are an entirely different matter naturally. But I've made several thousand dollars for my own use, I've seen some really interesting people and situations, I've had an orgasm or two, and I've even gained some good insights into a few personal problems. No, I wouldn't call myself exploited [*laughs*].

As a matter of fact, I've never before been in a position in which I had such complete control; I'm able to totally regulate everything that goes on, and sometimes when I'm stoned I start to see the customers as these utterly vacuous puppets that I can manipulate for my own satisfaction, amusement, and profit. I know that sounds like creeping megalomania, but it's true. If I find somebody genuinely, totally obnoxious, I won't have sex with him at any price; and sexual frustration, particularly in a situation like that, can be a real bummer. But I don't enjoy puncturing men's egos, and I don't make a habit of it. First of all, I don't want to eliminate my income, and, secondly, I'm just not that bitter. I prefer being pleasant—even on the occasions when I'm using my pleasantness as a weapon. Much more effective, and memorable, than a shrill yell and a grimace. I'm no Skinnerian, but properly applied positive reinforcement does make people, as well as pigeons, learn their lessons more thoroughly.

QUESTION: And faster?

ANGELA: [*Laughs*] Much, much faster.

QUESTION: But you don't feel any deep animosity toward men in general?

ANGELA: No, I honestly don't; although, of course, there are many things that I don't really like about the typical male personality, and in ways I do prefer the attitudes of most women, their emotions, and their sense of pride. Men usually lack a lot of confidence, and they may try to cover that up with a display of *machismo* and an effort to make a woman feel inferior even though they know it's not the case. They seem to need to establish an edge over the relationship that's being established, so that they feel in control. I recognize the fact that those actions are just defense mechanisms, but they're very unnecessary and unpleasant; and they're not too effective either.

QUESTION: Do many of the men who come into the massage parlor act this way?

ANGELA: The majority of them don't, no; some of them put on an air of very nervous bravado, out of an attempt to make themselves feel more comfortable in the situation and even as a way of half-pretending to themselves that they're in some other, more ego-gratifying arrangement. They try to fantasize that I'm just someone they've picked up, and in doing so they come on with the usual behavior that they'd use to approach any female. Judging from what some of these people seem to consider an effective approach, I'm not surprised that they have to come to a massage parlor to get laid.

Most of the men, though, not only don't lay on a heavy *macho* number, but they walk in feeling as though *I'm* the one in the superior position, knowing that I'm in control. They're openly embarrassed about being there and actually look up to me in a lot of ways. They see me as a sexually experienced person, which is something that holds a great deal of importance for them—to be relaxed, to know a lot of "technique." They see me as a knowledgeable, gutsy, and sophisticated sort of woman, and they enjoy the idea of me being superior to them in that way. I simultaneously represent the nymphomaniacal fucking machine that their wives or girlfriends could never be and a better teacher of sexual "wisdom" than any of their male friends could be.

A lot of men even seem to see a visit to a massage parlor as an opportunity to relax their defenses and their various poses of "super-masculinity"; I'm sure that most men, when they're coming on with a lot of inflated *machismo*, don't really want to be doing that. They just feel that they have to in order to present a better "image" and to succeed sexually. But they're not really comfortable with it; nobody, male or female, can really be relaxed if they're madly pushing some shaky façade of "strength." Everybody wants to be appreciated for what they are, to have people know them and like them as a relaxed, basically defenseless person. And when they come to a massage parlor, they don't have to go through that stupid number; they don't have to make desperate overtures to some girl who's fighting back with the feminine versions of those same defense mechanisms.

They can just select a girl who fits their standards of sexual attractiveness and let her take over for a while. They know that some sort of sexual activity will take place, and that they don't have to try and persuade her, or even make the decision as to when it should happen. Everything is in her hands [*laughs*]. They don't have to do anything but lie on the table, relax, and enjoy. No commitment, no chatter over dinner, just a set fee, and they get what they consider a very pleasant luxury, with no hassles.

QUESTION: How popular is fellatio at this place, as opposed to intercourse?

ANGELA: Very—about a fourth of the sessions involve a hand-job, another fourth straight intercourse, and the other half is taken up with blow-jobs, or Frenches, or fellatio, or however you would like to most elegantly describe it.

QUESTION: Do you think that this is related to what you seem to see as a growing degree of, or desire for, sexual passivity among men?

ANGELA: Not in any negative or "perverted" sense, no; but I do think that all men secretly want to be able to be more passive than they usually are, and this does seem to be more commonly expressed nowadays, judging both from my experience at the massage parlor and from the men that I've known personally.

You were asking me about my feelings on Women's Lib; well, I think there's a very serious need for "Men's Lib," too. Everybody feels guilty and repressed and subjugated to some arbitrary standard, in different ways; women have certainly had a difficult time of it, but so have men. They're the ones who have traditionally carried the responsibility in almost every situation, including sexual ones. Responsibility is a nice thing, but when it's pushed on you in that heavy a way, it's hard to cope with. There's very little choice involved there. I'm sure that most men would like to have a lot of those responsibilities shifted; but admitting that, and actually having that shift take place, is a different thing than secretly wanting it to happen. It's nearly impossible for a man to be able to say, "Well, I really can't deal with all of this"; because they've been raised to feel that they should be capable of dealing with everything, no matter how rough it might get. Keep your lip to the grindstone and a stiff upper nose, and all that crap. I really feel sorry for anybody who's had to put up with those kinds of pressures, and most men have.

QUESTION: And you think that prostitution is a useful outlet through which men can let go of those feelings of responsibility and pressure?

ANGELA: Yes, I certainly do. It's too bad that they can only let go of them temporarily and can only manage that through something like prostitution; but in this society, as it's currently structured, I do see that as one of the good things about prostitution. It's not just the ugly men or the sexually unsuccessful ones who go to massage parlors; this goddamned *planet* is sexually unsuccessful, but for no good reason, and afraid to admit it. Until that changes, we'll have prostitution and we'll *need* it.

QUESTION: Do you think that you would have become involved in prostitution if the massage parlors hadn't been available and so well publicized?

ANGELA: No, very probably not; I wouldn't necessarily have been against the idea, particularly after my experience with swinging, but I just wouldn't have known how to go about it. I certainly wouldn't have just gone out on the street, and you can't exactly look up "brothels" in the Yellow Pages; or, at least, it used to be that you couldn't. All of the better New York massage parlors are in the Yellow Pages now, generally with a very businesslike display ad.

I would've enjoyed the experience of working in a high-class "house" in an apartment in the city; but I doubt that I ever would've done it, because I had no idea where to look and I would've been afraid to try and find out. Knowing of the existence of the massage parlors, and the fact that they advertise not only in *Screw* but in places like the New York *Post* made it much easier to get involved. I wouldn't be surprised if some of these places were listed with employment agencies in a couple of years; they ought to be.

QUESTION: Do the girls talk much about their personal backgrounds at work?

ANGELA: Not a lot; even though there is an unusual amount of pretty immediate honesty about things like sexual matters, there are some questions you just don't ask. A lot of the girls don't want to talk about their lives because they may have come from very unfortunate circumstances and don't even want to *think* about it: girls from the ghetto, or with a history of addiction, or whatever. Some of them have had some fairly heavy lives, and to them, working in a massage parlor is a way to keep up an aura of some kind of worth or decency. You're a *pretty* girl, you're making money now, you can begin to have some more hopeful expectations about yourself, whatever their basis in fact; you want to project that kind of image. And you certainly don't want anyone who's more attractive or otherwise better off than you standing around saying, "Well, what did your life consist of?" And you have to dredge up all these hideous memories of prison or something. There's about a fifty-fifty split between the poorer girls and the middle- or upper-class ones, although the proportion of "girls next door" seems to be increasing very fast; so there are some potential tensions there. I never pushed the "niceness" of my own background on anyone else, and I never pressed them for details about their possible misfortunes. If any of the girls felt like confiding in me, and they often did, I'd listen with a very sympathetic and helpful attitude; but I'd never think of grilling them or lording it over them.

QUESTION: Do many friendships form at a massage parlor, girls that you might see socially outside of work?

ANGELA: Sometimes; but, fitting in with what I was saying earlier about the jealousies and so on, it's not a good idea for cliques to be established among certain girls. That would create "in-out" group hostilities: the blondes *versus* the brunettes, or thin girls and plump ones, or racial groupings, or whatever. Any situation like that could make things difficult at work. Your shared experience tends to revolve around just the work situation; if you're seeing someone as a friend outside, you don't talk about it a lot or some of the other girls might begin to feel that you're kind of "ganging up" on them, in one way or another.

QUESTION: Would you say that there are fewer friendships formed among the girls at a massage parlor than among a group of girls in, say, a secretarial pool or salesgirls at the same store?

ANGELA: I'd have to answer that in two ways: The feelings and understandings you have about each other are somewhat deeper and stronger, but there are fewer strictly social relationships. You may not talk a lot about your past lives or your hopes for the future, but you do discuss many feelings that you can share within the experience of the moment; and that's a pretty gut-level experience to be sharing. There's quite a bit of communication about each other's sex life and some very basic emotional feelings, whereas in an office girls might see each other more often for drinks or at parties, but they might not get around to talking about as many really important attitudes or emotions.

At times we've come close to establishing an almost familial sense of group trust and caring for each other; for a while at Mademoiselle's the personalities of the girls who were there blended together to create a friendship experience that's rather rare to the massage parlor scene. I'm sure I'll always feel very close to some of these people, no matter what happens.

QUESTION: Is there ever any discussion of lesbian feelings?

ANGELA: Oh, yes; there's even some occasional lesbian activity going on: kissing and petting in the dressing room, that sort of thing. That all came out in the open one night; it was a slow evening, there were only two or three customers in the back, and one of the girls suggested that we all undress in the lounge because she thought it would be funny to see the customers' reactions if, when they came out to leave, we were all sitting there on the couches in the nude. Some of us were a little freaked out by the idea, particularly if a cop happened by. But she went ahead and stripped and kept teasing the rest of us about it, and nobody wanted to seem "chicken," so we all started slowly taking off our clothes; she even got the manager to undress.

It was funny when the customers came out; one of them didn't know what to do—he just ignored what was happening and left immediately. Another one really got off on it and started to get undressed himself; so we had him leave, and by then it was closing time, about three in the morning. The door's locked and we're all a little drunk, a little stoned and naked; so Brenda, the girl who'd started the whole thing, suggested that we give the manager a Christmas gang-bang. By this time a couple of the girls were getting sort of uptight and didn't know what was happening, so they got dressed and left for the night. That left me, Brenda, two other girls who were very smashed, and the manager. So, with very little convincing necessary, we took him in the back, onto one of the water beds, and did this whole number on him; in the process of which, very naturally, we started getting into some lesbian things, too. We . . . what can I say, we had a good time [*laughs*].

It was from that experience that I started to develop an interest in having a lesbian relationship with this one girl in particular, Brenda. Like I said, I'd had homosexual experiences before at parties and I'd already considered the idea of a steady thing with another girl; but this all took me by surprise, in a pleasant way. She's very cute.

QUESTION: Did your husband know about this?

ANGELA: Yes, of course; I told him all about it. He did have some slightly funny feelings about it at first because this was someone that I liked and wanted to have an ongoing sexual relationship with, not a customer or somebody at a party; and it was another girl, which was odd. He didn't object to it at all, though. His main reaction was that he wanted me to bring her home for dinner, with a view toward a possible *ménage à trois* situation.

QUESTION: Did this happen?

ANGELA: It did, eventually; I approached her with the idea of coming home with me, and she was a little hesitant at first because she had originally been interested in just a relationship with me. But my husband is very nice and very good in bed; the three of us have had several very enjoyable evenings since then, and I continue to see her now and then on my own, outside work. It's fun because there's a real shared interest with Blair and me; I'm not in the least masculine-oriented, but it's sort of as if we're two guys having fun with the same girlfriend: Juliette and Jim, you might say. Brenda's a petite, bouncy little blonde, totally uninhibited; and in a way it feels like she's a toy that Blair and I can play with together.

QUESTION: A toy?

ANGELA: That sounds terrible, I know, as if we're just into *using* her; but it isn't that way at all. The three of us get into a lot of different sexual combinations, but the most common one is for me and Blair to both be doing things to turn her on: like maybe he takes the bottom half and I take the top half, or vice-versa [*laughs*]. She loves it; it's really a trip to have that much attention paid to you all at once. Brenda's a very happy toy.

QUESTION: Do you feel that there's any sort of causal relationship between prostitution and lesbianism or bisexuality?

ANGELA: Not really; it's not that uncommon a phenomenon at massage parlors, but I don't believe that either one leads to, or drives you to, the other. It's certainly not a matter of turning to lesbianism out of satiation or disgust with heterosexuality; and I don't think that there are more girls with bisexual leanings among prostitutes, just that the type of girls involved might be more willing to admit to it and do something about it. Most of these girls lead a pretty liberal sex-life even "off the job," and that sort of openness naturally tends to include at least some bisexuality.

I would say that prostitution does lead to an understanding and acceptance of some fairly "bizarre" sexual preferences:

masochism, transvestism, fetishism, and so on; and a little bisexual fun on the side starts to seem rather ordinary by comparison. But it's not anything perverse or jaded; it's just being honest enough and relaxed enough to extend your pleasure-options.

QUESTION: How has your experience as a prostitute affected your involvement in swinging or your feelings about it?

ANGELA: Not at all, unless you count the fact that now, when I get stuck with somebody at a party who isn't too great, I feel like asking him for my fifty bucks [laughs]. The two are just separate things that I do for entirely different reasons.

QUESTION: Would you say that group sex is a healthy thing for other couples to get into?

ANGELA: Don't point that question, it's loaded. No, seriously, that's a very difficult thing to answer in such general terms; sure, I think it's extremely healthy to be able to break through some of the old repressions and hypocrisies that have surrounded marriage and the idea of "infidelity" or "adultery"; but there's a lot of hypocrisy in the swinging scene, too—repression, even. A good percentage of the people involved are very straight, and this seems to be their only concession to any sort of personal liberation. And, obviously, you've got to have a pretty stable relationship with somebody to begin with; it's certainly not something to get into in order to patch up problems you might already be having, any more than having a baby is a solution to those problems. If there are any insecurities in your relationship, chances are those fears will just be aggravated by swinging. But for couples who have some knowledge of where they're at and what they're doing, I do think it's a good thing on the whole; and it really can put a lot of spice and just simple friendliness back into your relationship. It's fun to talk about other people that you've been with; I enjoy hearing my husband talk about the girls that he's gone to bed with, and his excitement about seeing them again, and so on. The best fucks of all are when you get home from an evening of watching each other make it with other people; that can be a real turn-on, as long as neither one of you has any big self-confidence hang-ups.

That's another whole thing about being a married prostitute, too; I imagine most men think it would just absolutely kill them to have their wives do something like this, but the degree of their jealousy is directly related to how much they freak out over their own masculinity. It's a combination of worrying that the woman is going to find somebody who's a better lover and also a fear that that sort of experience is going to unleash her sexual potential on the husband himself, which is really a dumb thing to be concerned about. Practice makes perfect, and an experienced woman is a thousand times better in bed, but a lot of men just aren't too sure they could handle that. They're afraid of the power of female sexuality, they're actually in *awe* of it—I see that all the time in their reactions to me at the massage parlor—and they want to keep their wives from realizing that power, even at the cost of having lousy sex to come home to. They say they come to a massage parlor to get a good blow-job because their wives won't do it, but I think, in a lot of cases, the truth is they won't *let* their wives do it. It sounds weird, but I believe that's just another way they have of keeping "their" women submissive. If I were going to start a Women's Lib group, I think I'd begin with lessons on how to give a decent blow-job. *There's* power for you; they could turn their husbands into whimpering ninnies. But it's a nice kind of power; everything gets equalized and everybody has a good time. If men could just relax and stop worrying about who's king of the mountain, they could have a hell of a lot more fun and probably live longer, too. Jealousy's just an excuse for fear and weakness, but it's totally self-destructive.

QUESTION: Have you and your husband known any couples who got into swinging and then broke up?

ANGELA: A few, but I really don't think that was the basic cause of their splitting up; it just speeded things up a little, but the process was already at work. They might have stayed together a little longer otherwise, but that would've just meant covering up a lot of their problems and emotions for more time than was necessary. Swinging does have the effect with a lot of people of making the problems that they're having together more apparent, of really bringing things up front. You have to confront a lot of things that are always there but are usually hidden; and if the relationship isn't strong enough to maintain itself under long-range "normal" circumstances, then swinging simply makes that obvious quicker. I tend to think that's basically healthy; if the relationship is fucked up and isn't going to bring any great fulfillment or even fun to these people by continuing it, then I think they should discover that before they're forty-five or fifty and completely stuck in this mire.

A lot of the breakups we've seen have actually just involved a regrouping of people in potentially more workable combinations. I'd be very interested, ten years from now, to see a study done on the state of *second* marriages brought about through swinging; I'd be willing to bet that they last a while longer than might be expected.* Strict monogamy, as it has been, is full of shit, obviously; but a primary one-to-one relationship, one where the bonds are both mutual and permanent, is still very desirable, very reassuring. The honesty in a relationship like that has to be *total*, though; there's no room for lies to yourself or your partner about your genuine emotions, particularly on a subject as supposedly crucial as sex. But the main point of swinging is the discovery that sex *isn't* crucial; important, yes, just like any other aspect of your being, but crucial? No way. And if you can't see that, then you've got no business staying in the relationship that has oppressed you to that point.

QUESTION: Do you think you and your husband will continue to be involved in swinging for a long period of time?

ANGELA: Well, we go to much fewer parties now than we used to. We've both gotten a little tired of the "scene," and

*No second-marriage statistics are currently available, but studies have shown a lower rate of divorce among swinging couples in general.

we were never that obsessed with the need for steady orgies anyway. They're still fun now and then, and I'm sure we'll be going to two or three a year until we're ninety-five; but when you've been to your fifteenth, you have a pretty good idea of what the sixteenth will be like.

I've also saved as much money as we could reasonably need for some time to come, and I'll be quitting my massage parlor job at the end of this month. Our sexual activity from this point on will continue to be a very freely structured thing and will certainly continue to involve other people; but we're more interested now in building that around a few people that we know and like in a variety of ways, and as a result of our experiences we have a better idea of how to go about arranging that. Literally every one of our friends, including those who were so freaked out when we tried to approach them a couple of years ago, are now into or considering swinging or something like it; and all of our newer friendships have been formed with at least a tacit understanding that the relationships might come to include some form of physical intimacy. That really seems to be establishing itself as a new social norm, and I think it'll continue long after all the "swinger's clubs" have disappeared.

I do think that some very healthy and long-lasting changes in human relationships will come out of all this trial-and-error experimentation. Not group-marriage communes, because a twenty-person household just multiplies the problems of a couple by ten; and not weekly orgies with strangers, because that's . . . it's not even "dehumanizing" or anything as strong as that: it's just boring, after a while. But once enough people have understood the range of possibilities that exists, some really good things can start happening; a lot of them have already started, as far as we're concerned. Is the tape running out?

QUESTION: Yes, it is; is there anything you'd like to add?

ANGELA: Just that I hope I haven't come off sounding too Utopian or analytical or absurdly positive about either swinging or prostitution; I never got around to talking about some really funny things and also some real downers. None of this has been a hundred percent good *or* bad as far as I was concerned, but there are some widespread negative stereotypes about some of these things that either never were true or are in the process of changing very fast, and I wanted to get that across. It would be silly to pretend that *any* of this—swinging, prostitution, bisexuality—has been smooth and simple all the way; but I'd like to say that I am a basically very happy person, and I've found the problems much fewer and much easier to deal with than I ever would have imagined. I don't regret anything that I've done, and I'm pretty excited and optimistic about the future. Mine *and* the world's, believe it or not.

3. Babs

BABS is, in a word, "bouncy." Her ample but well-proportioned body is constantly in motion, dashing helter-skelter around her apartment to pour drinks or change records or just to move for the sake of not sitting still. Her accent and razor-cut blond hairdo are precisely those of a thousand or more flirtatious barmaids in the pubs of Kensington and Chelsea.

Babs has never worked in a massage parlor as such; she operates out of her own East Sixties' apartment, receiving customers there or visiting them in their hotels and offices in a manner similar to that of the traditional call girl. She regularly places her own display ads in Screw for "Private massage," and her entrance to the business came about through her response to a Help Wanted ad in the same publication. It is no longer necessary for a new girl to pay hundreds or thousands of dollars for a meticulously compiled list of clients, or for a budding new-breed pimp to kidnap teenaged recruits into bondage off the bus: one column inch in the sex industry's trade paper is more than sufficient to elicit a steady stream of reliable customers or attractive young women in search of easy work.

Despite her pixielike manner and her frequent laughter, Babs seems more inhibited than any of the other girls I interviewed, and this tension obviously carries over to her personal sex life. She appears to derive little enjoyment from sex, which at first led me to the conclusion that I had at last uncovered a case of professionally induced frigidity, a destruction of someone's basic sexual responses caused by her occupation as a prostitute. As I questioned her more closely, *however, it became clear that Babs' sexual difficulties predated her work by many years, with their roots lying in the repressive British social and moral structure to which she was subjected from childhood. Though she was somewhat reticent on the point, I believe that the cause-and-effect relationship between Babs' frigidity and her work are the reverse of what I had originally thought: that is, her externally deadened sexual sensitivities made her initiation into prostitution easier in certain ways, and she may well have been attempting (with only partial success) to thereby achieve an otherwise totally elusive satisfaction.*

* * *

QUESTION: What sort of family background do you have?

BABS: My father was a business administrator in a little North Country English town; he had quite a responsible position, nearly sixty men under him. He always earned a good living, by English standards, though of course it'd be thought peanuts in America. My mother's a housewife, my brother's an executive in the civil service, and my sister's a housewife with three children; all quite respectable, you know.

QUESTION: Did you get along well with your family as you were growing up?

BABS: Yes, very well indeed. I was the youngest of three children, so naturally I was just a bit spoiled; but still, I was trained in all the virtues and always encouraged in school . . . there's absolutely nothing in my background to indicate why I should be doing this. It isn't as if I've seen people used to easy money: any money my parents had, they worked for it. Nor was I accustomed to associating with the "lower elements" in England: My town was very proper, and Soho was more a legend than a reality. I was never involved in any of this at home; I hardly even knew it existed outside naughty books.

QUESTION: What kind of work did you do in England?

BABS: I was a primary-school teacher in what would be

the equivalent of your second grade. I spent two years at that, and it simply wasn't leading me anywhere; I can only take so much of rambunctious kiddies, and the best I could hope for was transfer to another primary school in London perhaps or marriage to some up-and-coming young solicitor. I was right sick of England, to tell you the truth, and there seemed to be so many more opportunities here in the States. My family thought I was crazy when I up and told them I was emigrating; none of them have ever even traveled on the Continent a great deal, and they were a bit frightened by the news reports of all the violence in America; but they could see it was what I wanted. So I used my savings to come here.

QUESTION: What did you do when you arrived?

BABS: Well, the money I'd come with was running out quickly, and I didn't want to go home and say I'd failed; so I followed every possible avenue to getting work, which wasn't very easy. I wasn't qualified to teach here and couldn't have done at any rate: the Board of Education gets rather sticky about work permits and that sort of thing, which I hadn't been able to get as yet.

Finally I located a position as secretary with a film concern; they were a very informal operation and didn't make a fuss over seeing my papers. Compared to English standards, the money seemed very good: I was making about one hundred and sixty-five dollars a week, but after tax it only comes down to one hundred and twenty. Any halfway decent apartment is a minimum two hundred dollars, so you've fifty a week in rent; then there's your gas, your electric, telephone; you need to be reasonably dressed, visit the beauty parlor . . . and that one sixty-five is [*snap of fingers*] gone. It sounded like a lot to me at first, but it really isn't so much when you come down to it.

So I just thought I'd make a little extra money in my spare time; I knew this girl who was supplementing her alimony by doing massages, though hers were fairly legitimate. The most they would've gone to would be a hand-job. I expressed an interest in the business, and we got to talking it over at lunch one day, and she told me she'd seen an ad in *Screw*. Well, I'd heard of *Screw*, but I never . . . you know, it isn't the type of thing that women would normally buy. But I bought a copy that afternoon, and I saw an advertisement which particularly appealed to me, called "Playgirl Massage." It said "New dollies weekly," as if they were always wanting new people; so I phoned up, and said I was wanting some part-time work.

QUESTION: Did you go over for an interview?

BABS: Oh, it was all very cloak-and-dagger; I arranged to meet this guy the next day in a little park on Fiftieth between Second and Third. Naturally I was a bit nervous over that, but it was during the daytime and I thought I could always shout for help if there was any trouble. There was none at all, as it developed: I sat down on this particular bench that he'd mentioned, and waited for about ten minutes. and then along came George. He was about thirty or thirty-two, clean-cut, a fairly respectable-appearing young Jewish business type. I'd had my fears of there being your typical rough black pimp sort, but that wasn't the case.

So we sat and chatted; he'd brought along a chicken sandwich and gave me half; and he told me about himself and his business. He was college educated and had done a lot of different things, but was just dabbling here and there, this and that; so he'd just started this little girl service, mainly for out-of-town businessmen and the like. He handled all the appointments, which were mostly at the better hotels in the midtown area and the East Side. We talked an hour or so, and it seemed all right, so I decided to give it a go; I gave George my telephone number and told him I could do appointments in the evenings, after work.

QUESTION: What was your first experience with a customer?

BABS: It was two days after I'd met George, on a Saturday night. I'd been a bit jumpy since that meeting on Thursday, not absolutely sure just what I'd let myself in for; I was anxious to get the first time over and out of the way, and also trying to put the whole thing out of my mind, as if it wasn't really going to happen.

I was napping when George phoned me that afternoon, and when I answered I'd half forgot who he was for a moment; it took me a few seconds to wake up and collect myself and realize that this was *it*. The appointment was for eight thirty that evening at the Summit Hotel on Lexington at Fifty-first. George gave me the name and room number and said it was a businessman from Ohio.

I must've started getting ready three hours in advance and changed clothes six or seven times before I went. I wanted to seem attractive and sexy, not as if this was my first time; but I didn't want to . . . look the part too much, you know. Finally I settled on a quite ordinary pink and blue jumper with a little matching jacket, and I swept my hair up in the back.

All the way over in the cab, I kept thinking, "Bloody hell, girl, what are you *doing*?" And walking through the lobby of the hotel, even though I looked quite conservative, I was utterly positive that everyone there knew exactly what I was about. I could feel their eyes on me and hear them whispering as I went past, and I half-expected a troop of police to stop me at the lift. Going up, I kept seeing pictures of my family at home, and what they'd think if they knew . . . and then I was at the door, knocking, and I thought "Run! Run, while you've still a chance!" But my legs were quivering too much to move, and suddenly the door was opening.

I felt better straightaway when I saw the guy: he was a well-dressed, smart executive type, very well-spoken, and a little younger than I'd expected. He invited me in very politely and offered me a drink, and we sat and chatted about his convention; which all made me feel much more at ease. If he'd been one o' these who jump on you, I'd've probably run off, but he was very nice. Then he gave me the fifty; and I remember as he passed me the fifty-dollar bill, I thought, gee, it hadn't really occurred to me what *easy* money it was. We went to bed and I was back out of bed and dressed within about twenty minutes. I was just amazed at how simple it was, and as I was dressing I kept thinking how as a secretary I'd've had to work a full day or more for that money and jump to work at seven o'clock in the morning and all that . . . I just gazed in the mirror where I was combing my hair, and I thought to myself, "Well, luv, this isn't half bad."

QUESTION: What was the arrangemen. with George in terms of fee-splitting?

BABS: The price to the customer was always fifty dollars, and it was a fifty-fifty split, which I thought was quite high; George got twenty-five dollars and I got twenty-five dollars. I later found out that *was* rather high; the proper rate is forty percent for the agent, which would've been only twenty dollars. George was very nice, but he could be a bit greedy; I had to get cab fares, and once when I got a twenty-dollar tip, he even wanted a cut of that, though he'd previously told me my tips were my own.

So it didn't take me more than a week or two to realize that George was getting fifty percent for doing nothing more than answering the phones and saying, "Right, I'll send somebody over." So I thought, well, what was to stop me from going down to the *Screw* office and putting my own ad in? At that time they were fourteen dollars, now they're twenty-eight. So I mapped out this little ad; you know, you don't have to advertise very ingeniously or subtly, you just say "Beautiful blond masseuse"; and I put "Residential Only," though I didn't realize at the time that that meant you wouldn't accept them at your own apartment, whereas there was no reason why they couldn't come there.

Still and all, I was amazed at the response the ad had the very first week; there were dozens of guys phonin' up, and, of course, now all the fifty dollars was mine, so the profits were jumpin' up sky-high.

QUESTION: Did you have any problems in breaking away from George?

BABS: Oh, no, no . . . even though he was greedy, he wasn't vicious. There was none of this "pimp" sort of thing; that's for the girls in the streets or else only in the cinema. George never even tried to approach me sexually. It occurred to me that he might try and get laid one day when he came over to collect his commission, and I wasn't about to give him any of that sort of extra commission. I decided that if he tried anything, I'd say "Well, give me the twenty-five back," and I knew he wouldn't do that . . . George would always grab the money. But he didn't try anything, and there was never a hint of him threatening me or like that.

No, the biggest problem I had in first going on my own was learning to deal with all the phonies and the bullshit artists on the telephone; I don't know why, but there are many, many guys who get their kicks that way, and it's more a bother than it might sound. If they phone up from a hotel, I always call back and verify it with the hotel desk. With an apartment, it's a bit more difficult, though I always try and check them in the phone book, and I always phone them back. Some of them don't want to give their full names over the phone, but I have to insist on it. You can tell some of the phonies right off, like if they say they're on Fifty-fourth Street and they give you a Queens number. Others may try to convince you they have an unlisted number so you can't check it, and then they give you the address of a police station or a vacant lot. A few of them give the name of a friend they're playing a joke on; I fell for one of those once, before I learned to call back every time and I went to the apartment. The name and the address were correct, but when I knocked the man's wife answered the door and was most frosty with me, as you can imagine. Then some will give you a phony name, often obviously so; I had one guy phone up and say his name was Harry Bigcock*. Naturally I hung up on him straightaway, but then he kept phoning back, mad as a hornet, demanding that I check it out; and sure enough, there he was in the directory. He became one of

*This name has been changed from an equally improbable double entendre.

my regular customers, even though he didn't quite live up to his name.

You get a lot of these guys who'll make appointments to come here that don't turn up, that's bad enough; but when they have you going out on a wild-goose chase, you lose twice as much time plus the round-trip cab fare and the calls you've missed while you were out. I'd say that out of ten calls, maybe one will materialize. Aside from the outright phonies and the heavy breathers, you have what I call "shoppers," guys who phone up and say, "How much do you charge for a massage?" and when you tell them "fifty dollars," they say, "OK, thank you," and hang up. I'm not as annoyed by that because at least then you know, all right, the fifty's too much; you know where you stand, and you're not out any time or money.

But you only need three calls that turn out to get your hundred and fifty a day, so it isn't too bad.

QUESTION: Is that what you average per day—one hundred and fifty dollars?

BABS: That's the minimum average I set. On the numbers that I do myself I actually end up averaging more like two hundred or two-twenty-five. Then I have a few other girls that I arrange things for, and those commissions come to another hundred a day, say; so my total income from the business is around fifteen to seventeen hundred a week. Before *and* after taxes [*laughs*].

When I first started doing this full-time, I used to lounge around during the day and do nothing, and then I'd have to do everything at night: my social life, the work, it was all crammed in. Now I try and have a more evenly distributed day, and make seven or eight hundred during the afternoons and evenings in three or four days; then I have the rest of the week to ease off and make the rest, up to the thousand mark for my own tricks, at a fairly leisurely pace. And once in a while, if I've been out to the theater or had some people over to dinner and I'm home alone by twelve or one o'clock,

I'll put the phone back on and take a late-night call.

A lot of calls do come in after twelve, although now the Hotel and Motel Association of New York have laid down a new law that single men registered in a hotel can't have women coming up after midnight, which is stupid; as if nothing could happen before the "witching hour." But this is what they're doing, especially hotels like the Beverly at Fiftieth and Lex, because that's a big prostitution area, a street-walking area; they stop anyone going in there, even at nine o'clock you'll get a cold look. It just depends on how the security happens to feel; sometimes you can walk in at two A.M. and they won't say a thing; other times they'll be pretty nasty and occasionally make you leave without going up. I always try and avoid a confrontation, like in the way I dress; somehow or other, passionate purple see-through hot pants just don't make it in the Waldorf lobby.

QUESTION: You said you have other girls working for you now; how did this come about?

BABS: Well, George . . . remember George? He decided he was going to California because too many of his girls were refusing to put up with his fifty percent commissions. So for a hundred-dollar "introduction fee," I got a girl who'd been working for him, and she was happy to go with me because I only charged her the standard forty percent commission. Then another trick that I went to got me two girls. One of them's a little Japanese girl, very demure; she really turns the guys on—she was a big smash right off. Then there was another one that I've only spoken to over the phone, which is very risky. . . . I send her out on assignments unseen, and she hands my forty percent to another girl to give to me. The guys say, "What does she look like?" and I say, "She's beautiful, you'll love her"; but I'm thinking, My God, I've never seen this bird, I don't know if she looks like Dracula's daughter. But she's going out all over, and she gets repeat business, so I guess someone's pleased with her.

I've got most of my girls from tricks who'd say, "I know a girl in this business," and they've sent them to me. Some of these girls just haven't known what they're about; they've been doing numbers for twenty or twenty-five dollars on the street, so they're happy to have someone make all the arrangements for them, and they get thirty dollars. I've had no trouble getting people. Other girls just want to do a trick now and then; they don't want to put an ad with their home phone number; they don't want to have all that bother, or else they're married and don't want their husbands knowing how they pay for all those new outfits. They come and go, but I generally have five or six girls that I'll make appointments for. It doesn't come to all that much extra money, and I'm not tight about my commissions; I really do this half as a favor to the girls, and what money I get from them fairly covers the risk and the bother I go through making the arrangements and placing the ads.

QUESTION: What is your average clientele like?

BABS: I'd say for the most part they're upper income, especially the out-calls, the hotels; they're nearly all out-of-town businessmen, executives. Then there are a lot of professional men, doctors and lawyers; a couple of diplomats . . . mostly middle-aged, married, upper-income types. The average younger guy, on say two hundred a week, well, after tax that's one fifty, then with the rent . . . out of the remainder, fifty dollars could be half of his money for the week. It's really quite a bit for maybe . . . well, over the phone I always say it's an hour session, but they're never here an hour; they aren't in bed ten minutes. I've even thought of cutting that down further by getting some blue movies to project on that wall, and by the time they got in the bedroom [*claps hands*] they'd be so excited they'd be out in ninety seconds.

But most of the men I have are fairly well-to-do, if not wealthy, and don't seem to mind the prices. I went to the Waldorf on a double with another girl one time, and he just wanted my girlfriend and me to dance while he watched and jerked himself off; we didn't even touch him, and for that he paid a hundred and forty dollars. Christ, he could've gotten laid nearly three times for that; he was out-of-sight.

Then there are others, you'd never believe how stingy they can get; there's one who lives on Central Park South; he's rich as a bitch . . . but you should see him with the money! He won't give me a fifty-dollar note—he'd give me fifty ones if he could get away with it; he gets out his wallet and goes "Five . . . ten . . . fifteen . . . ," like every dollar is making him bleed. I mean, really, you wouldn't mind when people haven't the money, but when you know they do . . . still, they're sometimes even tighter with it. I reckon that's how they got it all in the first place, by being tight; but now they can't enjoy having it, it hurts so much to spend.

QUESTION: Have you ever gone out with a customer socially?

BABS: Now and again, if they're nice enough and they seem able to pay for a good evening on the town, with dinner and a show. If I like them, I won't charge for going out with them; but so many of the guys ask, practically all of them in fact. You're never quite sure if they really like you or if they just want to try and get something for nothing. I keep two books, a blue one and a black one: The blue book's the social book, and the black book's the trick book. Every one of the customers that I see more than once is always trying to go from the black book to the blue one. They do seem fascinated somehow with the idea of dating a prostitute.

Then you also get all sorts of people offering you "deals" of one sort or another to get laid free or cheaply. I had one man call and say he worked at the Roosevelt Hotel and that he'd set me up with the men who came in there on conventions and the like, without taking any commission. He just wanted to get laid, to "test me and my girls out." Can you imagine—the gall? And another guy kept phoning up and sending me letters; he said he ran a "computer dating service," but he didn't have any computer and what he was arranging wasn't dates. He wanted to set me up with these guys who thought they were just getting a girlfriend, and I'm supposed to tell them there's a fifty-dollar charge for getting laid! I thought that was a bit cheeky, and I said I wasn't about to go along. But this guy just kept phoning and writing; he really wanted to get laid himself. I don't think he'd ever had a freebie in his life.

QUESTION: What sort of notations do you keep in your "black book"?

BABS: Basically just the guy's name, number, and address, plus their fee. They're all at least fifty dollars, but I have a few who'll go seventy-five, a hundred, or even more—particularly for special services. If there's anything in particular that they want I'll write it in parentheses, like "enema" or "discipline" or "TV," so I'll be prepared. Then with some of them I put down "P.A." for "Pain in the Ass," so when they phone I'll know to either avoid them or send them somebody who's willing to put up with them; or "C.B." for "Cheap Bastard." Some of them just carry on and on about the money and say things like "If I get you three other customers, can I get a free lay?" And other guys will try and do an exchange, a trade-off, with their professions or their businesses: dentists who'll offer to clean your teeth, or boutique owners who'll offer you a jacket or a skirt. I don't go for that sort of thing ever; it's strictly cash or nothing.

QUESTION: What do you do with the money you make? Do you keep a savings account?

BABS: I used to have a savings account—still do, but I don't put most of my earning there anymore. My bank was in the same building where I'd worked as a secretary, and it got just a bit suspicious when the same tellers I'd been handing my paycheck to for three months are suddenly seeing me deposit hundreds of dollars at a time, all in cash. Finally one of the girls just looked me in the eye and asked, very curious, "Are you still working upstairs?" And I had to tell her, "No, no . . . I'm . . . not doing too much of anything these days" [laughs]. The very next day I went to another bank and rented a safe-deposit box. I put my money in there every week now; there's quite a bit saved up, over twelve thousand dollars. And some I cable back to England, to bank there; I've three or four thousand in a bank in London.

QUESTION: Obviously, you don't pay income taxes?

BABS: No, of course not; why should I? I don't believe they'll bother my safe-deposit or check out the account in England. I may end up paying taxes on about a third or a quarter of the money, though, just to keep them off my back; I think you can just put down "self-employed" without being any more specific, so long as you give them a share. Still, I worry on that score; if I pay no taxes, they can eventually find me out for that, but if I *do* pay taxes, they can deport me for working without a permit [*laughs*]. It's a regular Catch-22, isn't it? I mean, how in hell do I go about getting a work permit as a prostitute? So I'm still not decided just what I'll do; I'll make up my mind come the morning of April fifteenth, most likely.

QUESTION: Have you ever had any problems with the police?

BABS: No, not the slightest. I worry about that possibility from time to time, but then I'm very careful. I always try and suss the customer out before making any commitment, and I always have them undress first, there's a law that a copper can't strip off in the line of duty.

QUESTION: Do you think that prostitution will or should be legalized?

BABS: Naturally, for all the usual reasons. It is a victimless crime when it's done like this, and the standards of the society are changing so quickly now. I honestly do believe that prostitution is a good thing, a desirable thing, particularly for these guys with certain types of sexual wants that they just can't tell their wives or their girlfriends. Or just ordinary guys, who want to go with someone different now and again, without the problems of meeting a girl and chatting her up and spending twice as much as it would cost them just to come and get laid right off.

I do have some mixed feelings about it being legalized, though, because then I'm sure there would be quite a lot of new laws about licensing and paying taxes on the income and so forth; I'd be left in the cold, I'm afraid. Most likely the first thing they'd do would be to put up an embargo on foreign talent [*laughs*]; so, for the moment, I'm happy with the situation as is. But I would like to see them stop harassing girls, and eventually it should be made legal.

QUESTION: Does your landlord know what you're doing here?

BABS: Yes, he does, as a matter of fact; when I was working as a secretary I had a much less expensive place in the Murray Hill district, but then as things developed I realized I needed a nicer flat, particularly if I was going to be taking tricks in my own place. So I checked all the ads and went to this one agent who controlled several buildings. I told him what sort of place I was interested in having, and when he began asking for references and telephone numbers at work I got a bit concerned, thinking, "What on earth can I tell this man"; but he recognized that straightaway, and after a bit of conversation he said, "You know, you can be honest with me; we've a lot of 'unemployed' single girls in our buildings, and they always pay the rent on time." So finally I told him I was a "masseuse," and everything was fine; he understood right off. He told me that as long as I did things discreetly and was regular with the rent, he didn't care what I did or how I made my living. From what I understand, that's not uncommon among the landlords in New York; prostitutes, so long as they're quiet and well-mannered, are often considered quite desirable tenants. We're surely not interested in creating any sort of conspicuous disturbance, and there's no question of our being able to come up with the monthly rent.

QUESTION: What is the normal routine when a customer comes here to your place?

BABS: Well, after the appointment's been made and they've come up, I try and make them feel at ease; sometimes they're very nervous, so I offer them a drink. Then we sit and chat for a bit, usually about their business. Most of the guys who come here are New York residents who can't receive a girl in their apartments because of their wives, and they don't want to pay an extra twenty for a hotel room.

Then, after we've chatted for a couple of minutes, I ask

if they'd like to go into the bedroom, where I have them strip off first, to make sure they're not a cop, and then I ask for the money. Unless I really know them, I always ask for the money in advance, and I never accept any check except a traveler's check. I had some bum experiences with checks in the beginning: one guy not only didn't have an account, the check was printed on a nonexistent bank!

Oh, and one wretched man a month or so ago said he'd left his money in his car because he'd been mugged at another girl's place; so he told me he'd leave his watch as security and come back up with the money. The watch is still here and probably only worth about ten dollars, though it had the look of an expensive one. So I've finally learned my lesson: unless they're regulars, it's cash in advance—no watches, no checks. And then, once they're undressed, I always make the excuse I'll go turn the telephone off, and when I come out, I hide the fifty underneath that sofa.

Once they've gotten laid and have gone to the bathroom to wash up, I always get dressed immediately; if they see you nude, it turns them on again, so I try to get them out of the bedroom before they decide to hang around for a while longer. If they start putterin' around, I'll give them a gentle hint, like "It's time for you to leave." That usually sends them dashing off because they figure I've another customer coming, and they don't want to meet.

QUESTION: If there is more than one customer waiting in the living room, how do they generally relate to each other?

BABS: Quite nervously. They hate to see another guy here, I suppose it makes them jealous [*laughs*]. Seriously, though, they often phone up and ask, "Is it strictly private?" A lot of the guys I see are ones that feel a bit of guilt and would be afraid or ashamed to go to a regular massage parlor, where it's much more public. When it's very busy and I'm doing something with another girl, and there's two men here at once, we usher one into the bedroom and open that sofa up into a bed. But there's only one bathroom, and when they're done, they try and sneak into the bathroom and say, "You look out first, see if he's about"; and the other trick's out in the other room or crouching in the kitchen, saying, "Has he gone? Has he gone?" And they're peeking around corners looking for one another; it can be quite a comical scene. I think they mostly get shy if they're here for a whipping, or if they don't want someone to see them who knows they're married; though, God knows, every last married man in this city is doing this at one time or another, and anyone else who's here likely hasn't come up for tea and cookies himself.

QUESTION: How do you personally feel about the fact that most of your customers are married? Do you feel that you're helping them to "cheat" on their wives?

BABS: Not a bit of it—I don't think they're doing anything wrong. Not unless they have four or five children and they're in a bad financial way, and here they are spending fifty dollars just to get laid; that's where the only wrong might come in. But most of my customers are right well-heeled, and this seems to be a good outlet for them.

Some do feel a conscience themselves because they'll come in and say, "Well, I'm a *nice* guy . . . I've been married nineteen years, and I've only been unfaithful four times." And they'll go on telling you about every one of the four times—who it was with and what they did; or all about World War Two, what they did as GI's—as if I really gave a damn—or their wives, for that matter.

But a lot of the wives don't know how to satisfy their husbands, and they're not even aware that their husbands need some outside source of sexual pleasure. Many of the guys say their wives won't even give them a French or make love in different positions; and the men with certain peculiarities, like the masochists, have the hardest time of all. They're frightened silly of saying anything to their wives or girlfriends. A few have said they've asked them and their wives have thought they were crackers, they haven't understood at all; some have even asked for a divorce in that circumstance. But I can understand their reaction; if you're not in the business, and you haven't that much experience . . . and then your husband suddenly hands you a whip and says,

"Flail me a bit, dear, that's what I crave" . . . it might well be a difficult thing to accept, for some women. Everyone's frightened of something they can't understand.

The transvestites have the same problem, even more than some of the masochists. They couldn't just strut about the house wearing their wives' knickers and dresses without provoking a row. They tell me they often wait till their wives have left to go shopping, and then they dress up and prance about. But if they've children, it's difficult, and they don't want to live in fear their wives may come back early. They like to come somewhere they know they won't be laughed at, and where they won't be disturbed for three-quarters of an hour, and just freely live out these fantasies of theirs.

QUESTION: Do many of the men want to talk a great deal, ask you about your life, or tell you about theirs?

BABS: Yes, a goodly number do . . . they want to get laid, certainly, but they also really want to just sit down and chat; some of them are really quite lonely. My best customer's this guy from New Jersey who's come at least once a week for six months; he putters about the flat and pays sixty to get laid once, but he dearly loves to talk. He tells me all about his wife in Georgia, and what he's done that week, and what his kids are doing; it's talk and talk and talk some more. Sometimes I wonder whether he's really paying the sixty to get laid or just for the chance to talk; he's quite sad, actually, because his family have gone and he's no one who cares what he feels or thinks. A great many of the men seem that way, to one extent or another; they don't need a psychiatrist and they'd feel odd visiting one, but they do need someone to chat to regularly, someone who'll be nice and listen. I always act as though I'm interested with guys like that, so long as they're not too much of a bother.

Then quite a few ask about me and how I got into the business; I suppose nine out of ten must ask that. And several have wanted me to talk to them while we were in bed; that's always one of three things: Either they just want me to say a stream of naughty words, or they want me to tell them stories, to make up fantasy situations for them. The men who want that are often very hesitant to tell you so, which is most annoying; they just beat around the bush and waste both our time. I don't know if they think I'm a mind reader, but I'm not. There was this one man about sixty-five years old, who took three separate visits to tell me that storytelling was what excited him; and once he finally said so, he was so hard of hearing that I practically had to shout loud enough to be heard on the street below. Most of them are satisfied with quite simple stories, generally about the guys I've been with and sometimes about me being with other girls. Often I'll make up some interesting tales about my wild and wicked past in Swinging England [*laughs*]; it's funny, but these men have finally, after many years, realized that they do prefer being with an experienced girl, and the idea that she is experienced does excite them. They've fallen for the old double-standard thing and married themselves a real or pretended virgin; but after the supposed "glory" of the wedding night, what good's a virgin? It's just funny that it takes them so long to realize that.

But I really do much prefer if they simply tell me outright what they want, for I've no way of knowing, particularly with the stranger requests. Some of them even get uptight if I simply say, "Tell me what it is that you want"; they think I'm going to suddenly divine their deepest secret, something they may have hidden from everyone they've known, from their wives, their girlfriends, even themselves . . . perhaps for many years. It's more than a little difficult for them to immediately express that to a stranger; but it really would be much easier for me, and better for them, if they'd just go ahead and tell me. It's not as though I'm about to be shocked by something they want; they couldn't really think they're going to show me something new [*laughs*]! And I don't give a damn what it is they want; I'm being paid to perform a service and "The customer is always right." Of course, there are certain things I don't care to do . . . but not that many, and in any case it's always better to know right off. It's best if they tell me at the very start—before I even take the money or either of us has undressed—because if it's something I can't do, like Greek or something, I'd sooner have them know that before any commitment had been made.

QUESTION: Do you have a regular boyfriend that you date?

BABS: Yes, I have a steady boyfriend who's a lawyer in Brooklyn; he's thirty-six, and he hasn't a notion of what I'm doing. He's not the type that could take it; he's very straight about this sort of thing. He's Italian and believes very much in the old "virginal" images of women . . . that whole great split between possible types of girls, that they're either all innocence and adorability or else they're complete and utter whores. His family'd driven that into him so thoroughly that there was no compromise or mix of those things conceivable, that he never would be able to deal with that, the fact that the girl who is, at least at the moment, his "ideal of femininity" is at the same time a *literal* whore. He's just not ready for that, and I'm not about to tell him—not now, anyway.

I've been through that experience once before, in the worst possible way; my last boyfriend, a budding young Madison Avenue type he was—account executive, I believe. We'd met at an East Side party of some mutual acquaintances and struck if off right well—dinner twice or three times a week, long and serious conversations after the cinema, me helping him decorate his flat, and some right good times in bed. There'd yet to be a mention of marriage as such, but neither of us was in any particular rush on that score; but there was an obvious building toward that level of involvement, you know. Whatever they're calling "love" these days, this was at least near to it.

So we got to know one another well, in most all the ways two people can, but still I was having to always be hiding one of the biggest parts of me, the way I make my living and spend most of my waking hours either doing or arranging for. The number of lies, and lies to explain earlier lies, or pave the way for new ones that had to be told . . . they just kept mounting. Excuses for how I could afford this flat and for why he couldn't call me at "work" . . . I told him my family had some money and that I was assisting in a photographer's darkroom, never knowing when I might be able to be reached on the phone. Then when he'd come here, I'd always have to take the phone off the hook, saying that I had so many friends who might call at odd hours and that I didn't want us to be disturbed; and I always lived in fear that some regular john may try and phone me and get so drunk that he decides to just stop by without setting up an appointment. I pictured the scene so many times: me here sweetly pouring another glass of wine for my adoring suitor, when suddenly there's a crashing storm of knocks on the door, and some man screamin' "Open up, Babs, I've come for me whippin'!"

That never happend, all the better for my heart, but what did was worse. One of my other girls, Tina, was handling the phone while I shopped in the afternoon, and she set me up a series of appointments. The first was around eight that evening, and it was an old customer; so we hung about and chatted for a bit after he'd had his lay, and I lost track of the time. Then the buzzer sounds, and I press the button automatically, knowing I've another date coming. I told my first customer to sit and relax for a minute but that he'd have to make himself scarce soon after the other man came. I didn't mind them meeting, and I knew this first guy would be nice and put the other to ease right quick; so I retired to the bathroom to freshen up. I went back and straightened my eyebrows, put on some fresh lipstick, and this and that; and while I was there I could hear the other man come in, and my regular talkin' to him, saying, "This your first time here? She's quite a girl, gives a good time," and so on. This is all fine with me, I'm happy he's giving me a nice little buildup; so I come sauntering out in my low-cut gown, a sensuous look on my face to greet the new business . . . and there sits my boyfriend, quivering angry! Of course, he'd known ever since he called that afternoon and got the address from Tina . . . but now there he is, getting the word on my performance from my latest customer and seeing me emerge from the back all set for action. It was quite a bad moment, as you can imagine. Not as bad as it could have been; after all, he had been calling to set up something with a girl himself, just not knowing it was me; I have two phones, and the number I advertise is different than the one I use for social calls. But he wouldn't listen to any of that, it was all me that was at fault, me that was the dirty, cheating one . . . so he's gone now. I often think that I should tell my present boyfriend or should find another guy who'd understand; perhaps I will, someday, but that's not easy. So many men have these images, and as a woman, you're only supposed to fit *one* of them; even though the men desire *all* of them, and if you love someone you're meant to fulfill as many of their desires of what they'd look to find in another person as possible. Why do so many men get married and then look for other types of enjoyment outside that? You'd think they could accept it all from a single person, would like the fact that someone could at least begin to be all the things they really wanted . . . but they're so uptight about their sexual wants, they want to put those aside in some corner and have them satisfied by someone they don't care about. It's an odd approach.

QUESTION: Do you have any "straight" girlfriends who know what you're doing?

BABS: Not really; most all the girls I know now are in the business. I do socialize with the other girls, and we go out for drinks together; it's easier, all knowing and sharing what you've been through. Same thing as with the boyfriends, only it's so much easier to find other girls who understand.

Once or twice I've met girls on an outside basis and talked them into the business; they see your flat and say, "Oh, what a lovely place"; and they see your wardrobe full of clothes and hear you're off for the South of France on vacation . . . and they'll say, "Gee, I'm sitting in my little studio wearing rags, and I can't afford to go to *Jersey*; how are you *doing* it?" So I just mention it very casually, make it seem quite natural. Sometimes you think people are so broadminded, and then they'll be horrified when you say what you're doing; others seem totally straitlaced, and they take it with perfect ease. Once I tell them it's fifty dollars a go, for what may be fifteen minutes' "work," they're usually pretty interested; and they start doing it part-time, while they're still working as secretaries or saleswomen during the day. They'll say, "Well, just an extra hundred a week, wouldn't that be nice?" And that extra hundred or two, clear, on top of your salary . . . that can make quite a sudden difference in your life-style. That's another five or ten thousand a year; you can have money in the bank, a nice holiday abroad . . . but, you know, it always ends the same. They come and say, "Well, I'm wasting my time as a secretary; have you any numbers?" [*laughs*]. And I've had girls come, saying, "I want to get this apartment, and I've a month's rent to put down, the security, the broker's fee . . . how long will it take me to get a thousand?" And I tell them, "Oh, a week or two"; and they say, "Fine, I'll just do it two weeks, till I get my thousand to set up the apartment." Then later they'll say, "You know, I really could use a new stereo or a color TV . . . just one more week." After that it's a new wardrobe or a certain set amount to have in the bank: "Well, just one more month, then I'll definitely quit." But by then they're never out of it. They get used to the money so quickly, it's so easy to earn; it's frightening how quickly you do grow accustomed to the finer things in life, and once you've had them, even for a few weeks, you don't want to go back. They *can't* go back, not to the old struggling, being a secretary-bird. They're in the business.

I was only going to do this a couple of weeks; all I wanted was two hundred dollars [*laughs*]. Then when I had my two hundred, I thought why not two thousand, and when I had two thousand, it was ten thousand . . . it just goes on, and you're never through. None of the girls I know are on hard drugs—none but the hardest drug of all, money. We're all addicts to it . . . but so's the whole society. Addicts and prostitutes, every blessed one of us, man and woman alike; it's what we're taught and it's how we live. I'm just honest with myself about it, that's all. And my business dealings are often a little stranger than most [*laughs*].

QUESTION: What are some of the odder customers and requests that you've had?

BABS: Oh, now *there's* a book, luv; I've done just about every type you can picture, and many of them have been quite interesting.

The first time I ever saw anything out of the ordinary was this guy in an apartment on East Thirty-eighth Street. It was quite a nice flat, but spookylike from the minute I walked in. He'd all these odd pets, some running about and some in glass cases: Every manner of reptile he had. Alligators, iguanas, lizards of every description, and snake after snake. I was a bit queasy right off because, as I undressed, I could see all these little leathery eyes lookin' at me, like as if they might be preparing to dine; and he the same, quiet and sort of slithery, watching me just like his pets were: I get goose bumps yet, just to think of how it all first struck me!

So I took off my clothes, and as I'm goin' to lay beside him on the rug—he had a big, thick fur rug—he says, "Not yet" and tells me to put my *shoes* back on. I did and then it develops that he wants me to walk around the cages, touching them and putting my body up against the glass. I could hardly stand it, the glass was so cold and all the tiny eyes and teeth and claws moving what looked like right up against me; but he was paying well, and I was curious, so I kept it up—just sort of turning and rolling against the glass and running my fingers over the places where the snakes and the lizards were. They watched, but only a couple of them snapped or anything. Meanwhile, he's layin' back on the rug, propped against the sofa and playing with himself. Then he tells me to reach *inside* one of the cages and pull out this great black snake; and I thought, "Well, here's where I draw the line; I haven't come here to get myself snakebit!" But I didn't want to seem frightened, so I just looked at him real cool and said, "I'm sorry, but that would involve quite a substantial extra fee," and he says "How much?" I told him "A hundred more," figuring that ought to get him off this track and let us get on with business; but instead he says, "All right," and reaches for the hundred! Let me tell you, my heart was going to beat all at that point 'cause I'd committed myself, I'd named a price, and I had no idea what this man might do if I backed out then. I never said I was frightened, I just told him I'd not had that much particular experience dealing with snakes and might there be another that wasn't dangerous. He got up then and showed me how to open the cage and lift the snake, and said the black one wasn't any danger at all, no matter how fierce he might look; and he did look right fierce. The guy even put his fingers in the snake's mouth to prove to me; so I thought, "For a hundred and fifty, if there's no chance of harm . . . " and I took the snake from him.

He wanted me to dance about with the creature first, sliding it over me here and there; and then to come at him with the snake, to make as if I was threatening him. The thing was hideous slimy, and I felt strange standing there shakin' it in his face; but I did what he asked. Now he's startin' to moan and groan, you know; he's cringin', but he's moaning happy, like a pup with his barker and his wagger working at the same time. Finally he has me slap at his thighs and his belly with the snake's tail, and at this the snake's getting a bit upset, which didn't please me any, even though I believed he wasn't one to bite. The guy understood this, so he had me go to a big chest on the side of the room and take out a great black whip, a cat-o'-nine-tails it was; and he rolled about on the rug while I held the snake and beat him with this thing, hard—I couldn't believe how hard, but he's sayin', "Ah, more, darlin', harder!" till finally he comes all over himself and I'm left feeling silly, naked with a snake and a whip in my hands. Oh, I wish I had a picture of it; I kept my composure, but the look on my face must've shown some of my feelings. Once it was done I didn't know whether to laugh or cry, but when he handed me the one-fifty, I knew which. That much, all for half an hour of playing this funny little horror-show game; and I'd never even had to lay the guy! He was my intro to the S & M scene, and quite an intro he was.

QUESTION: Have you done many other S & M sessions since then?

BABS: Quite a number, yes; I even include that as a specialty in my ads now: "The English English" [laughs]. From that customer, and one or two more right afterward, I realized how much money was to be made doing that sort of thing, and I've invested some equipment. Here, have a look. . . .

[NOTE: At this point Babs went to a closet in her bedroom and took from it a variety of sadomasochistic paraphernalia, including several whips of different sizes and types, two large dildos, lengths of rope, a set of professional-looking hand-cuffs, a thick flat paddle, and various leather and rubber garb. An offer to demonstrate the equipment was politely made and as politely declined.]

BABS: I got these things at The Pleasure Chest—they've quite a selection and the prices are fairly reasonable. All this lot only set me back two hundred at most, and that's including the hip boots that I got elsewhere. It all more than paid for itself in only a few days.

QUESTION: Do customers ask you to use specific pieces of equipment on them?

BABS: Some do, if they know what I have available; with others, I'll make a choice myself and start in, then if they don't care for it I can switch to something else.

Of course, some ask for things I don't have, like chains, or for things I won't do, like . . . well, we had this one guy last week, another girl and I together. He said he wanted the two of us to whip him and for us to be smoking cigarettes while we set to; one would whip him and call nasty names and curse, while the other of us bent down sneering and blowing smoke in his face. This was all fine, up to when he asked us to burn him in the balls with the cigarettes.

We didn't, of course; some of them like you to hit them in the balls, and I'll do that up to a point; but burning them with lit cigarettes? I couldn't do that, I'm sorry. He went off in a huff, and we gave him half the money back; I hope he finds someone to oblige, but it won't be me.

Lots of them want you to play a particular type, to act out a little theater, like; these are the masochists in particular. One of my most popular is "Madame Binh"; I make out like they're a pilot that's been shot down and is being interrogated by the North Vietnamese. Every time they won't answer a question, or if I'm not "satisfied" with their answer, I'll hit them or spit on them or ram something a little farther up their rear. The way they love it, it makes me wonder how many of these guys would *want* to have been prisoners especially if they could have women interrogators who were good and mean. I've taught the act to Kiki, my little Japanese girl; she's tiny, but she does a good show; the men love it when the girl really *is* Oriental and hands 'em a karate chop now and then, right where they'd feel it most.

I've found all this of particular interest, being English; they say it's our national kinkiness, and I wouldn't doubt that a moment. I was never involved in anything like this while I was there, of course, but looking back ... when I think about the treatments dished out in school to girls and boys alike—we do have quite a hang-up about discipline, it seems. I don't know just why that is, but it does seem to be a characteristic, and since seeing all this, I've wondered now and again about my dad and my bro, just what they may be into. Though I can't quite see my mother wielding the cat-o'-nine-tails [*laughs*].

QUESTION: Have you ever been paid to have sex with two or more people?

BABS: Several times, now that you ask. There do seem to be quite a few couples calling and more guys wanting two girls; it's popular nowadays.

Somehow that sort of scene always seems to bring out the voyeur, man or woman; either it's the couple watching two of us girls, or the husband watching me and his wife, or her watching me and him. . . . There's invariably some very intense *looking* in those situations. Often the couples are just beginning to experiment with different things and want to try them out in a "safe" situation, with someone who's hired for the purpose and knows what she's about: the wife going with another girl may intrigue them, or maybe they just want to taste a tiny bit of S & M, say.

It was odd for me, the first time going down on a woman. I'm not that way at all, it just doesn't turn me on, and I'd had no experience along those lines. But I knew what ought to be done, and I'm paid to perform a good service, so . . . then it was strange again, the first time doing it with a girl I was working with, as a show. We knew each other quite well and never a thought of having sex between us, before or since: unless we're well rewarded, and then . . . ah, well you've never *seen* such passion! [*laughs*].

This other girl, Kathy, and I— we had a session the other night: a terribly attractive, soft-spoken young couple from Atlanta they were, called Bob and Laurie. We all four got to chatting over drinks when they first came up, and they were very curious about everything, asking about what type of customers I had and all . . . so I happened to mention the whips and things, and they got interested. Laurie was all agiggle the whole evening and said very little; but Bob said they'd like to see a bit of what was done with the leather goods, and we all took our drinks to the bedroom and undressed. First they had Kathy and me lash each other lightly, taking turns and then together, like as if we were fighting. Basically, they just wanted to make it together themselves, while we did various things. Kathy and I would be kissing each other while they were making love, or we'd caress the both of them, or Laurie would kiss me while she was screwing Bob and Kathy was eating me . . . all sorts of combinations, but usually revolving around the two of them together. At one point Laurie decided Bob should go with me; but when he started to, for some reason he lost his hard-on, and was very embarrassed. He'd seemed all in control of everything up to that point, but then it was obvious that he was even more nervous than Laurie, despite her giggling. She pretended to get annoyed with him then because she said she'd wanted to see him and me together, and she had me hit at him with the whip a little, though not too hard. Finally they suggested that Kathy and I go down on the two of them at once, and we did; that's how they came, lying there holding hands and watching each other get eaten.

Then once I was paid to attend an orgy. This guy phoned up and asked what I charged for an entire evening, so I told him a hundred and fifty; then he said, "Now, is that by the number of hours, the number of screws, or the number of guys?" At that, I was prepared to call him a name and slam the phone right down; It sounded like he was hiring me to minister to a bloody rugby team at flat hourly rates. So I said, "I don't do stag parties, chum; try the corner of Forty-second and Broadway"; and as I'm putting the phone down. I hear him shoutin', "No, no, dear; it isn't what you think at all!" Well, that put my curiosity up, and I reckoned it couldn't hurt to hear him out over the telephone; so I asked him just what he *did* have in mind.

The story was that he'd an invite to this orgy—"swing," he called it—and his wife wouldn't go, so he'd talked her into letting him go alone; but the party was for couples only, and he had to bring someone, a girl. He explained that I'd not have to do anything I didn't care to and that there would be lots of other women there for me to talk to. I was a bit dubious about it all, but he'd a good answer to every question I could think to ask. The party was in a good suburban neighborhood, I could call and check it out with the hostess so long as I didn't tell her just who I was . . . and the best argument he had was that he offered to pay me another fifty, two hundred all told, for not saying how he'd found me. So I agreed to go with him that Saturday night.

Saturday came and by midafternoon I was having second thoughts: What if he's lied to me, perhaps he's a dangerous type who'll just kill me in the Jersey woods, or maybe he's taking me to be raped by eleven hulking gorillas. The whole setup seemed odd, and I'd never done any work outside Manhattan before; maybe it was a new type of police trap to get me to cross a state line. . . . I'm not that familiar with all the American laws, it just could be. I worked myself into such a state of nervousness, just imagining all the bad possibilities; and finally I called the office number he'd given me, to say it was all off. But he'd left for the day.

Very well, I decided, I'll just tell him when he shows up that I've an old friend from out of town visiting or an emergency call. . . . I settled on all manner of excuses and discarded them all. By the time he rang the buzzer, I'd determined to tell him the truth: that I didn't trust the situation and would rather pass it up. If he attacked me, I'd stay near the phone and be right ready to call 911. So there I was, all prepared to ring the law and the fire department if necessary to save me from this mad killer when in walks the mousiest fellow you could hope to imagine, five-five and balding, with glasses and a bow tie. I had to stop myself from laughing—he made such a silly "abductor"—so I offered him a sherry, and he perched there on the very edge of the sofa, more quivery-nervous than most of my masochistic tricks. Now I was totally convinced all over that his story must be true but for one particular: His wife hadn't refused to go along; I couldn't fancy the poor little man *having* a ruddy wife, let alone asking one to an orgy! He was one o' these that comes across all rough 'n' tough 'n' manly on the phone, but then when you see them . . . so, anyway, I'd lost my fears.

He'd parked a station wagon about a block from my flat, and we drove the whole route to New Jersey listening to WPAT and commenting now and again on the number of trucks on the road. At last we parked on a quiet, residential street, and as we got out of the car, he turned to me, very jumpylike, and said, "Remember, don't tell them who you are," as he passed me my money. I felt like bloody Mata *Hari*; but he'd paid and paid well, and here we were out in the country, so I went along to the door of the house with him.

It was a fairly nice house, one of these expensive but very typical American places, all flat and solid. A woman answered the door, very polite and proper, wearing a simple cocktail dress; she showed us in and introduced us around, and the trick is grinning and bobbing about, telling everyone I'm his "fiancée." There were about twelve or fourteen other people there, all couples and all in their late thirties or early forties. Everybody had a drink in their hand, and a couple of snack trays were set out, with pretzels and crisps and onion dip. It was all a perfectly normal social gathering, until the hostess came strutting out from the kitchen stark nude and struck up a casual conversation with one of the little groups of people.

In less than five minutes, everybody else had stripped off, and various people kept leaving the room or heading to a soft, dark corner. . . . I'd long since lost track of my customer; he'd wandered off with some woman in a half-slip. I undressed with the rest of the crowd and was soon off in a back bedroom with one of the men I'd been chatting to over drinks ten minutes earlier. It struck me kind of sad that he was a john and didn't know it; but I'd promised not to say a word and didn't. Still, it doesn't seem quite right, what that little mousy man was up to; as I understand it, one of the main things about those parties is that it's "share and share alike"; but if you're not *offering* anything that's important to you, if you're not there with someone you care for or, at least, *know* . . . I couldn't call that honest sharing. I'm not necessarily convinced that what these people are doing is a good idea; but if you're going to be involved, it seems you should be honest with everyone.

However it may be, I got two hundred dollars that night for just two lays and one short thing with a woman; so I couldn't be too upset, not personally. Right nice company they all were, though; I'm glad they didn't know why I was there, and I wouldn't do that again. It seems cruel somehow.

QUESTION: What are some of the other strange individual customers you've had?

BABS: Well, there's always the TVs; I was very naïve at first—I didn't take them seriously when they'd phone up. They'd ask, "Have you any women's clothes there?" and I'd think, "Well, what do you think *I* wear, you ninny?" But then they'd be asking, "Will they fit me?" and I'd just hang up. I thought they were playing tricks on me, I very honestly did; at that time I thought TVs and homosexuals were one and the same thing, and why would a gay guy be calling a prostitute, a girl? So I just dismissed it.

The only thing I knew of men dressing up in women's outfits was as a comedy number; that's much more common in England, you know. Every musical comedy or revue has at least one female impersonation routine, and even the comedy shows on the telly are always tossing in some man in drag when things get slow. The TV TVs [*laughs*]. Seriously, one of the biggest of the West End theaters, the Palace in Cambridge Circus, has a permanent show like that: "Danny LaRue at the Palace." P'raps that's another of our royal historical kinks; I'd hate to advertise my home country being populated by poufs, but there is an exceeding amount of interest in the TV thing there, even if it is presented as a joke. After all, jokes are only thought funny when they're about familiar subjects, isn't that so?

So, as I say, I never believed them when they'd call; but one day I just got exasperated with these foolish jokes being played on me, and I told one to come on over if he'd like. I was sure no one would show, but sure enough, here comes this big masculine brute of a man, acting humble and apologetic. He paid me the fifty right off, and then he went back to look through my closet; I knew none of my dresses would fit him—he was at least six foot—and I figured, "What he rips, he pays for." But he was very careful with my things and didn't put on anything that was small enough to be damaged.

Before I knew it, here he saunters out in one of my bras, panties and hose, and a wig of his own; he sat by the dresser putting on make up and talking to me about what dress he should wear "to the dance." He went on and on like that, combing his wig and applying gobs of makeup, all the while having me call him Joanna, while we discussed which beauty parlor was best and what were *Cosmopolitan's* latest hints for the single girl. He never even wanted a jerk-off; we just talked "girl-talk" for nearly an hour and he left.

After he'd gone, I thought over the number of calls like that I'd got and realized this must be quite a good market—not as big as the masochist trade, but nothing to be sneezing at either. So I've since laid in a full stock of very frilly girls' things, blouses and skirts and underclothes, plus one long formal gown . . . all in extra-large sizes. It's been quite a popular wardrobe, I must say.

It is odd how they love to just talk and have you talk back to them as if they were really just another bird. *Some* of them must be gay, and wish they were female all the time; but the majority just like to do an occasional role-switch and otherwise are as normal as can be. They're usually quite anxious to prove that to you and are forever showing you photos of their wives and kiddies, who naturally enough don't know what's going on; it's sad that they can't be totally accepted by their families because they're almost always so *nice*; and what they're doing isn't really all *that* strange.

QUESTION: Have you had any customers who requested something outside the "normal" range of "perversions"?

BABS: What a funny combination of words . . . I'm sorry, but that just struck me.

QUESTION: That is a pretty odd concept; I was trying to put all the quotation marks in my tone of voice, but maybe they didn't come across.

BABS: No, I understood how you meant it; still, it's a strange way to put something.

QUESTION: So it is. Anyway, have you had any other particularly memorable "different" kinds of customers?

BABS: Some, of course . . . oh, yes, there was this one old man. He had a lovely cooperative apartment on Riverside Drive. It was always a bit weird just being there because he had this series of photos covering the walls—of him and his wife. They started about fifty years ago, and it was like a movie . . . you could watch them both age, from their wedding day through their honeymoon and their first children, then their first grandchildren, right up to now: she's around seventy and he must be seventy-four or -five. Sometimes I'd walk backwards through that hall, and it was like a gradual time-trip to the past, with this one man and woman. And it was doubly odd knowing the man, both simply knowing him as an *old* man and also knowing him in the sense that I did.

His thing was vibrators; it was long past the time that he could have his fun without some sort of artificial aid, and the vibrators were ideal. All he wanted was some sort of stimulus, something to make him feel alive yet; so we'd just strap these two vibrators around our waists, and he with an extra behind him, and I'd have to hold him for an hour or so, telling him how I loved him and so on. It was just affection that he needed, that and *some* sort of stimulation; between us, the vibrators and I seemed to supply it. I don't know if he ever actually came, but whatever happened he considered it worth a hundred and thirty a visit.

Sometimes he'd want to walk with me outside and would pay extra for a walk. I'm sure I know which was his favorite of the walks we took. Strolling along the Seventy-ninth Street Boat Basin one day, he suddenly handed me the end of one of his ties and asked me to lead him along by it. Only it wasn't about his neck, you understand; it was stuck out through his fly. He'd apparently tied it on himself hours before, in anticipation of this great moment; so I led him around like a pup on a leash, and he never stopped grinning the whole hour. I must say, we got some funny looks from passersby; but he seemed to enjoy that and I didn't mind so long as I was paid.

His main thing was still vibrators, though; he's only discovered them the year before, and he said they "made his old age worthwhile." He once gave me an extra eighty dollars for going with him to St. Patrick's Cathedral; what we did there was we got down on our knees and we prayed thanks to God for vibrators.

He was a very nice old man, really; he died about two months ago, but I know he died happy. He'd discovered how to enjoy himself once again, even if it was with the help of a machine.

There was another customer you might like to hear about; he called and said he'd like to box with somebody. I took him to be another of these jokesters, so I just humored him and said, "Sure, come on over." Well, he did come, and he'd brought a pair of boxing gloves in a big cloth case. I wasn't about to start fighting with him, even in play, because you never know . . . so I told him I'd give him a little show shadow-boxing by myself, or I could call in another girl. That excited him, so I had him wait out front while I called Kathy over. Then we took off our clothes and put on the boxing gloves, while he told us what to do. Once we'd got the hang of what he wanted, he didn't have to tell us—we just went on with it. We did a whole pantomime of being in the boxing ring, dancing about and striking at each other . . . jabs to the vital areas particularly excited him, since we were both nude but for the gloves. He was watching this and masturbating all the while, and finally he told Kathy to "knock me out"; I pretended to take a heavy blow, and I fell down moaning as if I was half-unconscious, writhing my body about on the floor while Kathy jogged about above me, throwing punches at the air; that's when he came, without us ever touching him once. He told us afterward that he'd seen these films in Germany of girls boxing, and it really turned him on; it certainly seemed to, at any rate. It's amazing the number of different fantasies that these men like to live out.

QUESTION: Do you feel that you've had an opportunity to live out any of your own fantasies by being a prostitute?

BABS: Yes, to a great extent. . . . This has been a hell of an increase in income, and I never dreamed I'd be able to afford a place like this, and have all these clothes, and go abroad every three months, and still have loads of money in the bank. It has been almost like a dream, definitely.

QUESTION: I meant sexual fantasies; how has this business affected your own sex life?

BABS: Not that much, really; I'm not that way out sexually myself. It has all made me a bit more tolerant of other people's desires though; and it's caused me to wonder—when I see ordinary businessmen on the street or at a party, I think "Hmmm . . . I wonder if you're a masochist, a straight French, or maybe a TV." You can't tell by appearances, not in the least.

QUESTION: Do many of the customers want to perform cunnilingus on you, or do they seem otherwise interested in getting you excited as well?

BABS: Some do; but I usually try and get around it because I haven't met one yet that knew how to do it right . . . and I don't like being bitten [laughs]. Eat if you must, but please don't bite.

Speaking of which, a few get into trying to leave marks on you, like biting your shoulders or something; I don't know just why, but I certainly don't want to get marked up like that. Perhaps that's the same sort of mentality that leads people to write on walls and subway cars, so they can somehow establish their own existence or identity by leaving traces of themselves behind. I suppose they'd like to write "Kilroy was here" in tooth-marks on my bum if I'd let them.

QUESTION: Do you ever get turned on with a customer?

BABS: No.

QUESTION: Never?

BABS: Very, very seldom. . . . Oddly enough, one of the best times I've ever had with a customer was with this guy who was really a bit gay, I think. We didn't even have any sex as such, no intercourse or Frenching, just . . . well, the guy was slightly masochistic, and what he wanted was to wash my feet, which was nice anyway because I walk around the place barefoot a lot and my feet are always a little dirty.

He was acting a little girlish, so I acted girlish too, and

said, "Oooh, that's a nice idea," when he told me what it was he wanted to do. I took off my clogs and my skirt and led him into the bathroom, and I sat there on the edge of the bathtub wearing a little blue top and a pair of knickers while he carefully washed my feet. Then he began to kiss my feet, which was very nice, licking and sucking my toes and caressing my legs . . . it was quite pleasant, though it tickled a bit, and I was laughing and giggling while he did it. Then he asked if I had a razor, and he shaved my legs for me, very delicately and smoothly.

After that we went into the bedroom, and he put some Jergens lotion on my feet and legs; then we took off the rest of our clothes, and we just lay on the bed. He put his arms around me and held me and told me how he hadn't been with a woman for a long time. He asked if I thought he was strange, and I told him he wasn't strange at all, that he was very nice and that he was quite the gentleman, which I appreciate. He just hugged me and kissed me for a while, and that was about it; it was really very nice, and I genuinely enjoyed myself. He seemed to get something out of it, too, though he never came or even tried to. He was such a nice guy, really much cooler and more relaxed in particular ways than most of them; he wasn't so much into "Me, me, me!" and yet he also wasn't one of the real sick ones that want to be beaten and kicked and burned or something. I actually felt guilty about taking his money, he was so nice; I told him so, but he said he'd enjoyed himself immensely and that it was worth it—he insisted I take the money.

QUESTION: Have you ever had an orgasm with a customer?

BABS: No. But then, I've never had an orgasm full-stop with anyone . . . so I don't think that would mean anything. Still, it would be more difficult with the customers even if I could. So many of them seem to think of you as just an elaborate masturbation machine. I think of it as a job, a service for which I'm hired; but I don't like to be thought a machine, nonetheless.

QUESTION: Do you attempt to purposely detach yourself

from the sexual experiences you have with customers?

BABS: I reckon you'd have to say so, yes. I'm usually thinking about something else. I hate to admit it, but sometimes I'll even watch the telly over their shoulders, particularly if it's one of my favorite programs; they don't mind it being on in the background, but they get quite annoyed if they catch me looking at it [laughs].

QUESTION: How old were you when you first had intercourse?

BABS: Sixteen.

QUESTION: Did you find it pleasurable?

BABS: I was slightly disappointed. You see, I was brought up very conservatively; sex was never mentioned in our house, and English television at that time was very staid, and none of my friends knew what was about. I suppose I over-glamorized it before the fact; it had always been kept so "hush-hush," and I had a notion that it must be fantastic to be kept so secret. I was quite disappointed.

QUESTION: Approximately how many men had you had sex with before you became a prostitute?

BABS: I would say a dozen at the outside, which by today's standards isn't that much. For a time I was still searching out that "fantastic" experience I'd imagined, but I never really found it. I've always been a bit disappointed in sex and still am. Maybe that's why I'm able to accept it so easily as a job; that's what it's always seemed, more or less.

QUESTION: Do many of the customers you see have sexual problems themselves, particularly with impotence or premature ejaculation?

BABS: Yes, a good number do; if they come too fast, that's all right. It just makes things easier for me. But the others, them that can't get it up ... frankly, they're a pain in the ass. They come in and they look rarin' to go; they tear off their clothes and they can't give you the fifty fast enough ... but then, nothing. It's so awful, I don't know just what to do sometimes. I don't like Frenching for a long time, which is the only thing that turns some of them on;

and if you talk about it, that just makes them worse. They always, without exception, say, "This is the first time this has happened to me in my whole life!" and I think, "Who are you tryin' to kid?" I know it's usually just that they're nervous, and they need a bit of sympathy. . . . I'd like to feel sorry for them and help them, but after so many times I find it hard to give a damn. That sounds cruel, I know; but this *is* a business, and that sort of thing gets wearisome if you don't like the person to begin with.

QUESTION: Do you ever plan to get married?

BABS: Someday, no doubt. It isn't likely I'd tell my husband what I'd been doing, though; most of the men I know wouldn't understand a bit of it. I'll tell him I made my fortune playing the horses [*laughs*].

QUESTION: If you were married, would you be upset at discovering that your husband had been to a prostitute?

BABS: Probably not; it would depend on the situation. I'd like to think that by now I'm able to do anything that might please a man, though; it would be a trifle funny if I found my husband was out paying for it once a week, and he said, "Well, I was wanting a bit of S & M, and I couldn't ask *you* . . ." [*laughs*].

QUESTION: Do you have any misgivings or regrets about having been a prostitute?

BABS: None at all.

QUESTION: The experience hasn't emotionally affected you in any way?

BABS: No; just that I think I'm a bit more tolerant nowadays, that's all. Otherwise . . . I haven't let anything affect me badly. If I think something might, I just shut it out.

QUESTION: How do you feel about the Women's Liberation movement as it applies to yourself and what you've been doing?

BABS: I don't keep up with them that much, but from what I've read I imagine they'd be opposed to prostitution. I doubt they'd think too highly of me. Still, what they're saying is that a woman should use her intelligence, and I think this is the most intelligent thing I've ever done. Anyone who'd say otherwise is ignorant or not very realistic, to my mind. Should I have spent my days in a Yorkshire schoolhouse? Or stayed a secretary? Or sold myself into marriage? Not bloody likely.

QUESTION: Do you plan to remain in the United States?

BABS: Yes, I hope to stay here indefinitely; it's a much more exciting country than England, though I'll always enjoy going back home on holiday. One reason for me being extra careful about how I conduct the business is that I would like to apply for American citizenship at some point, so I'm doubly worried about any problems with the police or the tax people. But my luck's held thus far, knock on wood.

QUESTION: So you do plan to continue working as a prostitute?

BABS: Yes, as long as I'm single; if I go on for another year-and-a-half to two years, I could have close to a hundred thousand put away. There's certainly no other profession I'm qualified for that could earn me that; it would be stupid to quit at this point.

4. Joanna

JOANNA *is perhaps the most widely experienced of all the subjects interviewed in this book; she has worked in practically every aspect of commercialized sex in New York City, from live sex shows and pornographic films to Eighth Avenue massage parlors and "model studios."*

An advocate of Reichian sexual psychology, the basic tenet of which is the maximization of orgasmic experience, Joanna makes an often-successful attempt to find pleasure in her sexual labors. She is contemptuous of that supposed 99 percent of prostitutes who dutifully and purposefully negate their own emotional and sexual sensations "at the office."

Joanna is easygoing, bright and talkative; there is little or no defensiveness in her attitude, and she seems eager, though by no means desperate, to befriend almost anyone with whom she comes in contact. She does not fit any of the prescribed stereotypes of Jewishness or prostitution, and her degree of relaxation and self-acceptance is both surprising and enviable. She is quick to laugh but never giggles; seriously introspective but far from morbid; active and alert but by no means manic. Joanna might be considered out of place in any one segment of existing society, but she has gathered together a variety of apparent contradictions to create her own inimitable niche. Though her future seems highly unpredictable, Joanna will undoubtedly find some strange way to make it work.

* * *

QUESTION: How did you get your start in prostitution?

JOANNA: About four or five years ago I needed some money, and there was this older man who liked me, so I started giving him blow-jobs for ten dollars. It was just a one-to-one, personal kind of thing; I didn't go out into the street. I just knew this one person and I'd go to see him from time to time.

QUESTION: How did you meet this person?

JOANNA: I met him through a friend of mine who had known him socially, through her parents as a matter of fact. He had sort of come on to her when her parents weren't around, and when she gave him the brush-off, he offered her money. The perversity of the idea must have appealed to her, and she needed the bread anyway, so she did it. Then afterward she told me about it, and she said, "If you need some extra money, why don't you give him a call," and I did.

That was when I was still living in the Midwest. Then, when I came to New York, the first thing related to prostitution that I did here was this sex show. Simulated sex, naturally; you just had to get up there and pretend like you were balling and so forth, and make it look . . . you know, interesting.

It was a pretty seedy little joint, a little theater kind of, with about ten rows of old theater seats, all spaced pretty far apart so the customers couldn't get each other too wet [laughs]; and then this little stage, with a platform on it about the size of a bed. I'd come out on the stage and undress, pretending like I was getting ready for bed, you know, and then the guy would come out already naked . . . I guess they didn't want to watch *him* strip . . . and we'd just start right in, making out and feeling each other up, and finally writhing around and moaning and groaning up on the platform. That was a pretty uncomfortable platform, just this wooden thing with a red blanket and some pillows thrown on it; but still, every once in a while you'd forget about the people out front and actually start getting turned on.

One of the guys I worked the sex show with was pretty nice, and one night we were both really excited and just started actually balling; which ruined the show, of course. Real sex isn't half as good to watch as make-believe sex, and I think the audience was kind of disappointed that night, although none of them would've believed that they were let down because they finally saw what they'd come to see. The manager got a little upset, both because he didn't think the show was all that good and because he was uptight about the cops. So he told us if we had to fuck for real, to do it either before we came out or after we went offstage. We never did though; it was just a spontaneous thing that one night, and I also think we were both at least a little turned on, if only subconsciously, by the idea of actually doing it with all those people watching.

There was also a sort of "massage parlor" in the back of the place; the guys would get all turned on from watching the performance, and then they could go back to where some of the girls who appeared in the shows, plus a couple of others, were tricking. I wasn't doing any of that at the time though; I was still just working onstage. Even still, I made a good bit of money doing that—over three hundred dollars a week for four hours a night.

I eventually got fired from there, though, and things started to go downhill for a while; so I made a few pornographic movies and posed for some magazines, and then finally I went ahead and got into the prostitution gig.

QUESTION: In a massage parlor?

JOANNA: Not at first; I started off just doing it on the street, which was an incredible bummer: real heavy freak-out time. I didn't like the idea of standing out there with all this stuff on, tight skirts and sweaters and so forth, saying, "Look what I do; this is the role I play." You were just as open to the cops or the dangerous sickies or jealous pimps, as you were to the potential customers. Most of the girls in that scene run on a really high adrenalin level; they play all sorts of sick games. They chase people down the street with knives, and people chase *them* down the street with knives, and they get busted twice a week . . . forget it!

So after a couple of depressing weeks of trying that, I started working at various different massage parlors. They were called model studios in those days.

QUESTION: What would happen at these "model studios"?

JOANNA: The customers would pay a certain amount, supposedly for a photography session, and then they would have to pay extra if they wanted a camera and so forth. And, of course, they'd have to put on this front most of the time, that they wanted a camera to take pictures of the girl. Once in a while they'd take pictures, they'd get turned on to spread shots and things like that; but most of the time they just wanted a blow-job or something. Naturally, in any of these places, what you pay out front is nothing; you don't get anything for it except maybe a few pictures, and if you want anything else you have to pay more for it.

But there were a few guys who just wanted to take pictures, and the pictures some of them wanted were pretty strange. They were really into spread shots, and a lot of times they'd just get right down on the floor about ten inches away and have you pull back the sides of your pussy until they could see clear up to your uterus, practically, and then they'd take close-up pictures of *that*. A lot of men just seem completely ignorant of, and fascinated by, what a woman's genitals look like, even way up inside; I think about twenty or thirty percent of all middle-aged men are frustrated gynecologists [*laughs*]. Then there were some guys who'd act like they were shooting a centerspread for *Playboy* or something, and they'd have you do all these little "artsy" things with veils and stuff; I guess trying to pretend to themselves that there was some kind of "socially redeeming value" to what they were doing. They couldn't just relax and get off; they had to justify it all. A lot of men were just so fantastically nervous, they couldn't even bring themselves to ask you to pose in any certain way; they'd just sort of stand there and silently shuffle around, madly snapping pictures of anything you happened to do, like scratching your foot or something.

QUESTION: Was body painting also offered at these studios?

JOANNA: Oh, yeah, the body-painting trip; that was ridiculous, because you have to just sit there and let all these guys, one after the other, put all this paint on you. Which also gets pretty weird because those little brushes really tickle, and sometimes it's hard to keep from laughing too much, although they really dig it if you giggle a little bit and act sort of girlishly ticklish. Usually they'd just paint some quick, big circles or stripes or something around your legs and your stomach, and then they'd take forever doing all these careful, intricate little curlicues on your breasts and your ass. Once in a while they'd do some funny things, like they'd "label" all the parts of your body, put little arrows and captions like "cunt" or "nipple" in the appropriate places. One guy painted a polka-dot bikini on me, with painted straps and clasps and everything; if I'd shaved off my pubic hair I probably could've worn it to the beach and gotten away with it. Then a couple of people got into making little cartoons and faces, like using my pussy as a beard, and so on. One or two of these places were really straight—you really couldn't do too much else there, you know; and you have to sit there and let somebody put all this paint on you, and you have to wash it all off, for like a five-dollar tip [laughs]: oh, God.

But even at five-dollar tips, it beat straight jobs. I used to do secretarial work because I was very, very . . . cowardly, I think, would be the word. I was so conditioned to security and "respectability" that I was afraid to do anything else. Then finally I got into waitress work, and I saw that at a decent waitress job you came out better because you didn't have to buy clothes—you wore a uniform, plus you got one or two meals a day. Whereas a secretary, even a good secretary at a good salary, has to have this whole wardrobe for the office and spends a fortune on lunch and coffee breaks . . . but it took me quite a while to get away from that, even to go so far as waitressing. And then I saw that, wow, I could make at least fifty dollars a night in these places, so it's ridiculous to do anything else.

QUESTION: How many of the model studios involved prostitution in addition to the photography and body painting?

JOANNA: Ninety-nine and nine-tenths percent [*laughs*].

QUESTION: What sort of facilities did they have?

JOANNA: Well, in the photography rooms they actually had lights set up, for proper exposures [*laughs*]; and in the body-painting rooms they often had a black light, and as the person painted on your body it would glow.

This one idiot came in—he had to be a cop; he offered me a hundred dollars if I would meet him later . . . and you just don't come into a place like that, you go to a call-girl service if you have that kind of money to spend. Well, not always, once in a while you'd meet guys like that through studios, but not *that* place. It was on Eighth Avenue, you know, and *God.* . . .

QUESTION: Where in the model studios would the actual sex take place?

JOANNA: In the same room as the photography or whatever; there was usually a mat of some sort on the floor, and you could turn down the lights in the photo rooms; the black light in some of the body-painting rooms was kind of erotic itself. They'd just close the door, and what you'd do behind the door was your own business. Like I said, some of the guys actually wanted to take pictures; and if that was the case, and it didn't look as if you were going to get the price of a blow-job or a fuck out of them, then some of the girls would say that they would only do certain poses, and if the men wanted spread shots or anything, then they had to pay more for that. And, of course, watching some of those poses would get the guys more turned on than they had expected to be, and it was pretty easy then to talk them into something extra, which cost quite a bit more. So some of the guys got conned into paying twice as much for the same blow-job they could've had if they'd just asked for it to begin with. They really got "tricked" [*laughs*].

QUESTION: How much would be charged for various sexual services at the model studios, and how would that compare to the prices now at the massage parlors?

JOANNA: I think the money was better in those days because of the fact that there were fewer studios. And there was less differentiation, you know; like, you might take twenty or thirty for whatever the guy wanted, whereas now they have this thing where it's ten or fifteen for a hand-job, twenty or twenty-five for a blow-job, and thirty-five or more to ball.

I really don't see that much other difference between the model studios and the massage parlors, except that some people at the model studios actually wanted to take pictures and some people now actually want the massage. But I'd say maybe fifty percent want the massage, that's all; and usually only about five minutes' worth of that, before you get into the sex.

QUESTION: What was your first reaction to doing this sort of work; did you go through any traumatic sort of thing?

JOANNA: Not really; the number of guys I screw, or the reasons I screw them, is irrelevant. I basically just feel sorry for all these guys because most of them are really fucked up. No more problems than the average person, but that's not saying a hell of a lot. They're really uptight, and they generally don't relate to their penis at all; it's a separate object to them. Like "Is *it* in?" or "*It's* going to come." Really. And if you actually do a massage on them, their muscles are so tight it's incredible. Of course, most people are a lot tighter than they know they are. They're so accustomed to their tension that they're not even aware of it anymore; they honestly don't know what relaxation is. Some of these guys, before they ejaculate, *tighten up* instead of letting go. Can you imagine?

So I usually just feel sorry for them and often try to help them learn to permanently relax, or, at least, to relax while they're with me. That's not to say that I take any shit from the obnoxious ones, of course; a lot of guys pinch me on the ass and I just pinch them back, hard. Once a guy actually bit my clitoris; he said it was accidental, but if he'd done it again, I would've kicked him in the balls or something. Some of the girls seem to have a very low self-image, and they'll put up with more stuff like that from guys; but if anybody starts fucking around with me, I just . . . well, I've slapped a couple of guys, and I'd do more than that if it came to it.

QUESTION: Have you ever had a masochist as a customer?

JOANNA: Oh, yes, I've had masochists a few times. The first one I had wanted to be stomped on with my boots and kicked, so I did that.

QUESTION: Did you enjoy it yourself?

JOANNA: It was a little freaky, but interesting; yes, I *did* enjoy it, in a way. But, you see, I have a problem with that; I'm not very good at controlled hitting, which a lot of people are. Most people, when they get into physical combat of any sort—people who habitually do it— have "game rules." Preconscious game rules, like hillbillies have this thing about when you draw blood, that's the end of the fight; things like that. So guys who habitually go into bars and fight or who do the sadomasochistic thing, generally control it pretty well, take it to just a certain point, and that's it. But I'm afraid that I'll flip out and really do somebody some harm. Now it's true that I'm small, but that's irrelevant; you know, if somebody flips out, he can have the strength of ten people. At first I was so afraid of hurting someone that if I did it and somebody said, "Oh, that's too hard," then I'd do it lighter; and finally I talked to a few people about it, and they said, "Well, you're supposed to do it *harder* when they say that; just say, 'Shut up, motherfucker' and whack 'em again" [*laughs*].

One time I did draw blood; I was spanking a guy with a hairbrush, and he sort of freaked out; but some guys even like that. Some people are just so conditioned to pain, you know, that they literally can't accept pleasure; the only way they can enjoy themselves is if they're being hurt, because they just can't accept the idea of enjoying themselves freely.

Sometimes there are people who get off more on words than they do on acts. Answering the phone at one of the studios or at the drug hot-line service I work with, people will say things like "How's your cunt? What are you wearing? Tell me about the last time you had sex. So you like your pussy eaten? Do you like to give blow jobs?" And the more four-letter words you say, the more they like it.

QUESTION: Do you usually hang up on these callers?

JOANNA: No, because I kinda feel sorry for people if the only way they can get off is to talk on the phone. Actually, the first time somebody did that, I freaked out, and I said, "Oh, I can't do that," and I really felt bad about it. And the next time they did it, I got very turned on myself and just went through this whole verbal fantasy number for them. Yeah, I've actually gotten turned on by these things; I can get into talking about sex sometimes. But then after you hear five hundred or two thousand of them, it gets kind of boring. You answer the phone, you say, "hello," and somebody says, "How much hair do you have on your pussy?" and I think, "Oh, God, not another one" [*laughs*].

Some guys, customers or not, are really obnoxiously demanding. This girl and I once went to this place where this guy had advertised that he was making a movie, and he was having auditions, casting people for the movie, and he would pay fifty dollars for the auditions. So naturally we went to the "auditions"; I went a couple of times. Strangely enough, he never called us about the movie [*laughs*]. But, anyway, after that this girl and I were talking about various sexual things, and she said, "Do you like cunnilingus?" and I said "Sure"; and she said, "Well, 1 have this friend who *loves* to eat pussy, and I'll introduce you." So she set it up, and I went over to his place, and it wasn't too bad at all; he was going down on me, and I was sort of really getting into it and relaxing, just like getting really relaxed and calm and digging it, because he was pretty good; and then all of a sudden he jumps up and says *he's* not enjoying it, because he wanted somebody to talk to him, to say, "Oh, yeah, suck my pussy" and all this kind of shit. Which I don't necessarily always get into doing; sometimes it's a lot better to just let go and even half-forget where you are and who you're with and what exactly is happening . . . just lie back and relax, you know? So I said, "Well, I feel that if somebody's doing it to *me*, then they should do it the way *I* want; then if I'm doing it to *them*, I'll do it the way *they* want it." And it developed into a kind of an argument; we just didn't click, you know, so he took me home. There are a lot of people like that; they put ads in *Screw* and so on, and they have these specific fetishes, and they really don't care who the person is. I'm not saying there's necessarily anything wrong with that, I've been in moods like that myself; but it is kind of weird when the fetish is *always* more important than the person or the act. If they're into women wearing pink shoes, they don't care about anything else—she could be ninety-five years old and missing both arms, as long as she still has feet to put pink shoes on.

QUESTION: Have any of your customers ever been fetishists in the classical sense, hung up on shoes or underwear or something?

JOANNA: Not really; sometimes they came around, but I really didn't work with them because I never had any of the "props." I can't stand all that stuff; to me, putting on a "persona" like that is like a big pain in the ass and always has been. I used to do it because I was conditioned by society to be hung up on it. I wouldn't go out of the house without my makeup and all this, you know. Now, if I go out in the street, I'll still put on like minimal makeup because people still think, especially in New York, that it's a necessary part of your outfit if you're a woman, and it's hard to *totally* break away from all that programming. But as far as going to all the trouble of trying to fit into this role, wearing black stockings, garter belts, and things . . . if a guy was paying me a hundred dollars for it, I could see doing it, maybe; but maybe I wouldn't. I mean, I wouldn't put on those spiked heels for five thousand dollars because I've already ruined my feet just from walking on concrete with *regular* shoes.

QUESTION: What were some of your experiences in making pornographic movies?

JOANNA: Well, let's see; the first one I did was really nice. First of all they had me do one by myself where I was masturbating; I smoked a couple of joints and I really felt good. I really got into it; it was kind of weird doing it with these three guys just wandering around, all dressed and just watching, and with the camera, you know . . . but not so weird that I couldn't get myself off. It wasn't even a matter of trying to blot out the reality or anything, because that reality can be very sexual. Just knowing that you're doing this supposedly very private thing, and these guys are here watching you do it, and it's being recorded on film to be blown up on a screen and hundreds of other people will be watching you do it, and they'll all be getting off at the same time. . . . I can get turned on by exhibitionism, at least sometimes.

So we finished that, and then I just relaxed for a few minutes while they changed the film and so on, and then they brought in this guy that I'd never met before—a young, fairly good-looking guy. He and I smoked another joint and then started making love, and it was really far out. I knew nothing about him, he knew nothing about me, but sexually we just clicked. Maybe they should turn all these stupid singles bars into porn studios; it can be a pretty good way to meet people sometimes. That didn't work out for long though; we really dug making the movie, and we decided to spend the weekend together; but we took some acid that weekend, and I found that I had great trouble relating to him intellectually. Physically, he was interesting, but intellectually, forget it; we were like two poles apart. We took the acid, and it was like one of the heaviest trips I've ever had. I was totally out of my body, and it was like ten billion electric volts. I felt totally in synch with myself, with humanity, with the macrocosmic and microcosmic universe. . . . But he just couldn't begin to understand the things I was flashing on; he couldn't make the connections. It was too bad because I felt really fantastic. I really wanted to ball, but he said he couldn't ball me because I wasn't the same person I was the day before; the day before I was "a girl who was looking for something"; and I said, "Yeah, and I found it." He obviously like the negative parts of me, he liked me as a "seeker," or as someone who wasn't there yet; he liked me as a human, but he didn't like me as a god. That's the only way I can put it because that's really what the difference was. It was really funny because we'd gone through this whole thing and it was so great, you know; and then suddenly I'm into this other thing, which is also fantastic, and I wanted very much to be able to put the two together into a greater whole, but he's saying, "Wow, I just can't relate to that," and he kicked me out.

So that was the first movie I ever made. I've only made two or three in all; I did another one which involved about three or four people. It's kind of funny because first of all the guy has to keep an erection long enough, but he can't keep it *too* long or they'll run out of film. Everybody's just really stoned out of their minds, and sucking everyone else off, and fucking everyone, and . . . these were like "loops," you know, sixteen millimeter silents. Really idiotic things, with ridiculous little story-lines just to have some kind of plot; ten seconds of establishing the scene in the beginning and ten seconds of resolution at the end, with half an hour of straight sucking and fucking in the middle. Sometimes you could really get into it, and then all of a sudden the director says, "Cut! Okay, change positions" [*laughs*].

I also did a couple of posings for magazines, and that was really funny; the positions they got you in, no one could ever, ever do anything in those positions *except* pose. And these guys were really genitalia freaks; they'd have a guy who'd be bending over, and they'd look at his penis and they'd look at his balls, and they'd say, "Wow! Look at those balls, the way they hang; isn't that perfect?" It was really a whole 'nother fetish thing, you know; and that's what the people who read those magazines dig. They don't really care about anything else; they just want to look up somebody's pussy.

QUESTION: What was it like at the first massage parlor you worked in?

JOANNA: The thing about massage parlors is, a lot of it

depends on the owners, how they run the thing; and the guys that ran this one were absolute idiots. They expected everyone to work like ten hours a day, six days a week; the manager was late half the time, and he'd rip off money from the guy that owned the place. He wouldn't put a session down, and then he'd keep part of the session money and the girl would get part of it; and he'd want blow-jobs and stuff, but he'd pay something for them, you know. A lot of managers have that attitude or worse; some girls think that in order to keep the job you have to give the guy a free blow-job, and it's often true.

QUESTION: Did you ever encounter this while applying for jobs at massage parlors?

JOANNA: Oh, definitely, absolutely, at a lot of the places; that was their "audition," so to speak. You'd almost always have to go back and take off your clothes for them, and very often you'd have to give them a blow-job or ball them. And at one place, after I got through with all that, he told me he wouldn't hire me because they already had too many girls! "Gee, you're really good, but. . . ." Several places had you do that; there was one place I didn't mind 'cause I liked the guy; but that doesn't happen *really* frequently. I've heard some girls say, "Well, I'm not gonna give the guy a blow-job just to get hired"; which I think is insane. I mean, really; because you're doing it anyway, you're doing it for money; why wouldn't you do it to keep the job? Of course, if the guy gets too obnoxious about it . . . you know, if he wants to do it all the time or something like that, it's a different matter.

QUESTION: Do you have to wear any sort of costumes at the massage parlors?

JOANNA: Some of 'em you do, some of 'em you don't. Often a lot of the girls would wear leotards and tights and maybe pants over that; some of them, they'd wear short skirts, or see-through things. For a while practically everybody was wearing see-through tops and little halters and things. They still do some, but a lot of them now, if they want to decorate the place a little bit more and get more money and be a little bit higher class, they wear more like dresses and things, pretty much normal street clothes, which I think can be even sexier than some of those weird costumes, the harem-girl outfits and shit like that.

QUESTION: Have you ever encountered a policeman while you were working?

JOANNA: Well, not one that arrested me [laughs]. If I was ever the least bit paranoid about it, or if the manager was the least bit paranoid, he'd say, "This is a straight session, don't do anything." And sometimes it was really obvious because they'd come in and ask all these questions about what you do and all this kind of stuff, and they wouldn't say anything. They'd wait for you to make a move, you know, stupid game. But I've always won, so far.

QUESTION: What are the average customers like?

JOANNA: It depends on the parlor, of course; at the really crummy ones, you'd have mostly workingmen, so to speak; some businessmen, but they didn't have too much money. At the more expensive ones, you'd have just about all businessmen who made a lot of money. The average one is a mixture; and a lot of times, too, the workingmen, particularly the construction workers, spend a lot of money.

QUESTION: What sort of age range do the customers represent?

JOANNA: I'd say the average age is about forty-five. But you also find some little old men who can still get it up, and, surprisingly enough, you run into some really young, good-looking guys; I couldn't believe it. Sometimes I'd get turned on, and sometimes a guy that wasn't that great looking would turn me on, too. But I would sort of wonder what the guys were doing in there, really; except that in a nice place, or if somebody comes to you, it can be considered sort of a luxury.

But I've run into some really pathetic guys, too. There was this one guy who worked up above the massage parlor, and he'd come down at least once or twice a week; wow, he was so . . . he had something wrong with him, where his semen would go back into his balls and they'd be like really big. I think he needed some type of operation, but he didn't want to have the operation because then he'd have to give up sex. He was so pathetic; once in a while I'd give him like a hand-job or something, but he would pay me ten or twenty dollars for a half hour just to hold him, to hug him because he'd never been held by anyone before. He was really pathetic; I don't know what happened to him.

I think a lot of the girls really get disturbed by some of those customers, but they purposely turn off any potential empathy because it would completely freak them out if they didn't. They'll say like, "Oh, God, the guy was such a creep"; because it wouldn't be cool or they couldn't stand themselves, if they admitted how much his pain or his lonelinesss had actually affected them.

QUESTION: How did you feel about having sex with someone who was genuinely repulsive in appearance or deformed in some way?

JOANNA: Well, I had one guy who was an amputee; I didn't see that it made that much difference. The only thing that would really repulse me would be someone who smelled really bad or something. Oh, God, we had some of those; there was this one guy, he was really fat, and I forget what it was . . . maybe he didn't wipe his ass or something, but he had a really terrible smell. He was a residential customer, and every girl that ever went over there would go only one time; they'd never go back to him. This guy had money—he wasn't any hobo on the street or anything; he stayed at one of the best hotels, and he would have people over quite often. I used to feel really good about maybe helping some of the more pathetic people enjoy themselves, like I was really helping them out; but after a while it just gets to be kind of a drag.

QUESTION: Has any customer ever gotten violent with you?

JOANNA: No, they haven't; I don't know whether it's just because I've been lucky and seen only nice guys or what. If I was ever in any situation where I felt the least bit paranoid, I would just leave, because I trust my intuition. I'm not saying that I don't have some irrational paranoia, but I would rather leave those decisions to the paranoia side than to the trusting side of my personality. But nobody ever tried anything like that; they really didn't; not even in a hotel or anything like that.

QUESTION: Did you ever have a sadist as a customer, someone who wanted to pay to beat you?

JOANNA: People have asked me, but I've never done it, and I wouldn't.

QUESTION: Has anyone ever "stiffed" you, had sex and not paid for it?

JOANNA: Yeah, I was really naïve for a while; I used to actually not get the money first sometimes, and that's really stupid. You'd agree on a price and go ahead and do something, and then the guy would say something like, "Oh, gee, I thought I had such-and-such and I don't; isn't that a shame"; and what can you do, call the police? So now I always get the money first unless I really, really know the person, you know, if he's like an old reliable customer.

QUESTION: How many different massage parlors have you worked in?

JOANNA: I guess about six or seven.

QUESTION: What was the worst of them like and why was it the worst?

JOANNA: The worst one was a place which was really cheap and dirty and crummy, and the managers fought with each other; they got into some kind of fistfight and all the girls freaked out and ran downstairs. I never went back there, but I think the rest of the girls got a kick out of it. They were fighting so hard, and so oblivious to everything that they almost ran into me, and that's when I said, "Fuck this shit."

QUESTION: What about the best one you've ever worked at?

JOANNA: There were a couple of them that were all right; this first place I was talking about, where I only did the sex show, that was one of the best as far as money, even though I wasn't tricking. Then there was another place that

was really good, too. The managers would check the customer's ID in the beginning to make sure he wasn't a cop;
some of the prices you'd get were really good and some
of them weren't, but it averaged out very well. It was a place
where there were a lot of girls to choose from, but there
were a lot of customers; it was in a very convenient location.

QUESTION: What sort of facilities were there in these places?

JOANNA: Usually there's a main room when you come in,
and then there are several small rooms that have sessions
in; some of them have showers and a few, but not many,
have saunas. Some of them have water beds, which is very
difficult to give a regular massage on, but . . . [laughs]. Most
of them have massage tables. They usually have carpets on
the floor and drapes and . . . like anything else, it depends
on which one you're talking about in terms of ,how nicely
it's decorated or something. Mostly they're fairly dark inside,
and some of them try to look plush; a lot of them have
dark red drapes and things. Most of them have doors on
the rooms, but sometimes there's really not much privacy
at all, just a loose curtain or something, which kind of bothers
some of the customers.

QUESTION: What is the most commonly requested form
of sexual activity?

JOANNA: Well, blow-jobs are really popular and hand-jobs
sometimes; lots of the men seem to prefer that to fucking.
I really prefer giving blow-jobs myself 'cause it's easier on
me; and if you were gonna get any kind of disease from
someone, there aren't very many things you can really catch
orally. I guess you can catch gonorrhea, but there's a lot
of vaginal diseases and things that women can catch, like
trichomoniasis, which is not considered V.D., but . . . I usually
wouldn't ball anybody except for a lot of money; it's also
a lot of trouble to have to go and wash up and spray all
that stuff in, unless a guy uses a prophylactic. So I prefer
doing blow-jobs, and most guys prefer them, too, because
they can just lie back and relax and let someone do it to
them, for a change.

QUESTION: Have you ever had V.D.?

JOANNA: Yeah, I had the clap one time.

QUESTION: Did you get it at the massage parlor?

JOANNA: I wasn't working at a massage parlor then; I got it from a boyfriend.

QUESTION: What precautions do you take against getting V.D. again?

JOANNA: Usually you try to make the guys use rubbers; but if I need money, and somebody offers me fifty dollars to ball and he doesn't have one, then I probably won't insist on it.

Your actual percentage chances of getting something aren't that different than if you just ball a lot of people for the fun of it, or if you ball somebody else who's with a lot of people. I think the ratio of V.D. spread by prostitutes has even decreased; the "epidemic" has been caused by the number of people just fucking for the fun of it. From my own experience, and from other girls I've known, a prostitute tends to take better care of herself than most girls and isn't so uptight about going to a doctor when she needs to.

QUESTION: What was your childhood like?

JOANNA: I was a spoiled brat basically. I was raised by my grandparents to be a nice middle-class girl. I had certain things I wanted to do, like sing, but I worked in the meantime as a secretary or a typist for eight years because I was so inhibited. I was really unable to do anything else; I was even too inhibited because of this whole conditioning to security and the "right" ways to achieve it to even try a waitress job, because there might be a few days I wouldn't make a salary, and I was conditioned to think that anything like that was "beneath me"; bullshit. Nothing that I can make this kind of bread doing is beneath me or anybody else.

QUESTION: What kind of religious training did you have?

JOANNA: Well, I really didn't have much religious training, except the usual bit about God being "in the sky" rather than in yourself, and all that shit. I remember seeing a picture of Abraham in this comic-book-form Bible and refusing to believe that it was anybody but God because that's the image of God I had from their description: the whole anthropomorphic father-figure thing.

Later I went to a Christian Science church for a while, but when I got to be about thirteen and realized I was going to start menstruating, and these people were trying to tell me I didn't really have a body, and I thought, "Hey, that's not right . . ." [*laughs*].

QUESTION: Do you have any religious beliefs now?

JOANNA: Well, now that I've experienced myself as infinite, and as God, and as the universe, it sort of supersedes everything else I've ever been told. As Alan Watts would say, "We're It"; that's all there is, us and our awareness. The group to which I belong now is sort of like Zen, but it's from this country. There are a lot of Eastern methods of enlightenment, but our methods work better on Americans; we're into getting people *in* their bodies as well as outside them, so we take it from all sides. You can have the experience of your soul as part of the universe, but if you're not in your body, why bother? You're gonna have that out when you die anyway, so you might as well live now.

My philosophy is that people should do whatever they want to, as long as they don't hurt anyone else or interfere with somebody else's choice of how he wants to live. I feel that the way I manifest myself in life, knowing that we're all one, is by helping people—anyone who asks me, with anything that I can. I feel that I have a lot of useful information about how the world, and the mind, and the universe work. What religion really is to me is returning oneself to the place you were at before you were born, before looking at the world through other people's eyes; being reborn and starting over from there. If you go against yourself, if you fuck people over, you fuck yourself over. You're going to feel bad about it eventually; you're going to have, quote, "bad karma." You can run and run from yourself, but you're always there; so what I'm working on is getting in touch with myself, my original self, and letting that lead me. I find that if I don't go against myself, I always come out all right. But I've had a hard time following my real instincts because it's something I didn't originally have any faith in; like, the first time I ever had sex, I just completely split off from myself in a way: not to the point where I would be classified as schizophrenic, but I do remember thinking that this "wasn't me" 'cause my concept of a nice, middle-class girl just did not include fucking [*laughs*].

QUESTION: In other words, you were detaching yourself from your own sexuality in your original experiences with sex?

JOANNA: Right.

QUESTION: Do you do that now, within prostitution?

JOANNA: I've gone through various stages, you know; like I said, I didn't get turned on a lot at first. Basically, what it amounts to is that if I'm turned on within myself; if I'm feeling good and really aware of my body, feeling sexual feelings within me, then I get turned on pretty easily. But if I'm uptight or something is wrong, or if I'm sick and don't feel good or something, then I'm usually turned *off* pretty easily. The last time I was doing it was really a drag; I just wasn't in the mood, and I sort of felt a cold coming on, and I had a lot else on my mind.

QUESTION: But you do sometimes enjoy the sex you have as a prostitute?

JOANNA: Oh, sure. I think I'm one of the few people that do, at least to hear what some of the other girls say. It really surprised me, when I'd run into a guy that was really attractive and young; it'd be far out. Before I did it, I expected that everybody'd be a fat, bald old man, and that's all there was, you know, 'cause who else would go, right? But it wasn't that way. I enjoy it a lot, sometimes; other times it's a bore really.

QUESTION: Do you have any difficulty in achieving orgasm, either in prostitution or in your private life?

JOANNA: Oh, well, now we have to go into what orgasm is; according to Wilhelm Reich. Very few people in this society are capable of achieving real orgasm 'cause what happens is not only total pleasure, but also total ego loss, at least for that period of time: total merging with the universe. Otherwise, it's only a partial orgasm, or with me, a lot of times, it's just ejaculation; most men are used to using the word orgasm for that, and most of them think it's the same things.

Most people run on tension, and they have sex to relieve that tension, just like they'd play tennis. They're just not capable of relaxing every muscle in their body, which you really have to do to have a total orgasm. Men think they've had an orgasm if they ejaculate, but a man can build up just so much tension, so much sperm, and he *has* to let it out; it's a very mundane biological thing, not an orgasmic event at all. And as I said before, a lot of men don't even relate to their penises; they talk about them as "it," like they're a separate thing. They're really so insensitive it's amazing. It's like a habitual behavior pattern, you know: "I-go-in-here-and-I-say-this-and-I-do-this" and "whoops!" Out it pops, and that's it. They really don't pay that much attention to what they're feeling. If a girl has big boobs, that turns them on, or if they like small boobs and a big ass, that turns them on . . . but most people never really experience actual orgasm, I don't think.

QUESTION: What degree of impotence have you encountered with your customers?

JOANNA: Very rarely; hardly any at all, in the true sense of the word. I've had guys who couldn't come because they drank too much, and I've had a couple of guys who couldn't get it up, also usually because they'd been drinking a lot of alcohol. But, as I said, most men never have a genuine orgasm; they just ejaculate—so I suppose you could consider that a nearly universal "impotence" of sorts.

QUESTION: Have the religious feelings you now have in any way affected the way you feel about prostitution; have they caused you any guilt or anxiety?

JOANNA: No; like I said, my practical philosophy is a pretty basic "live and let live." Actually, what the organization I'm with is doing is not only enlightenment; we're also performing a function, and we feel that you would do whatever you need to do in order to get done what you need to get done, as long as you don't hurt anyone else. Prostitution is an agreement between two adults; and an agreement for a person to do certain things to your body or to have you do certain things to their body, as long as it's freely made and no one is harmed, is really no different than an agreement to type something on a typewriter: both involve renting your time and your skills, and even your body, though I did use my fingers a little more in typing that I do in prostitution [*laughs*].

I really don't see anything wrong with it; you can't have black without white or good without bad, and you can't have Puritanism without prostitution. So when *that* no longer exists, when people are no longer trying to tell other people what to do, and they no longer have the concept that they or their bodies are evil or dirty, et cetera, then there'll no longer be any need for prostitution because people will be willing to help each other fulfill their needs . . . and feel free to admit their own needs.

QUESTION: So you believe that prostitution as it now exists will eventually disappear?

JOANNA: Well, if the world changes and evolves into that, which I think it will . . . because if no one were sexually repressed, you just wouldn't have any of this stuff—you wouldn't have war or anything else. And you wouldn't have people projecting themselves, their essences and sexual energies, into money, as we have now; there wouldn't be any need for it. If everyone grew up without somebody telling them what to do and what not to do, and they felt like having sexual experience when they reached puberty, they would go ahead and have it; and it would be very easy to find people to have it with, because nobody would be so inhibited.

Aside from *whether* they can have sex, people also have unnecessary preconscious structures in their heads about *who* they can and can't go to bed with. If you're an upper-class WASP, you just wouldn't go to bed with a Mexican, say; or people that look a certain way, people that look like your mother or your father, or people that *don't* look like your mother or father. And people get really freaked out if someone from outside their particular categories turns them on;

they just can't deal with that, and they try their best to shut it off, and they get fucked up as a result; whereas if they relaxed and went ahead with their own feelings, they could just get plainly and happily fucked.

QUESTION: Then you believe that sexual repression is one of the primary problems of the human race?

JOANNA: Oh, definitely; there's this whole Mechano-Mystic dichotomy, as Reich called it, where the soul or essence or spirit is supposed to be something above and beyond the body, but never really a part of it; this is where most people are at. Then there's the idea that the body is something "animal," and that's supposed to be terrible and bad, debased and horrible; rather than understanding that God, spirit, nature, essence, sexual energy, and soul are really all the same thing. All energy is sexual energy in the sense that it's bioenergetic cosmic force; it's universal orgasmic orgone energy. We *are* energy; it's all one and the same, body and soul and sex.

There's more to it if you're going to work on a person therapeutically because just working on the body and not anything else doesn't make it; people have concepts of themselves, and the problems basically start from that. If you have an inaccurate concept of yourself, everything else is gonna go wrong from that. If enough people tell you you're "so-and-so," then your whole life is going to be based on "so-and-so"; you can do this and that, and you can't do that and the other . . . you can't fuck, or whatever, or only in certain positions, or whatever your preconscious is telling you. If you put a person in a situation where they can release their sexual energy, and they don't understand what's going on, they'll just run from it and tighten up again; so it's not the only thing to be worked with in helping people, but it's certainly one of the major things. If you don't work with your body at all, it's just as ridiculous as working with *only* that . . . and there are a number of supposed methods of "enlightenment" in which they get the person out of their body, and they're at one with the universe, but they never get back in the body; they control it like a puppet, which is both sad and a little frightening.

QUESTION: Do you feel that your work as a prostitute enables you to offer a useful social service or even a form of therapy?

JOANNA: I feel that I do, but I don't think that's the case with all prostitutes. If I'm really turned on, then because I've been through a lot of this program that I'm in, there's a lot more of my actual essence being used than there is with most people. I think some of my customers may have learned something important from me, even unconsciously, even if they didn't know it. I do think I'm capable of offering them something unique and valuable that they, hopefully, can retain in their own lives and in their own relationships. I think that way a lot of times, if I'm in a giving mood; if I'm uptight, I don't feel that way—I just think, "Oh, God, let's get this over with."

QUESTION: Then you often attempt to inject yourself as a person into the experience?

JOANNA: Yeah; I find that completely detaching myself from *any* experience leads me around in a very vicious circle; if I'm really in my body, just about anything is groovy. I've found that shutting myself off is just a total bummer; I think that anybody who says otherwise is really kidding herself or himself, at least to a great extent. Usually what happens is that a person has so much pain in their body that they detach themselves because they don't want to feel it; but I've found that it generally hurts more to do that than it does to go through the pain and relive it and get rid of it, get it out for good.

QUESTION: You've said that you hope prostitution will eventually disappear, as sexual repression is eliminated; in the interim period, do you think that prostitution will or should be legalized?

JOANNA: I think it probably will be; by that time I doubt if I'll be into doing it, so I won't be personally involved, but I think it'll happen. And I do think that the legalization of prostitution, just like the legalization of marijuana, would be good, because it would be a step in the direction of people being able to do whatever they want to do with their own lives, and that's really what counts. Sometimes I think that everything is really evolving and happening, and it's beautiful; but, on the other hand, we have people like B. F. Skinner writing books like *Beyond Freedom and Dignity*, and we have people who want to try doing lobotomies again. Their concept of a human is that it's a potentially evil thing that must be repressed, or else it'll turn into a monster; whereas, actually, the monsters result from being repressed in the first place. They just want to turn people into robots, even more than they already are.

QUESTION: What do you think of group sex?

JOANNA: Whatever turns people on, they should do. I think it's probably good; there are times when I've really turned on, and I was attracted to everybody, it didn't matter whether they were male or female or what they looked like, especially if I was with people I liked as people. I believe that anything that breaks down inhibitions is good; and if that's what breaks down inhibitions for somebody, then they should follow it through. If they've never done it, and they want to experiment, then they shouldn't be afraid to try it out and see what it feels like. Of course, people play a lot of unnecessary and potentially destructive games, even within something like that: suburban couples playing "wife-swapping" and stuff. They're just creating new sets of definitions and restrictions and aren't really freeing themselves at all.

QUESTION: Have you ever had any lesbian experiences?

JOANNA: Yeah; I never really thought about the sexual part of it as a child but always knew that such things existed: you know, women living together and acting like men, and so forth. I had a couple of cousins who were lesbians. In some ways I'm very inhibited about it, even though my upbringing about it was very liberal: but I've always been attracted to other women. I tend to think it's a natural way to be. According to Freud it's just one of the normal psychosexual stages of development, and if you're "genitally mature," which very few people supposedly are, you wouldn't want to have sex with a person of your own sex. But I've always felt that when I'm turned on, everybody's attractive. A lot of the girls in the massage parlors are bisexual—a really large number of them. Once you open yourself up to the idea of a great variety of sexual partners, even paying ones, a more open attitude toward things like bisexuality just seems to naturally follow.

QUESTION: Have you ever had a customer request that you and another girl perform a lesbian act for him?

JOANNA: Oh, yes; basically the main thing involved is practicing cunnilingus on each other, and the guy usually ends up balling one of the chicks or both of them. Or a guy wants to be eaten at the same time a chick's eating another chick, or something. A lot of guys like to have two girls; it's very common. It's interesting, too, that a lot of guys get turned on by two chicks making it together but not two guys. Most men are terribly afraid of their homosexual side; and it's so obvious that the ones who fight it the hardest are the ones who'd really like to do it, but their conditioning, their concept of themselves, says, "Oh, no, no; you're a *man*, and a man doesn't do *that*." I had this one guy who said he liked to go beat up faggots in the park, and he was just *so* vehement about how much he hated them and all that you could really tell he was actually dying to try it himself; but those feelings frightened him so much, he had to channel all that energy into hostility and beating up the people who represented what he was most afraid of in himself.

The concepts of sex that we have in this society are just amazing—they're so rigid: the strict definitions of "man" and "woman" and what each is supposed to do or not do, think or not think, enjoy or not enjoy. Also, our images of sexual attractiveness can be so simplistic. . . . At one massage parlor, I got the job and then I went back the next day to go to work, after tripping the night before; I was still rather spaced out, and I didn't have much makeup on, and I was wearing something that was comfortable but not too sexy; and I got like one customer in two days. All the other girls had a lot of hair or wigs, and they had on pretty leotards; so I went out and borrowed somebody's long blond wig, and I got a little lacy blouse you could see through and hot pants and boots and tights and all that; and then I made like a hundred dollars a night. It's such a stereotyped thing, it's just amazing. In a massage parlor, this blond wig thing is insane; they don't see anything else. I worked in one where there was this blonde who wasn't nearly as good-looking as most of the girls who worked there, but the men would come in and see her and say "I'll take the blond," and that was it. They have such stereotyped ideas, like in the type of questions they'll ask you and so on.

QUESTION: What kind of questions do most of the men ask?

JOANNA: Just really stupid and straight, a lot of the guys; they ask you personal questions, like "Are you married?" or "Do you have a boyfriend?" A lot of the girls who work in these places work basically on the same principle that the girls on the street do, that they love their husband or their boyfriend, and they don't love anyone else or even really feel anything with anyone else; they say their old man would kill them if he ever found out that they did feel anything with somebody else. Then the same girl would come back a week later and be talking about how good her last customer could eat pussy [laughs]. But I think they really do turn themselves off basically; they feel they want to be "faithful," which to me is utterly self-defeating, self-destructive behavior. I mean, that's totally artificial, it's not natural; you can totally love someone and enjoy being with that person more than anybody else in the world, but love is infinite . . . and if you're attracted to that person, you're going to be attracted to other people. If you tell yourself you're not, then you're just kidding yourself. Even in a massage parlor, out of a certain number of guys, some of them are really gonna be good at cunnilingus or something. They don't all come there because they're too horrible to get girls, you know; some guys come there because they feel they have to get emotionally involved if they go out with a woman, or because the "dating" scene is often such a hypocritical, long-drawn-out version of prostitution; they'd rather just eliminate some of the time-wasting formalities of dinner-drinking-dancing and get what they're paying for right away.

It's really a shame that so many of these girls detach themselves the way they do. A lot of the girls who do this sort of work are really repressed. They have like really straight concepts, a lot of the girls; very straight and old-fashioned concepts about marriage, and about being faithful ... other than working in a massage parlor, they have a lot of inhibitions; it's like that's a separate part of their lives or something.

QUESTION: Do you have a husband or steady boyfriend yourself?

JOANNA: Not anymore; I was married once, but now I'm not into relationships with roles attached to them. I don't believe in having a relationship with expectations or requirements, and I don't have any desire for that.

QUESTION: What sort of relationship did you have with your ex-husband?

JOANNA: Well, as I said before, my first sex experiences were really bummers because I was so rigidly conditioned against enjoying myself sexually. For several years I was into the whole "petting" scene on dates, with very precise border-lines of permissible activity and places where I'd let a guy touch me or not let him touch me, all of that shit. So by the time I did go ahead and do "it," it was like a compulsive rather than a natural thing; if I'd just relaxed and done it to start with, it probably would have been fantastic. So for a long, long time I really didn't feel that much unless I knew in advance that I *wasn't* gonna ball a guy, and then I'd get turned on [*laughs*].

Then I got pregnant—and had the child adopted; so by the time I met my husband, I was really fucked up. We were very much attracted to each other immediately, but I still didn't find it easy to let myself go sexually; after a while, though, I did. I think that's why I stayed married to him as long as I did. We didn't have that much else in common, but he was really, really good in bed; he really turned me on and, more or less, opened me up sexually.

I sort of turned myself off when I left him, and it's taken me a long time to get those emotions back. What I want to do is to feel the same way, to love someone, without any of the hang-ups. At that time it was a whole traditional possessive thing, you know: "Where were you? Were you out with somebody? Why were you out so late? Why didn't you come home when you said you would? What were you doing looking at her? What were *you* doing looking at *him*?" and all this crap; really self-defeating. Pretty normal, I suppose; but "normal" isn't particularly sane or pleasant.

QUESTION: Does your ex-husband know what you're doing now?

JOANNA: I don't know what *he's* doing; I don't know where he is, and I don't really care.

QUESTION: Do the guys you know, or have affairs with, know about your involvement with prostitution?

JOANNA: Anybody that knows me really well usually does; it doesn't seem to bother them, and if it does . . . well, then I don't really want to know them anymore if they're going to be that hung-up about it.

QUESTION: How do you feel about the relationship between prostitution and Women's Lib?

JOANNA: A lot of the gung-ho Women's Libbers put down women who do it; but, to me, even though obviously certain laws and things have to be changed, Women's Lib is just a small part of *people's* lib—it's enlightenment, it's becoming totally yourself and totally aware. I feel that anything a person needs to do to get that way is natural, and in this society prostitution is a very natural thing; it's not necessarily a universally natural thing, but then this society's not exactly natural, is it?

When I think that I spent all that time sitting at a desk, bent over, wrecking my back and getting a flabby ass, and sat drinking coffee all day, ruining my pancreas, ruining my eyesight by typing eight hours for twenty dollars a day, just because I wanted to be a nice middle-class girl . . . I can't believe it really. That's an old joke, even—about the girl who spent five years at a desk until she realized she was sitting on a fortune.

QUESTION: So you don't feel that prostitution is exploitative of women?

JOANNA: No more than any other business, and, in many ways, less so. Just businesswise, there are some studios where you have to give the manager a cut out of your tip, which is ridiculous; and there are some that pay you part of the session money, but most of them don't, it's just up to you and the guy for what you get. But I don't see them exploiting any more than anybody else; they really are more liberal than anybody else, in terms of coming in late or taking days off or whatever. Some places exploit girls, like wanting them to go to bed with friends of the boss for not too much money and stuff like that; but, in general, I don't see that the girls are any more exploited than in a straight job. I'm sure that a person who works her ass off for two dollars an hour definitely feels exploited; and a secretary is usually expected to be more of a sex object than a prostitute, at a tenth the pay. So I really don't see that much difference, especially considering the amount of money the person's making. Of course, if you consider the amount of money that the people who *own* the massage parlors are making. . . .

QUESTION: What is your average weekly income at this?

JOANNA: Usually around three-fifty a week; I've made as much as six hundred a week, but not for quite a while, because there are too many people doing it now; business has gotten sort of bad.

QUESTION: What sort of drug use have you encountered in relation to prostitution?

JOANNA: A few people have joints if you go to their home or something; and a lot of guys, the younger ones, will bring a joint or two along to a massage parlor. I know almost no one who works in the massage parlors that doesn't at least smoke grass; most people are also into cocaine. A lot of them are heavy down-heads, and some of them are junkies; I'm not into that, at all.

QUESTION: How many of the girls you've known have been into prostitution as a means of supporting their own or someone else's heroin habit?

JOANNA: It seemed to me that it was a fairly small percentage of the girls, though I'm not that familiar with heroin, and I don't always necessarily recognize someone who's into it;

but I wouldn't say more than about twenty percent, tops. Maybe a little more than that among the street girls, and a little less at the massage parlors.

QUESTION: Have you ever had a woman as a customer?

JOANNA: Not alone; I've had couples, but never just a woman alone. I think that they just don't have the guts to come.

QUESTION: What would happen with couples?

JOANNA: They usually want oral sex; and a lot of the women dig being with other women, but only if the guy is there and they can project a lot of their feelings onto him. They say, "Oh, gee, I want you to enjoy this, too, I want you to get into it; isn't it a gas?" and things like that. But I've never seen a woman come into a massage parlor alone; women are just too inhibited right now, at this point.

QUESTION: Do you think that there should be male prostitution for women?

JOANNA: There is now, it's just more under cover. Older women, especially, will go to guys that advertise as masseurs, but I think very few women would go to a studio or massage parlor. You have that outward persona for men of "I don't do that kind of thing, ever"; then underneath that you have the fact that everybody knows damn well they *do*, and it's accepted in their peer group. Often, three or four men will even come in together, after an evening of drinking or something. But with a woman, it's not accepted in her peer group to do it; she can't just suggest to her bridge club that they all go out and pay somebody to fuck them. So women are usually sneakier about it; they don't go to massage parlors as such, but they might have somebody over to their house to give them a "massage" while their husbands are at the office—or while their husbands are in town at the massage parlor. And, of course, semipermanent "gigolos" have always been in demand, particularly in Europe, where everybody's traditionally been a little more open about their sexuality.

QUESTION: What sort of contraceptive do you use?

JOANNA: First I used the pill for a long time, but I stopped that because I gained a lot of weight from it and so forth; then I used an I.U.D., but that gave me a lot of problems. It gave me infections all the time, and it actually hurt; it was really ridiculous because I'd have to try and stop feeling, and if you're gonna do that, if you can't let go, why have sex? I really feel that some of the people who invented these contraceptive things were thinking of women in their traditional roles and were trying to keep them there. Most women are prostitutes anyway: the whole wife trip and all that is really a form of prostitution. And the attitude that people used to have about sex, that it was the woman's "duty" and all that; I think a lot of the people who work on the contraceptives still have some of that attitude because some of the problems that women have from these birth-control methods . . . it's like they're still being punished for their sexuality. In the last century there was even a huge moral complaint against the discovery of ether because it would take away the pain of childbirth: women who fuck are *supposed* to have pain and problems. Maybe I'm wrong, maybe the scientists are doing the best they can, but I really don't think so. I think any new medical discovery, any new law, any change in social structure or attitude that would make our lives more genuinely free and pleasurable, is purposely kept down and repressed . . . as a terribly sick method of revenge carried out by those very people, like Nixon and Agnew, who have been the most thoroughly repressed themselves. It's a bitter, vicious circle, but I hope to live to see it broken, and I'd like to think I've done all I could personally to help break it.

5. Tom

TOM is a male homosexual prostitute. Unlike many young men of his profession, Tom is himself admittedly gay. The combination of these two realities, in addition to his upbringing as a devout Roman Catholic and son of a New York City policeman, has caused him an unusual amount of deep personal problems: afraid to publicly declare his homosexuality, unwilling to admit the type of work that he has performed, and unable to break the moral shackles of his childhood religion, Tom is forced to live in a tortuous limbo of half-truths and fear of discovery.

On a casual first meeting, Tom would seem to be an extremely normal person with well-defined, easily attainable goals. A college graduate and qualified teacher, he conveys an immediate impression of articulate friendliness and deserved, if subdued, self-confidence. He is obviously popular with his students. Bright, witty, and open, Tom would be an asset to any high school class. Were the details of his personal background known, however, it is certain that he would never teach again.

Tom is by no means blatantly gay; his sexual preferences are apparent only in retrospect, after many hours of revelatory conversation. Then, and only then, does one begin to notice or recall a slight girlishness about his laughter, a subtle message in the way he sits or stands. To an impartial observer ignorant of the facts of his past, Tom would never be pinpointed as gay, let alone as a homosexual prostitute.

Tom's problems and opinions with relation to the massage parlor world are peculiar to himself as a male, as a committed homosexual, and as a Catholic; but his is a viewpoint shared by millions of other Americans who have never experienced these realities to such extremes as he. It is highly doubtful whether Tom will ever be a genuinely happy individual, but his story may be of immense value to other young men who are now undergoing some of the same torments that he describes.

* * *

QUESTION: When did you first realize that you had homosexual inclinations?

TOM: Well, you don't just wake up one morning and say, "Wow, I'm a homosexual"; it's a gradual process of realization that begins with various thoughts that often don't even have anything directly to do with sex: relationships with your parents, friendships or the lack of them, that sort of thing. I more or less resented my father and was a little too close with my mother. "Oedipus Regina"* right? I never really got into sports and was pretty much a loner; I generally saw myself as an observer of life more than a participant in it. Feelings like that tend to set you apart from the social mainstream of things in, say, junior high school.

Then, as I got a little older, I began to realize that I might be sort of different in other ways, too; high school becomes a period of very intense sexual self-acknowledgment. I found myself looking at other guys in gym class or guys swimming nude in the pool, which is really a very normal expression of curiosity, but I worried about it to the point of obsession. I'd still be thinking about it when I went home, and then I started thinking about it at night, and the next thing I knew, I was masturbating over those images. That sent me through these monstrous spasms of guilt, and I'd make great conscious efforts at putting it out of my mind; but sooner or later I'd catch myself again looking at a guy before I'd look at a girl, and I was gradually forced to a full awareness of how I actually felt.

* *"Oedipus Regina": "Oedipus the Queen"*

I went to college still without having done anything about those feelings. The school I went to was a very conservative one—Fordham in New York. Everybody was from the same social background, Irish and Catholic working class, strictly from the New York area; there were no dormitory facilities. Everyone had the same values, and if you didn't at least keep up the pretense of adhering to those values, you were lost. For instance, I joined a fraternity, which seems laughable now; but those were really invaluable experiences with straight guys, seeing how they lived and thought and conducted themselves in all sorts of situations. It helped me to reach an understanding of the heterosexual side of my own self, and therefore of other people who are one hundred percent straight, that I don't think I could've gotten any other way.

The fraternity experience also tended to delay my real entrance into homosexuality, which I think was good. Otherwise, if you come out too early . . . I think gay people get to be ridiculous. They think everything revolves around being gay: They go to gay restaurants, gay bars, gay movies, gay parties. . . . They just get carried away with these things, to an unbelievable point. It's like an Italian only going to Italian restaurants, and only having Italian friends, and only listening to Italian music. Racism and sexism work in several different directions, and I do think a lot of gays are very sexist.

QUESTION: When did you have your first homosexual experience?

TOM: Senior year in college. He was one of my best friends, an All-American football player type. We were an odd combination, the extrovert and the introvert, although anyone at Fordham who thought about anything other than sports in general and basketball in particular was considered introverted, if not an outright "weirdo." But Paul and I had a few hang-ups about our parents in common, and we shared some ideas about life, so we got to be really good friends. We took a couple of trips together, and it was on one of those trips, to Washington, D.C., that the sexual side of our friendship first developed, though in a very indirect way.

QUESTION: How was that?

TOM: We were sharing the same huge double bed in this hotel room in Washington, and he brought this beautiful French Canadian chick back one night. It was this really old-fashioned type of bed, in a very nice room, and he and the girl crawled into the bed and started screwing while I was lying there half-asleep. I think he knew I wasn't asleep, but the girl thought I was. I just kept my face more or less turned to the wall and kept breathing regularly, and listened to them making love right next to me. I could feel the bed moving, and every once in a while I'd feel one of them or both of them brush up against my back or my thigh. It was very stimulating, and I had a tremendous erection. I really wanted to sort of join in, but I didn't know how to go about it, or how either of them would feel about it, or who I'd do what to if I did, so I just lay there and pretended to be asleep. Then, when she left, I remember looking at Paul washing up in the bathroom, and he really turned me on. He was hung and he just looked fantastic. I had always been sort of afraid to see him without any clothes on; I think I knew I was gonna go crazy [laughs]. But I managed to control myself, and nothing happened that night; but I thought about it for a long time, and I replayed that scene as a masturbation fantasy about fifty or sixty times.

Then, about two months after we got back from Washington, we were at a bar in Brooklyn one night, tipsy but not drunk, and both of us bullshitting away about how horny we were and how none of the chicks in the bar were worth going after. So I said, "Did you ever think of going both ways?" and he just looked at me kind of funny and said, "What do you mean?" So I said, "Well, I just dig sex, period; when I get horny, it doesn't matter whether it's a guy or a girl." I was taking quite a chance, even though I knew I could trust him not to say anything to anybody else, even if he got pissed off; I was putting our whole friendship on the line, and I had no idea how he might react. I was scared to death that he'd just get up and walk away and never even speak to me again. But he was curious having been raised a good Catholic; it was something like Sodom and Gomorrah to him, and everybody wants to make a trip to Sodom and Gomorrah at least once, just to see what it's like, and then come back home again.

So I went home with him, and we went into his bedroom, and he took off all his clothes. I never even asked him to take his clothes off; I thought he would just drop his drawers or something. But he wanted to get nice and comfortable. He's a sexual animal, period, and if he was going to try this out he wanted to try it out right. I went down on him, and a few things like that; he didn't ask if he could screw me, which seems a little odd in retrospect, because I've found that that's usually what a straight guy likes to do.

So that's how it all started. I didn't really enjoy it too much, sexually, because I was afraid to; having faced my worst fear, I couldn't face the fact that it was all true. I remember going home that night, thinking, "Well, I've finally gotten that out of my system, and I don't have to worry about it anymore" classical attitude. Straight back to the closet. I was best man at Paul's wedding about a year later; we were very close [laughs].

QUESTION: How long after that was it before you had another homosexual experience?

TOM: It was in Miami, about five or six months after the time with Paul.

QUESTION: What happened in Miami?

TOM: I was there on vacation with my parents, of all things, and my father innocently happened to choose a hotel right across the street from a well-known gay bar. I sneaked over there and just started talking to some of the people. I was very nervous, and they knew I was just coming out, so they were extra nice to me; which was unusually lucky because gay people can be very unpleasant in that situation. There's a pronounced strain of bitchiness among gays; they're all playing some pretty desperate ego games and usually, when somebody's first coming out, they'll give him a regular "baptism of fire." They'll be polite, they'll even dance with you, but . . . it can be rough. Sort of an initiation procedure, which actually isn't a bad idea; if somebody's thinking of coming out, he'd damn well better find out fast that it can be a difficult life a lot of the time. He's not going to suddenly solve all his problems just by coming out, which is a natural subconscious expectation. You go through so many years of internal torment from denying it all that you tend to think giving in to your desires is going to make everything just simple and rosy for the rest of your life. I think it's pretty good for a gay person who's just coming out to have a little preview of the bullshit and the pain that can follow that action.

But I did meet a really nice guy at this place, and he took me home and showed me a lot of things [*laughs*]—yeah, a lot of things. Some nice, some not so nice; he tried to screw me anally, and I didn't like it at all. It was painful and just generally unpleasant; I still don't like it. Somehow that's like taking away the last vestiges of your masculinity; I don't even like to do it to other guys. But, aside from that, I definitely enjoyed myself: this was my first true, complete homosexual experience because it involved making out, snuggling up, just general bodily contact—everything I'd ever done with a girl. It really turned me on, and I didn't feel guilty about it at all; so when I got back to New York, I found out about a place called the Round Table and started going there when I could get away from home. I still live with my parents.

QUESTION: What are your parents like?

TOM: My father's a New York police detective, and he's very distant—a typical Irish cop, extremely authoritarian on the job and at home. Very strict, always very worried that the decadent neo-Roman New York society that he saw the dregs of every day would somehow influence me. His main worries were drugs and things like that, I suppose; I doubt if all this would have even occurred to him as anything that his son might be involved in.

My mother's Jewish—a weird combination, right? We had some pretty funny family gatherings, when the grandparents and uncles and aunts were all around; they all lived in the neighborhood, too. My mother pretty much ran the family, although my father tried to; I used to sleep with my mother until I was about eight or nine. It was a pretty typical Freudian version of the environment that's supposed to create homosexuality, I guess; I still can't decide how much of an effect it really did have on me.

My mother converted to Catholicism, and the whole family was fairly serious about it; my parents never would have considered a divorce, even though I think maybe they should have. I was pretty religious myself, even to the point of considering the priesthood when I was in early high school; then the sexual crisis—and I do mean crisis—more or less replaced my concerns with religion.

QUESTION: When did you first get into homosexual activity for pay?

TOM: Well, after I got out of Fordham I began teaching; I was in the city schools for six months, and then I received my license. In the same mail I also received a notice of a cutback in the schools, particularly in the field of Social Studies and particularly in my field. I was told that there would be no job available for me in the fall; I was terribly upset about that because I'd just finished four years of preparation for a job that I really liked and that I felt to be something worthwhile; suddenly I'm being told that "It's all over, go away and don't come back." This also blew my draft deferment, and I had number eight in the first lottery, which was held that year. I had been making about two hundred dollars a week, I'd bought a new car, I was fairly happy and my life seemed to have some direction to it; then it just fell apart.

I went to different job interviews all summer, in the city and upstate; I even thought of going to California, but they were having cutbacks throughout the country at this time, and I was low man on any totem pole, with a brand-new certification. I had car payments to meet, and I just had no idea what to do.

QUESTION: What did you do about the draft?

TOM: They called me in for a physical, and I pulled something that a friend of mine had done and gotten away with: When I got to the question of the form about homosexuality, I first checked it "Yes," then rubbed that out and checked "No," but left a very obvious smudge in the "Yes" box; that way, they couldn't officially put it on my record that I had admitted being a homosexual, but I hoped they'd just think I was a closet case and give me a 4-F or a 1-Y anyway; my friend managed that. But they said they wanted me to see an Army psychiatrist and come back in about three months. So it bought time for a while, at least; and I figured the freeze might be over in a few months and I could get my deferment back. So for the moment, anyway, that wasn't as pressing as the financial thing.

QUESTION: What did you do when it became impossible to find a job?

TOM: Well, at that time, *Screw* magazine was something new and exciting, like the most visible vanguard of the sexual revolution and so forth. I had started reading that, and I saw an ad in there that said, in essence, "If you're a half-way decent looking guy, call this number and find out how to make some bread." Now that was pretty obvious what it was about; and the first thing that entered my mind when I saw that was this kid I'd known from high school and run into at a gay bar after I came out. Even when we were in high school there was a rumor going around that he was selling himself on Forty-second Street on the weekends; and then when I ran into him he admitted that he really had been doing that, and that he still was, but on a higher level. I went up to his place for a party once; he had this fantastic apartment on the Upper East Side that he was sharing with another guy, and he kept kidding me about how I seemed shocked or hung-up over the fact of what he was doing; but he did seem to be relatively happy, and he had a lot of money around all the time.

So I thought, "Well, maybe I could do this temporarily," and I called the number in the ad. They told me it was a "massage parlor" opening up; and in those days massage parlors didn't have quite the reputation they do today. There weren't so many of them, and they weren't as blatant about their operations or advertising as they are now. But they told me that's what it was going to be, and that it was for an all-male clientele. I said that sounded all right, and I made an appointment to come down for an interview.

I sweated over that decision for the next two days, until the appointment; but I knew there was just no other way that I was going to be able to keep my car or have any spending money for the summer, and that I'd definitely quit if any teaching positions opened up again; so on that basis, knowing it was both necessary and temporary, I made up my mind to follow it through.

QUESTION: What happened when you went to apply for the job?

TOM: I came into Manhattan and found the address, and after walking around the block a couple of times, I went inside. It was really a pretty nice-looking place: It took up all of a three-story brownstone on the East Side, and it was decorated all right, with nice carpeting and drapes and so forth. There was a long hallway—with a closed-circuit TV camera for security, I later found out—that led into a reception area, with a desk and a couple of comfortable sofas and chairs and a color TV set in one corner of the room. There were a few paintings on the wall, mostly male nudes done on black velvet, that sort of thing.

When I first went in, there were only two guys there, two middle-aged Mafioso types; one of them was sitting at the desk, so I told him who I was and what I'd come for. He just glanced up and said, "OK, take off your clothes," which struck me as a bit abrupt. But they weren't even noticing me; they were just talking about business matters. So I got undressed, and then this obviously gay guy in his forties came in and started looking me over, making comments like "He has a nice body, average with a good solid build; he's hung OK . . ." and so on. That made me feel a little nervous, just standing there stark naked in this reception room while somebody looked me up and down and talked about me like I wasn't even there; but I kept my cool, and then he started asking me various questions. He wanted to know what sort of sexual acts I was willing to do and how much experience I'd had, how long I'd been out for; so I answered him honestly, told him I wasn't all *that* experienced, and that I really didn't care for "Greek" . . . and I also told him that my father was a cop. I had to bring that up because they wanted my home phone number, and I told them that was out of the question and had to explain why. They all laughed about this at first; then the one guy thought it over and apparently thought that having a cop's son in the place might help out if they got busted. I didn't say who my father was, or even give them my last name, but I told them what the story was, and they finally said it didn't matter.

So I was hired, and it was arranged that I'd work on a part-time basis, depending on how heavy the appointment schedule was. I'd call up every Sunday to check, and usually work Monday through Thursday; if it was a light week, I might take Thursday off, and if they really needed somebody extra, I'd come in on the weekends during the evening. I also told them that I really wanted to go back to teaching, and that I'd quit if a position opened up at a school. They thought that was pretty funny, too, and would say, "You're gonna be one hell of a teacher," and so on.

QUESTION: What sort of facilities did this place have?

TOM: Well, like I said, it was an attractive, three-story brownstone; the activities took place on the first or the second floor, and the third floor was just living quarters. Five or six guys lived up there, rent-free, and were on permanent call, twenty-four hours a day. On the first floor there was the reception area that I mentioned, and behind that there were two session rooms ; then there were four more session rooms on the second floor. There was no sauna or water-bed room like some of the places now have, but it was all roomy, clean, and private. The rooms were all just small bedrooms; there weren't any massage tables or anything, although there was heated massage oil around if any of the guys did want a little straight rubdown. Most of the rooms were pretty sparsely decorated and furnished, but not sleazy or dirty, and they were dimly lit, usually with colored bulbs in ordinary lamps. There was always a fresh change of linens after every customer; and if he wanted any extra "aids," there were some available. Pornographic homosexual magazines, vibrators, that kind of stuff—no whips or chains or anything, though. There were also pornographic films and an eight-millimeter projector that we could set up if the customer liked; and there was free liquor, up to a point.

QUESTION: What were the other people who worked there like?

TOM: Most of them were very nice-looking and at one extreme or the other in terms of type. Either they were very pretty and effeminate or they were extremely masculine, "butch"—either/or. Very little in-between, which I thought was ridiculous. Both the butch types and the effeminate types came on with this whole phony display of jaded sophistication; I tried to act more or less natural and honest which seemed to turn people on. I had more people come up and say, "Jesus, you'd never know you were gay." I never went in for the super-tight pants or bleaching my hair or any of the pretty-boy look—none of that, which even a lot of the butch guys did. The kind of masculinity they pushed was very fake, a very overdone sailor/cowboy kind of image. I did everything I could to avoid any of those very surface appearances and the catty ego-games and so forth; and I always said "he" not "she," and "guy" not "girl." Things like that just turn me off, and they turned off a lot of the customers, too. If they're gonna go up there, they'd like a straight guy or the closest thing they can get to a straight guy. I mean, if you're a homosexual, if you really dig guys, why should you want some drag-queen poor imitation of a girl? Or some sad caricature of a masculine guy? Why not just some nice, attractive, unpretentious, and fairly normal-seeming *guy*?

The other guys were all pretty easy to get along with, though, in spite of some of their fronts and affectations. We were all there for the same reason, and nobody was *too* snide or cutting to anybody else usually, probably even less so than in any random crowd at a gay party or bar. It was all very friendly, people taking turns to go out for sandwiches and coffee and so on. Most of the guys there were from small towns around the country, and they'd come to New York because their life-style just didn't fit in at home. Then they ended up at this place as a way to make a living, and most of them basically enjoyed what they were doing, a lot of the time, even though there was a certain amount of bitching and griping. Homosexuality is a very promiscuous way of life, anyway, and once a guy has come out I don't think there's quite the same kind of moral feelings attached to the idea of prostitution as there might be with a girl—unless the girl has come to recognize and admit how strong her own sexual drive is and has been pretty promiscuous herself.

QUESTION: Were all of the prostitutes working there admittedly homosexual themselves, or did any of them maintain that they were actually straight and just doing this for the money?

TOM: Most of them were pretty open about being gay, too, but there was one guy who was supposedly completely straight. He was working part-time, too, and wasn't living there; I think he had a job as a security guard someplace and did this in his off hours. He was married, but he just enjoyed having guys suck him and he liked screwing guys. There were some customers who did like that, to know that the guy was straight and they couldn't do anything to make him reciprocate; he wouldn't feel a guy up, or kiss him, or anything like that. This guy was also kind of a sadistic freak, and he'd enjoy it when some customer would ask him to take a leak on him or something. He got his rocks off that way.

QUESTION: What was the general level of education and class background of the people working there?

TOM: The educational level wasn't terribly high; most of the guys were pretty young, and they had either dropped out of high school or left just after. A couple of them had a year or two of college, but I was the only one with a degree. They were generally from middle-class or lower-middle-class homes, and several of them were bright enough to have gone to college. I guess they just preferred to ignore that and throw themselves into the New York gay scene as soon as possible, though. That goes back to what I was saying about coming out too early; you just get obsessed with the life and can't think or talk about anything else—it's a real waste sometimes. One or two of the guys were from poor families, but nobody ever really talked about that sort of thing much. None of the other guys knew my father was a cop, just the managers.

There were various cliques that formed, along class or butch/fem lines or whatever; and sometimes there would be some hostility between them, just bitchy comments and so on. I often came into a role as a liaison between the different groups and tried to patch up some of the problems. Guys like that are funny; if they have a grudge, they usually won't go down and tell the manager what's going on, not unless they're really pissed of and something comes to a crisis point. Otherwise, they'll just grumble to themselves, and they won't act properly in their work. And if a customer comes in, paying twenty-five or thirty dollars, he expects some pleasure out of the experience; you should at least have a nice pleasant greeting for the guy; but that's not the case with all these places or with all the guys in any one place. Some of them are very, very assembly line, but they wouldn't put up with that long where I worked. They told you, "If you don't like it, get the hell out. If you're tired or feeling bitchy, don't work tonight." Most of the customers were regulars, and they wanted to retain that repeat business. So you'd try to be very nice to them, ask if they'd like a drink or whatever; and if you came on too snotty or blasé with a good customer, you could be fired.

QUESTION: What if you were given a customer that you just couldn't stomach, sexually; were you ever able to turn a customer down?

TOM: Oh, yeah, if a guy really turned me off, I didn't have to do anything, although I'd put it in a nice, diplomatic way—maybe say something very kindly about "I'm not really sure if I could satisfy you, sir" or purposely act nelly if you knew he wanted somebody butch. But I was given more freedom than a lot of the others, mainly because I wasn't living upstairs rent-free. There were only a couple of other part-time guys, and we had more options than the rest; the guys who lived there weren't allowed quite as much leeway in turning customers down. Then there were a couple of guys there who didn't care what the hell they sucked up. Godzilla could have been sent up there or the Abominable Snowman, and they'd go to bed with him, too, as long as they got their fifteen dollars. That's their thing; it certainly wasn't mine.

QUESTION: What sort of prices were charged, and how was the money divided?

TOM: At that time it was generally around twenty-five or thirty dollars, but it wasn't up to me to do the bargaining; that was all handled at the reception desk. Whoever was at the desk would psych the customer out when he came in, to see how well-dressed he was, how he spoke, how eager he seemed to be, what he wanted, and so forth; then he'd be charged depending on all that and what he could pay. So there was just a single, one-time fee paid at the desk, and there weren't any "tips" or "extras" involved. The fee was supposedly split fifty-fifty between us and the management. Everybody . . . well, not actually *distrusted* the organization, but there was a sense of curiosity, of "Well, we *hope* that they're being OK with us." 'Cause let's face it: even if they're *not* being OK with you, if that's the only way a guy has to make money, he's not gonna start trouble and say, "I want more money" because they'll throw him out on his ass, and he'll be blacklisted; they really do that and it's an effective blacklist, too. The mob, or the Mafia, or whatever you want to call them, controls a lot of these things —particularly the homosexual places. The black guys in Joey Gallo's "family," the ones that shot Columbo, used to run all the gay places, bars and everything, around Christopher Street. There's a big business down there and also around Forty-second Street, in really young boys, like fourteen or younger; they call them chickens and the customers that ask for them are chicken hawks. It gets vicious, let me tell you.

We used to get paid by mail, anonymously; even the guys who lived upstairs would get their checks through the mail, and no one knew where it was coming from. They were cashier's checks, with only the name of the bank; nobody knew who was really paying them. Most of the guys got paid weekly, but in my case it was at the end of the month because I was only working part-time.

QUESTION: How much did you make?

TOM: For working three days a week, I'd usually make about one-fifty or two hundred; the guys who lived there would make around four or five hundred a week, plus free rent.

QUESTION: How would the customer go about selecting one of the prostitutes?

TOM: Well, first of all, nothing would be discussed over the phone; if somebody called up and started saying, "I want to get sucked," the guy who had answered would tell him that we gave massages, and if he wanted to discuss anything else he'd have to come down and do it in person. Then when they did get there, there was this book of photographs of guys in different poses, some of them dressed and some undressed. They were just Polaroids, not really pornographic shots or anything like that; every guy would try to pose in a way that got across whatever his particular "specialty" was, whether he was butch or whatever; some of the guys would wear different kinds of outfits, cowboy boots and jeans or something, and some of them were just stock kind of "muscle-beach" shots, and a couple of them were of guys in full drag, with an off-the-shoulder gown and all sorts of makeup. The pictures they had of me were usually fairly ordinary, just a head-and-shoulders smiling kind of thing, and I was generally fully dressed, though I did have a couple of barechested poses made; otherwise, they could have gone in my college yearbook [laughs].

So the customer would look through this book, and pick out the guy that he liked, and ask for him by name. If the guy he'd picked was there that night, he'd just go right upstairs with him; but they had pictures of everybody who ever worked there, so sometimes he might not be around, and the customer would either have to wait for him to get in, or pick somebody else, or come back at another time. If I happened to call in and there was somebody who wanted to see me, I'd go on over, even if I was busy that night; I'd just make some lame excuse and leave because I needed the bread. With the guys who lived upstairs, they'd always let the desk know where they were going when they went out, so if they were at the Round Table or Charlie's or some other gay place, they'd be paged there. Then the guy would look you over in person, and if he still liked what he saw, you'd take him upstairs; or you might go to his place, for an extra ten dollars, also paid to the desk.

QUESTION: How would the specific sexual acts that the customer wanted be arranged for?

TOM: He'd just tell the desk what he wanted; it was very businesslike and they didn't want to waste any time. The desk knew what everybody had the capacity or the willingness to do; they had a little file on you at the front, by your picture, with various code letters. The letters might mean that you did or didn't like to get screwed, or that you wouldn't get into drag, or that you were particularly adept at this or that; so there was a full range of choice, and the customer could just about always find somebody that would please him, both in terms of looks and action. There might be as many as fifteen or twenty people available; they had *fifty* working for them at one time. Guys up there like a troop of Boy Scouts [*laughs*]—Camp Fuck 'n' Suck.

QUESTION: So when you went upstairs with the customer, you knew in advance what he expected?

TOM: Oh, yeah, you both knew what was expected; it was all settled out front. But like I said, if the guy really turned me off, I wasn't forced to go through with it. And you'd never be set up to do something you weren't into doing, like getting screwed for me. That was all on record at the desk by my picture, and if a customer wanted to do that and selected me, they'd tell him he'd have to pick somebody else.

QUESTION: What was the average customer like and what sexual services would he request?

TOM: It really varied quite a bit, often depending on where they heard of the place. The younger people, the acid freaks, would come through the ads in the *Village Voice*—also the slightly hip "avant-garde" business types. Generally a nice class of people through the *Voice*, but not too wealthy. The well-dressed, middle-aged, affluent men would usually have found out about it through private connections; and you never knew *what* might show up through the ad in *Screw* [*laughs*].

As far as the average, or the majority, went . . . I guess most of the guys were fairly normal-looking businessmen around thirty-five or forty, who didn't really look very faggy at all. If they were experienced homosexuals, they'd usually either want to get screwed or go down on me. Also, they wanted to at least be able to pretend that they were with a guy who wasn't gay himself; I was supposed to go through a rap with most of them about being from the Midwest, and how I was broke and was only doing this for the money. I put on a fairly good straight act, just normal All-American Boy kind of thing, and that seemed to turn most of them on. It's sort of like a heterosexual man wanting to be with a virgin or the closest thing to it; only it's much more pronounced in the gay world.

QUESTION: Did you ever have any customers who were basically straight and just experimenting?

TOM: Oh, sure, it was a minority of the customers, but a relatively large minority. They were usually guys in their late or middle twenties, a lot of them married and suddenly no longer really sure that that's what they wanted. You could generally recognize them by the fact that they might be a little more conservatively dressed, hair a little shorter, nervously trying to act more manly than they were comfortable with in their speech and mannerisms, the way they'd walk. . . They usually said it was something they just wanted to "get out of their systems"; they wanted to see whether they liked it or not and were obviously hoping they wouldn't.

A lot of them, I think, really didn't like it; it depended. Like, most of these guys would either want to screw another guy, which I wouldn't do, or they'd want me to go down on them; and if the slightest thing went wrong or struck them funny, it would turn them off immediately. And they'd really be *happy* about not having enjoyed themselves, as they might have expected or feared. They'd actually give me a few dollars more if it didn't go too well because they'd think, "Gee, you saved my life." Unfortunately, most of them would be back again a month or so later—very short saving of the life.

QUESTION: Did you ever have any masochistic customers?

TOM: There were some guys who would come in and ask to be whipped or something, but I wasn't into that myself. I guess most homosexuals who are into that don't have too much trouble arranging to get beaten up anyway; and there are plenty of leather bars around where they can make contacts.

I was asked to take a piss on people a few times and refused; three times the customer got upset and reported me, but I just told them that he hadn't mentioned that at the desk in the first place, and he was given to somebody else. I didn't need to get money *that* way; it's just totally against all my values and conceptions of myself and other people. I just couldn't do it. I couldn't live with myself doing it.

I did have one guy who only wanted to wrestle; we'd get into the room and undress and just spend the time wrestling, with all the proper collegiate holds and timeouts and everything. He'd really get into it and work up a good sweat and then suddenly come, without my ever touching his penis. He was a damn good wrestler, too, always won. And he never even *mentioned* sex; we'd just wrestle until he came and then he'd thank me and leave.

Then there was another customer who'd come in and go through a long rap about all the chicks that he'd been to bed with in the last few days, and he'd want me to reprimand him for that, tell him how angry and disappointed I was that he'd been with females instead of with me or other guys. Then he'd apologize and go on and on about how terrible he felt and how wrong he knew it was, and have me screw him. I never figured out whether he was lying, fantasizing, or telling the truth. It was a very weird type of bisexuality, if that's what it was.

QUESTION: What were some of the other odd or unusual customers you had?

TOM: Well, a lot of guys were very voyeuristic; I think most men are anyway, whether they're hetero- or homosexual. They'd want me to pose for them, flex my muscles and so on, while they masturbated. There were also some gay films and magazines available, like I mentioned before, and sometimes they'd want to be jerked off or have me go down on them while they looked at these things, or they'd want us to sit and look at them together and rap about how we were both getting so turned on.

A couple of guys were just the opposite; they were very exhibitionistic. There was this one paunchy, balding old man who'd just strut around masturbating while I had to keep raving about his physique, which was really in horrible shape, and the size of his penis, which was practically invisible. Most homosexuals are very hung-up on the appearance of their bodies and very narcissistic, even when they have absolutely no reason to be.

Another one of my customers was this high-school football coach who must've been repressing himself for twenty-five years; he'd always act out a whole fantasy of me being one of his "boys" on the team and have me do ten or fifteen push-ups and jog around the room, and crap like that. Then we'd sit down together to "talk about the big game next week," and I'd have to act all innocent and football-playerish while he slyly put his arm around me and started to feel me up and finally went down on me.

QUESTION: Did any women ever come in?

TOM: No, not to the massage parlor; I guess they'd feel a little strange about doing that, going up to the desk and everything. I did have one transsexual customer though; he came to me a couple of times before the operation, and we'd sit around and discuss whether he should go through with it or not. He finally had it done, and he came back in about a month later; he was middle-aged and very dowdy-looking as a woman, but he finally seemed to be happy and at peace with himself or herself or whatever. Screwing this person, in the vagina that the doctors had built, was kind of strange; I had to use a lot of petroleum jelly for a lubricant, and it felt different somehow than screwing a real chick, different up inside: very tight, and more like external skin than the inside of a normal cunt. Generally speaking, the whole changeover was very effective though; they gave him hormone shots to raise his voice and stop his beard from growing and silicone breasts. He wasn't very pretty, but then he hadn't been very handsome either; and the operation really did seem to make him happy at last. I don't think there are many homosexuals who need to go quite that far, but in a desperate situation it can make all the difference to some people.

QUESTION: Did customers ever come in drag?

TOM: Yeah, there were a fair number of either super-nelly or even drag-queen customers. They generally didn't want to think of themselves as being in the "customer" role because it didn't seem too feminine an image; sometimes they'd prefer to have two or three guys come down and act like they were all making a play for "her," and then make a choice by coyly "submitting" to the guy they liked and letting him lead the way upstairs. They often liked to do things that way, or some variation of it, instead of just picking a bod out of the book and saying, "OK, I'll take that one"; that struck them as too masculine a thing to do, like some *macho* guy in a straight massage parlor.

Then there were several guys working there who were usually in drag or close to it, or they'd swagger around in cowboy boots and leather pants at work, and when they got off they'd break out the bras and panties and slips and stockings and stuff. Drag queens are really hung up on the straightest, most traditional sort of images of femininity, all the external crap. They're very big on bouffant wigs and fake eyelashes, purple fingernails and spike heels ... very nineteen-fiftyish, you know?

A lot of the customers who were half-straight, or liked to think they were, would choose these guys so as to ease their consciences and not feel too "queer." Also, I think there are a few genuinely heterosexual men who enjoy having a drag queen go down on them, for the same reason that a lot of girls go a little way into bisexuality: somebody of the same sex really understands what might turn you on the most and what feels best because he's lived all his life with the same equipment. So there are some men who want to see and feel a smooth, feminine face and a head full of hair, but still they appreciate an expert gay blow-job.

QUESTION: Did you ever encounter a customer who was someone you had known before?

TOM: Yeah, I did, once, and it really messed up my mind. Because not only was it somebody I used to know: It was a priest who used to give me counseling when I was a kid. He didn't come up there with his crucifix or his collar or anything, but I recognized him immediately. He didn't know who I was; he'd moved out of the neighborhood and hadn't seen me since I was nine; and he kept saying that I seemed more nervous than he did, and he couldn't figure out why. I used to go to this man with all my childhood problems—he really sort of represented a lot of wisdom and ideals to me; and suddenly he's just another customer, wanting me to screw him. I was pretty upset, but there was no logical reason that I could refuse to take him.

The whole thing put me in a very down state of mind for several days, an attitude of "Isn't there anything sacred anymore?"; which makes me think of my father, who's the biggest skeptic in the world. To him *nothing's* sacred or even particularly admirable. I hate thinking like him. I despise that sort of jaded cynicism, but I find myself getting more and more like him in a lot of ways, and it makes me sick.

Must be age or something, hardening of the arteries and softening of the brain . . . and other things [*laughs*].

QUESTION: Was the place where you worked ever raided by the police?

TOM: Yes, it was; fortunately, I wasn't there that night. I don't know what would have happened if I'd gotten arrested and they found out who I was; it would have practically killed my father, and he probably would have resigned from the force out of sheer embarrassment.

From what I heard, they sent in three or four really faggy-acting cops; I don't know where they learned their bit, but apparently they were pretty convincing. I'd warned the guys there that the cops were into that sort of thing because this was at the point where the cops were just starting to dress up like bums or priests or women and setting themselves up to get mugged: Halloween time for the N.Y.P.D. My father used to talk about it all the time. So I'd told them that some "undercover fags" were gonna come in there sometime and, sure enough, they did. Two guys were busted for soliciting and everybody else for loitering.

I was very freaked out by that; for the next two weeks I'd lie awake in a cold sweat for hours every night, just thinking about what might have happened if I'd been there and been arrested. That episode gave me the scare of my life and I quit working there right away. Which turned out to be a good thing because the place was busted again about a week later.

QUESTION: What did you do for money after you quit the massage parlor?

TOM: I did some things on my own, some private prostitution things; that seemed a little safer, a little less vulnerable than working at a known massage parlor. Know how I started? By advertising in the *Times*.

QUESTION: The New York *Times*?

TOM: That's right, the Sunday New York *Times*. Look in the classified section next week, under "Situations Wanted"; it's unbelievable. I mean, this is the good old prestigious New York *Times*, right? "All the news that's fit to print" and all that shit. And there's a listing for "models"—they usually have about fifteen ads; all guys, most if not all of them prostitutes. Some of these people have almost the exact same ad in *Screw*. In the *Times*, they always tack on "will pose draped," so it at least looks a little more legitimate, but everybody knows that's bullshit. They never have any ads for female "models"; I guess the *Times* won't print those. Apparently the staff over there doesn't realize there's such a thing as homosexual prostitution, but they advertise it every week.

The class of customers you get through the *Times* is pretty good, I'll admit that. I only advertised once in *Screw*; I didn't like the characters you'd get through them. And a couple of times in the *Village Voice*, they used to take ads for both "models" and "unlicensed masseurs," guys or girls; now they don't, they went "respectable" [*laughs*].

QUESTION: Did you use your home phone number for this?

TOM: No, I had a post office box, and anybody who was interested in the ad could send me his phone number. I used to have my own phone at home, but that was just too dangerous. If I was out, my father might decide to answer it or he might overhear me talking to a customer; and you'd never know what hour of the day or night it might ring. I couldn't act like a jailbird in my room: "Oh, my father the cop is here, cool it for a minute." He's a smart man; I'd always have to stay one step ahead of him.

All cop's kids are like that, about the simplest little things: for instance, do you know where all cops put anything important that they don't want their wives or kids to see? Taped between two drawers, so you have to pull the drawer all the way out and turn it upside down to see that anything's there. That's where I hide my dirty magazines and my grass; he'd never think I knew his own little trick. All us cop's kids would be damned good detectives, after spending our whole childhood playing James Bond to daddy's Dr. No-No.

QUESTION: What sort of experiences did you have in private prostitution?

TOM: Well, for one thing, I only went to people's apartments; I missed the whole hotel trade because I couldn't list a phone number in my ad. It was kind of strange because you never know where you're going really; it can get a little freaky now and then. A couple of times I've just walked away from guys or never even gone up if the building looked bad, but some of the people I've met were nice. One of the guys I met this way is one of my best friends now; it's not even a heavily sexual thing—we just have a lot in common.

QUESTION: Have you ever had any real problems with a customer?

TOM: Only minor problems, like them wanting to screw me and getting upset when I say I won't do that. I've never encountered any serious trouble or violence though, probably because I'm not willing to take what looks like a chance. Still, you never can know for sure; even somebody who's very respectable-looking, at a nice address, could turn out to be a nut.

That was one good thing about the massage parlor. They had a very good security system, with closed-circuit TV cameras in the hallway and one of the Mafioso types always around. Anybody who was thinking about causing any trouble at all could see right away that his ass would be thrown out of there fast, or even worse. The massage parlor was not exactly an easy place to "roll a queer."

QUESTION: What are some of the stranger experiences you've had in doing residential work?

TOM: Well, there was this one guy on West Eighty-third Street; he had one of these "inflatable females" you can order. It's like a life-size balloon in the shape of a woman: skin colored, with a wig and an outfit of women's clothes. Whenever I'd go ove his giant doll-thing would be there in a position to "ob ve us. sitting at the table, lying on the bed, wherever. He'd move it around as we moved. And while we were making it, he'd go through these numbers, and have me do the same, of *humiliating* the female doll: cursing it, verbally abusing it, sometimes even slapping or spitting on it. It was really sad, the degree to which he hated women, really very, very sad.

QUESTION: Did you ever have any women answer your ads?

TOM: A few times. A couple of them claimed to be virgins who wanted somebody to "break them in right," but those turned out to be fake phone numbers; the others were just very plain-looking middle-aged women. I only went through with the whole thing once, and it was a chore, let me tell you.

I also had a couple answer the ad once; I thought it was a put-on, but it turned out to be for real. They were in their thirties, not bad-looking, and the man wanted to watch me make it with his wife. It felt weird, but I did what they asked; the husband just lay there and jerked off—I never touched him. They were very friendly and nonchalant about it all, and they made me some coffee afterward. Apparently they did this fairly often, either with male prostitutes or with guys that he or she would meet in bars or wherever. The guy said they'd experimented with wife-swapping, but that he really just preferred to watch his wife doing it with a stranger.

QUESTION: Do you consider yourself bisexual?

TOM: No, not really, I can still objectively appreciate the fact that a girl may be very pretty, and I'm still capable of performing sexually with a girl, but . . . you might say that "my hard's not really in it." I'll always look at a guy first, it's just automatic. For instance, when I came in here, the first thing I thought was, "What nice eyes he has" [laughs]. I know that's gonna embarrass you, but. . . .

QUESTION: Well, thank you for the compliment.

TOM: Yeah, you do have beautiful eyes; you gotta be careful, you're turnin' me on [laughs].

Anyway, to whatever extent I may be bisexual at this point, it's basically just a front, a cover-up, like, I obviously don't want to make my family too suspicious, so there's one girl that I date fairly regularly. She's a very nice person, and I like her a lot, but . . . she just doesn't excite me. I'm always looking for activities that we can do that won't involve any sex, and when we do finally get around to doing something now and then, it's a very mechanical thing for me. Usually I just close my eyes and fantasize about Tom Tryon or Robert Redford

QUESTION: Your girlfriend knows nothing about your homosexuality?

TOM: No, she's very straight, she just wouldn't understand at all; it would hurt her quite a bit to know how much I've been deceiving her, and she would be terribly shocked.

That's one reason I'm very glad that I've been lucky enough to never have gotten V.D.; what would I say, "Don't get upset, honey, it wasn't another girl, it was a guy"? That would hit her pretty hard, particularly if I had to say it wasn't even just a guy, but one of my *customers*, for God's sake. I really have been incredibly lucky in that because most gay people are so promiscuous there's a real epidemic of V.D.

QUESTION: Do you think homosexuals are more promiscuous than heterosexuals?

TOM: More so than most heterosexuals, yes, even today. There's no real heterosexual equivalent to things like the dozen or so Turkish bath places in New York, where you just lie down on a bed in a tiny room and leave the door open, so a dozen or more strange guys may wander in and have sex with you; or the scene around the trucks in lower Manhattan, where people are just instantly dropping their pants for somebody whose face they can't even see, it's so dark; or the sex in parks, in bathrooms . . . it's really amazing, and I personally find it kind of disgusting.

QUESTION: Why do you think promiscuity is so prevalent among homosexuals?

TOM: For a lot of reasons; some of them, I guess, are tied up with the psychological things that supposedly lead to homosexuality in the first place, like lack of love as a child and so on. And I think it is generally more common for males, whether they're gay or straight, to be more outgoing, more nearly random in their sexual contacts; what was that poem that occurred to somebody in a dream, and he wrote it down as the key to the universe . . . then when he got up in the morning, he read it and it said, "Hogamous, higamous, men are polygamous; higamous, hogamous, women monogamous." There's really some truth to that, or at least there has been traditionally as a result of the way people are conditioned in this society. Also the fact that there isn't any legally or morally sanctioned type of permanent gay relationship available as an option tends to make it a more promiscuous group of people.

QUESTION: What do you think of the possibility of workable homosexual marriages?

TOM: Not much, to tell you the truth. That may sound like I'm contradicting myself, and I know it's gonna piss a lot of people off; but it really doesn't seem to be a very fruitful idea, if you'll pardon the pun. Even straight marriage as an institution is falling apart, so why should gay marriage work any better? There's no possibility of children; it'll take a long time to be totally accepted even if it's legal . . . only three or four percent of homosexual relationships work out on any long-range basis as it is, and I don't see why that percentage should increase.

The only possibility for any sort of long-term homosexual marriage that I can see would have to be based on an acceptance by both partners of the necessity for continued sexual variety; maybe that would work and maybe not. At any rate, that seems to be the direction that ordinary marriages are going, and if it's true for straights, then it's doubly triply, true for gays. The whole idea is kind of difficult for me to accept because of my religious background, so I just don't know what to think at this point. I don't see any other way out though.

QUESTION: Do you think homosexuality is caused by a person's genetic makeup or by environmental factors?

TOM: I think it's a mixture of the two, and I vary from day to day in my opinion of which one has the biggest effect. There have been some very convincing studies showing a correlation between the amount of female hormone in a person's system and the degree of his homosexuality; but there are also some elements of people's home lives as children that seem to be practically universal among the homosexuals that I know. I suppose it's about fifty-fifty.

QUESTION: What do you think is the general future of homosexuality in society?

TOM: Well, it's definitely on the increase, and I believe that could end up being a very healthy thing; it could have a good influence on the world. There is a lot of truth to some of the stereotypes about homosexuals, that they tend to be more creative, more empathetic, and so on; maybe we could do with a few more interior decorators and a lot less soldiers, to put it crudely. Ancient Greece did all right for a long time. The kids today don't seem nearly so hung up on maintaining the same old silly boundaries between masculine and feminine aspects of personality or behavior; they're more into establishing some kind of decent balance of the two. That may not be easy to pull off, but right now it looks to me like one of our best hopes.

QUESTION: Are you still working as a prostitute?

TOM: No, I've been doing substitute teaching since September, and that's fifty dollars a day when I work, which seems to be getting more regular all the time. My car's almost all paid off, and I got my deferment back, so I didn't have to hassle too much more with the Army; and the draft's ended now anyway.

I don't think I'd ever do it again, although I'm basically glad to have had the experience. It's a rough life, particularly homosexual prostitution; a girl can drop in and out of it more easily, I think, she can get married or whatever; but for a guy it can be a very degrading sensation. I see it that way, at least; my background, my goddamned background, still hounds me. I can't get away from it. Those Catholics, once they get it into you, let me tell you . . . [laughs].

QUESTION: Do you think the fact of your homosexuality affects your performance as a teacher?

TOM: Not in any negative sense, no. If anything, it makes me a *better* teacher. Like I said, homosexuals tend to be more understanding, more empathetic. I think I can deal more sensitively with many students' problems as a result of that, and even if some of my students were to suspect that I'm gay, it wouldn't hurt. The kids who are realizing that they're gay themselves would have a respected adult model to look up to and not see their future as absolutely hopeless; and the straight kids would learn more tolerance of individual differences. Not that they really need to—high school kids today are about the least prejudiced bunch of people you could hope to find. Don't get the idea that I'm about to openly declare my sexual preferences though; unfortunately, the Board of Education still has some pretty backward opinions about that sort of thing.

As far as me having any sexual interest in my students, that's an absurd thing for people to worry about. It's time everybody stopped having images of all homosexuals as slavering, perverted rapists; I'm not *about* to jeopardize my career in that way. As if I'd even think of approaching some immature, confused boy anyway. If I admire a handsome boy in one of my classes, that's no different than some straight teacher peering up the girls' dresses; neither one of us would think of following through with anything. Me even less so, because of the greater seriousness of the offense. The whole notion is just ridiculous; I'd have to be insane.

QUESTION: How do you see your own future?

TOM: I really hate to say this, but I think there's a very good possibility that I may cop out entirely, marry the girl that I'm dating, and continue to play around as a homosexual in private. Sexual freedom and Gay Liberation movements aside, I'm just honestly not in a position to come out publicly; I'm sure I'd lose my job, and I'm just not strong enough to handle the effect that it might have on my family.

Also, I'm afraid of being alone, and I'm afraid to get old; age is the worst thing in the world to a homosexual, whether he's selling himself or not. The older I get, the more I notice people standing around in the bars in this desperate, tragic parody of enjoying themselves. . . . I don't want to end up like that, forcing this hysterical falsetto laughter to draw attention away from the wrinkles on my face and neck, while I sit there feeling up the boys *I'm* paying to be with. I can't let myself do that; and yet I can't change my feelings. I don't know what I'll do in the long run; all my prospects are a little frightening, and I just don't like to think about it very much.

6. Sally

SALLY is a tall, very clean-cut and well-spoken young black woman. She is quite attractive, and she dresses with stylish understatement. Her general demeanor is one of friendly competence; a registered nurse, Sally seems capable of handling her work with precisely the right mixture of sympathy and efficiency. The highest compliment I can pay is that I would trust her implicitly with a needle in my arm.

There is nothing whatsoever in Sally's surface appearance or personality to indicate that she is, in fact, an expert sadist, a professional specialist in pain. During most of our interview, she sat gently stroking a fluffy orange Persian kitten. Her speaking voice is soft and melodic, her laughter subdued but abundant. It was difficult indeed for me to imagine this exceptionally bright and pleasant person with a whip in her hand, shouting obscenities and harsh commands at some cowering figure of a man twice her age.

Sadomasochism, a term which covers a wide variety of sexual deviations (and I do not use the word pejoratively), is one of prostitution's "gray areas." It constitutes a surprisingly large percentage of the business and is one of its more lucrative subfields. In many states, there is even some question as to whether existing prostitution laws are adequately written to cover this area.

A highly complex series of aberrations, "S & M" involves numerous social and psychological factors that are as yet only partially understood. Though shrouded in secrecy and innuendo for centuries, sadomasochism is nonetheless one of the more significant aspects of the human character, striking at the very core of our aggressive and self-protective instincts.

190

The people whom Sally describes in this interview have allowed their impulses to take them far beyond the "normal" range of behavior; but those same opposing urges of passivity and dominance exist in everyone, their relative balance affecting or controlling much of our daily lives. Indeed it is the tension between these perpetually warring internal forces which weaves the very fabric of our sexual and emotional natures, no matter what our individual orgasmic preference. Sally's incisive comments on her experience within the ultimate extrapolation of these universal phenomena thus form an important social document, with implications transcending their ostensible central subject.

* * *

QUESTION: What part of the country are you from?

SALLY: I was born and brought up in southern California; we lived in Watts until I was four, then moved to a temporarily integrated neighborhood in Pasadena. My father had worked as a delivery boy—until he was a thirty-three-year-old "boy"—for a dry-cleaning establishment, and finally saved enough money to open his own little laundromat. It was one of the few black-owned businesses in the ghetto at that time, and it was successful enough for him to open two more places like it, and when I was eleven, he bought out the white owners of the dry-cleaning place where he'd worked all those years.

My parents were middle-class with a vengeance: very uptight, understandably so, about racial things; very aware of class structures and appearances. My father never bought a Cadillac or a Lincoln, even though he could have afforded one and I know he would have liked to; but he was supersensitive about being thought of as "nigger-rich," so we always drove a two-year-old Chevrolet or Dodge. All sorts of things like that; he was scared to own anything garish or even colorful [*laughs*], and all our clothes or furniture or whatever were chosen very conservatively.

I was never particularly hung up about the racial thing

one way or the other, although I did go through a brief militant period in high school, but I got disillusioned with politics pretty quickly. My older brother and younger sister were pretty much the same way; he's a tax lawyer in San Francisco now, and she's a sophomore at my old school, UCLA, studying anthropology.

QUESTION: What were your main interests during adolescence?

SALLY: I got into a pretty heavy science trip, mostly biology. I was the only girl in my class who *enjoyed* dissecting frogs, and I was always entering projects in the science fair. One year I got a special award at the state science fair, for an experiment with the juvenile hormone; that's a substance insects secrete during their larval stage—it controls metamorphosis. You can extract it fairly easily from certain moths, with a centrifuge and a series of alcohol solutions; then if you just apply it externally, with a little brush, to caterpillars or whatever, they'll keep growing and growing until you stop giving it to them; then they immediately go into metamorphosis, and you get these real Frankenstein-monster insects. I raised a thirteen-inch grasshopper and a butterfly with a sixteen-inch wingspread. They die right away, of course, their exoskeletons, their shells, aren't designed to support that kind of weight. It's kind of pathetic but very interesting; and the hormone itself is beautiful. It's this deep golden color; you can really believe it's some sort of magic youth serum. Maybe I ought to market it as a face-cream; it wouldn't really do anything, but the rap you could lay on in the ads would bring in a mint [*laughs*].

QUESTION: What was your adolescence like sexually?

SALLY: Very normal. I dug sex, basically, but I wasn't obsessive about it. If you want the sordid details—I got deflowered by my steady boyfriend at a drive-in movie. I think it was *Thunderball* [*laughs*].

I slept with two or three other guys during high school and maybe four more in college. When I first got to college,

I'd planned to go on to medical school; but I realized I didn't really have the perseverance to follow that through, so I went to nursing school instead.

That was some trip: Nursing school is enough to prepare you for *anything*. Watching autopsies and operations all week, and parties with the medical students or the interns all weekend. It was a pretty thorough education.

Then, when I graduated, I worked for about six or seven months at a hospital in Los Angeles. But I was getting tired of California, and it was a drag being so close to all my aunts and uncles and grandparents. Even my mother kept showing up at weird hours to make sure I was a proper young lady, so I decided to split.

QUESTION: Where did you go?

SALLY: I came straight to New York and got a job with a private clinic on Long Island—mainly cardiac cases. I also filled in with some visiting service to a few outpatients, and that was the beginning of my final corruption.

QUESTION: How do you mean?

SALLY: Well, I had this one patient, an old guy named Harold; he was permanently bedridden, with heart trouble and prostatitis, and I'd go over to his house three times a week to make sure he was taking all his medicine and to bathe him, and so forth. He was always very happy to see me, and he'd make a lot of lecherous jokes about how well I filled out my uniform or ask me questions about my boy-friends—normal, run-of-the-mill stuff, all the male patients did it. I never thought much about it; I'd just kid him back and sometimes even tease him about the erections he'd get when I bathed him.

This went on for a month or so, and then one day while I was bathing him he asked me to scrub him harder; and after I'd finished, he wanted me to sort of slap him dry with the towel, you know? I didn't ask any questions, I just went ahead and did it 'cause I figured it'd probably get his circulation going better. It did that, all right; by the time

I was done, he had the biggest erection I'd ever seen him with. That turned into a regular routine, and every time he wanted me to do it a little harder than before; and then one day he asked me to give him a prostate massage while I was drying his back that way. I was very calm and cool about it; I just told him that that was for the doctor to decide and do, not me, but suddenly he started getting very insistent, and he said he'd give me fifty dollars if I did it. Now that was more than a fourth of my weekly salary, and I knew that it wasn't anything that could really hurt him; it would even be good for him. So I made him promise that he wouldn't tell anybody about it, and I pulled on a pair of rubber gloves—I was very fastidious in those days [laughs]—and stuck my finger up his ass. His prostate was swollen up to the size of a lemon, and it must have hurt like hell just to have it touched. But he started groaning, obviously with pleasure, as I rubbed it and squeezed it. While I was still slapping him on the back and shoulders with a corner of the towel. He ejaculated in about thirty seconds, handed me the money, and we both just acted like nothing out of the ordinary had happened.

I felt a little guilty about it when I went home because that type of "treatment" wasn't really in my province; but I bought a new dress and two new pairs of shoes with the money, and the guilt didn't last too long. He'd enjoyed himself, I'd gotten a nice chunk of money free and clear, and what I'd done was good for his condition. The next time I went to see him, there was a fifty-dollar bill lying on the table next to his pill bottles; he just sort of smiled at me when I saw it, so I pocketed it without saying anything and I gave him another session like the first one. This time he had me slap him even harder with the towel, so there was a row of red marks on his back by the time I finished; but he really dug it, and he seemed very satisfied.

Over the next few weeks we repeated this performance about a dozen times, and I was making a nice little pile of money out of Harold. It hadn't been all that difficult a thing to accept, for one thing because I was used to giving men enemas and inserting rectal thermometers; so it didn't gross me out too much to be putting my fingers up there instead. The slapping part was different, but it built up so gradually that I just got used to it pretty easily.

Pretty soon we graduated beyond the towel, and every time I went over he'd have a selection of small whips and belts laid out on the side of the bed. He'd stopped making lecherous comments, or grabbing at my ass, or anything like that; we never talked about what was happening—it was always made out to be a spontaneous, unplanned thing.

Eventually Harold mentioned in a very euphemistic way that he had a friend who would also like to hire a "visiting nurse with talent." I said I'd at least give the guy a call, and Harold gave me his phone number. He sounded all right over the telephone, and he lived in a nice neighborhood near my place, so I went over to meet him. This was the first time that I'd done anything strictly as a prostitute; I didn't bother to wear my uniform, and there was no pretense that I was there for anything other than some kind of sex.

This guy—his name was David—was also a masochist, only he was a little further gone than Harold. I was a little dubious about the situation when he told me what he wanted me to do: he had a pair of handcuffs I was supposed to chain him to the bedpost with and a very mean-looking bullwhip he wanted me to use on him. I just sat there in his living room sipping wine while he showed me these things, and he picked right up on the fact that I wasn't too sure about this. He said, "I know you don't usually do this kind of thing," and he offered to jack the price up to seventy-five dollars. That was enough to make up my mind for me, so I went ahead with the deal. I found out I could control it very well; he didn't want to be really tortured or anything, just kind of teasingly whipped, you know? He was very polite and friendly about the whole thing, not freaky or scary in any other way. I didn't even have to touch him at all; he just came while I was kind of flicking the whip at him.

That still put me through some heavy head changes; I mean, I'd been around, but I really never knew anything about this kind of stuff. . . . And all of a sudden—after all these years of being a nice little girl and being a gentle, thoughtful nurse—here I am cracking a bullwhip at some old man handcuffed to his bed. While I was doing it, I remember having all these totally irrational thoughts about being arrested, not for prostitution, but for *assault*. I started worrying that somebody might come by and I wouldn't be able to get his handcuffs off in time, or even that the whole deal was some kind of setup, that *he* might turn around and press charges against me if I hit him too hard; but, of course, none of that happened. He enjoyed himself, and I had seventy-five dollars and another semiregular customer.

By this time I'd bought a new stereo and a whole closetful of new clothes from my Harold-and-David money. Some of my friends were beginning to wonder how I was managing all this on my salary, and I told them my parents were sending me a little extra bread from California. I didn't really think too much about where the money was coming from myself; I kind of rationalized the whole trip as an extension of being a nurse—I was just ministering to these guys' needs, you know? I was making a hundred and sixty a week as a nurse, and averaging about one-twenty-five a week from Harold and David; and that extra one-twenty-five got to seem very natural—I started expecting it and counting on it.

Then one day David told me he was going away for the summer, and I was faced with a sudden drop in that income, so I asked him if he or Harold had any more friends that I might go see in my spare time. They didn't, but David showed me a copy of *Screw* magazine, which I'd never heard of, and said I might be able to find somebody through the classified ads in there. I didn't like the sound of that at all, and I was ready to just give up the whole idea and go back to living on my regular salary; but I leafed through *Screw*, and there were all these big display ads for various massage parlors. One of them was for a place called De Sade Studios, and it said they were hiring "buxom, dominant girls." There was a picture of this hefty black chick all done up in leather, scowling at the camera, and I thought, "What the shit, why not check it out?" I asked David about it, and he said he'd been there a couple of times; it wasn't bad. So I said I'd think it over.

It took me about three days to decide to look into the place, and I called up for an appointment. Some black woman, very friendly, answered the phone and told me to come by the next afternoon. I called in sick at the clinic that day, and I drove into Manhattan.

QUESTION: Where was this place located?

SALLY: In a kind of weird area; it was on West Nineteenth Street, a sort of warehouse district, with nobody around on the street except workers. I thought at first that I must've had the wrong address, but then I noticed a little sign on the front of this nondescript building and I went on in.

The studio itself was in a loft; you had to take a freight elevator to the eleventh floor. All these Puerto Rican dudes kept getting in and out of the elevator, lugging boxes of typewriters and things, and staring at me and commenting in Spanish. I was getting a little uptight, and by the time I got to the top floor I'd decided to just punch the "down" button and forget the whole thing; but when the elevator doors opened, there was no hallway or anything. I was directly facing the desk in the place. There were three or four girls sitting on couches next to the desk, and one of them got up and asked me if I'd come to see Ruby. I couldn't exactly say I'd wandered into that freight elevator by mistake, so I told her I had. She said Ruby'd be out in a few minutes, so I sat down to wait.

The place looked sleazy but clean; it was decorated in maroon and bilious green, really clashing. There were plastic draperies and old living-room furniture, and posters on the walls with pictures of girls in leather, girls on motorcycles, holding whips or chains. The girls who were sitting on the couches were mostly older than me and dressed in pants or leotards and boots. One of them was this frizzy bleached blonde with huge tits who looked to be about thirty-eight years old, and there were two black chicks, one of them

around six-and-a-half feet tall. I'm sitting there in my little
Bloomingdale's skirt-and-sweater outfit and my pink platform shoes, feeling *very* fucked up and out of place, you
know? I decided I had to get my head in the right place
if I was gonna pull this off at all, so I lit a cigarette and
started thinking about my experiences with Harold and
David, to convince myself what a tough-shit bitch I was. Then
Ruby came out, showing some shrimpy little guy with an
idiotic grin to the door.

We went into her office and sat across another desk from
each other, very businesslike. Ruby was very attractive, but
she was very large-boned; she was a black woman in her
early forties. We rapped about where I was from and so
on for a few minutes, and she made us both a drink. Then
she asked me if I'd ever done any S & M work before; I
ran a few more Harold-and-David flashes through my head,
for confidence, and I said, "Sure." She just sort of thought
that over for a minute, and then she started asking me a
whole bunch of rapid-fire questions about whether I was
familiar with all these different types of equipment, like "sus-
pension gear" and "rubber-wear," half of which I'd never
heard of before. But I kept nodding and saying, "Yeah, sure"
to everything she brought up. I didn't really know if I wanted
to go through with this, but I didn't want to make a fool
out of myself.

Finally she said, "OK, we'll give you a try," and she told
me to come back in two days with a black bodysuit, black
pantyhose, and black thigh-boots.

After I left, I went straight to a bar and had another couple
of drinks, and pretty soon I was really feeling like an arch-
criminal; I was the toughest thing in skirts, you know? I
had myself convinced that I was some kind of black Wonder
Woman, that I could handle any situation in the world.

The next morning things seemed a little different: I was
a *nurse,* for Christ's sake, I was a middle-class, well-educated,
professional young woman, not some hooker in a black outfit
with a whip in my hand. But the more I thought about it,
the more it seemed like a great goof: I could be *both* those

things, I could lead this amazing double life if I wanted to. The secrecy trip appealed to me, and I decided I would go back to Ruby's place on Thursday, just to see what would happen.

QUESTION: You didn't tell anyone you knew what you were planning on doing?

SALLY: Not a soul—not even Harold when I saw him Thursday afternoon. I might've told David—I probably would have—but he'd already left for Cape Cod, and he wouldn't be back for two months. So it was all my secret, my hidden double identity.

QUESTION: What happened when you went back that Thursday night?

SALLY: The area was a little freakier at night than it had been during the daytime, and I started having doubts again. But at least nobody was in the elevator hassling me this time, and I just went straight up. Once I was there, it was OK; I felt fairly familiar with the place since I'd been there before. There was a different set of chicks around, but the balance of types was about the same, and Ruby was sitting at the front desk. She showed me where I could go change, and then she gave me a fast tour of the other rooms.

Besides the lounge area and her office, there were four session rooms, all done in the same putrid color scheme, but with dimmer light, so it was less noticeable. Two of them didn't have anything but massage tables, one of them had a set of whips and chains on the wall, and the fourth room, the biggest one, was the "specialty" room. It had all this ceiling-suspension gear, a kind of rack, the main chain-and-whip collection, a shelf full of various dildos, a chest full of clothes . . . anything you could think of.

After she'd shown me around the place, Ruby told me to sit out front and rap with the other girls for a while, but not to take any sessions; she wanted to go in on a session with me first, and one of her regulars was coming by in an hour. So I sat down on one of the couches to wait for him to show.

QUESTION: Were the other girls friendly toward you?

SALLY: Oh, yeah, not *gushy*-friendly right away, you know, because this was an extremely different situation than if I'd been a new girl at an insurance office or something; but they seemed to accept me all right, and we got something of a conversation going right off. We just rapped about clothes and hair and so on.

Two or three customers came in while I was there, and one of them tried to select me, but one of the girls told him I was still in training. Then Ruby's regular customer came in, and she introduced me to him and told him I was going to take part in his session, and it wouldn't cost him anything extra. He seemed happy about that and just nodded and smiled. But it wasn't the typical sort of male nod-and-smile you might expect in a situation like that: no kind of looking me up-and-down, but instead he just looked meek and grateful, more like somebody that's been told to do some job they don't mind doing.

Ruby told me to come to the "specialty" room with her, and she jerked her thumb at him to follow us. The three of us went back to the room, and Ruby collected his fifty dollars. As soon as she'd pocketed that, she suddenly switched to a much harsher tone of voice and told him to get down on the floor and kiss her feet. He did that without hesitating, and then she told him to kiss *my* feet. He started pecking away at my shoe-tops, very daintily; I didn't know what the hell to do, but I wanted to make a good impression on Ruby, so I just stood there with my arms crossed and looked down at him kind of disdainfully, you know? Then she had him roll around on the floor a little, and she motioned me to help her push him around with our feet and step on him some—not kick him or stomp on him hard, just mash and nudge him a little. His suit was getting filthy and wrinkled, but he didn't seem to notice.

All this while she's insulting him, calling him a pig and so forth. After a while, Ruby ordered him to stand up and take off his clothes, but not to look at us while he did or "he'd regret it." While he undressed, she started talking to me, but all for his benefit, saying things about how skinny and ugly his body was and what a faggoty little pervert he was. I tried to join in on this, but mainly just said, "Yeah, right," and things like that. Once she caught him glancing over at us, and she said, "Sally! That little queer's *looking* at us, after I told him to keep his fucking eyes to himself; kick him in the ass!" So I kicked him in the ass, pretty hard, and he sort of bowed apologetically, but he didn't say anything.

Once he was naked, she gave him a push in the direction of this wire-and-springs contraption attached to the ceiling, and she started strapping his wrists and ankles into it. I followed her lead, and I put the straps on the other side. This whole time, she's keeping up a running stream of insults either to him or about him—calling him every name in the book, rapping about how weak and obnoxious an excuse of a man he is. . . . And he never said a word; he just stood there with his head hung down while we strapped him into this thing.

After he was all strapped in, Ruby gave a violent jerk on this pulley arrangement and he was hoisted up in the air about three-and-a-half feet off the floor, facedown, with his legs spread. If Ruby hadn't been there, I would've cracked up; he looked like Don Knotts all set to play Superman in the nude.

By the time we got him strung up, he'd started to moan and groan a little in anticipation, so Ruby started saying sarcastic things about his "whining" and said something like "We'll give you something to whine about, you cocksucking little pig!" Then she picked up a ruler and beat him on the back with it, and she even gave his penis a slap or two while I beat his thighs with a little leather whip. After a few minutes she switched over to a longer whip on his back while I kept on with the smaller one. I was getting into it more or less, and I'd yell something nasty at him every once in a while. Then she had me get a dildo off the shelf, and she rammed it all the way up his ass while I went back to whipping him, and then he came. She gave him another slap or two after he came, and then she let him down.

After he'd left, she smiled at me and said I was very good with a whip and that she was pleased to have me working there. Then I went back out front to wait for a session by myself.

I reacted to the whole thing very calmly; of course, I'd had a chance to work up to the experience through Harold and David, but, still, this was a pretty heavy scene. It all seemed very natural to me though, and it was obvious that I could handle the job. I had six sessions of my own that night, and I went home with close to two hundred dollars.

QUESTION: Were they all pretty much the same type of thing?

SALLY: None of the others involved the ceiling-suspension stuff; they were all pretty simple, straightforward whipping-and-humiliation numbers. Only one guy wanted me to jerk him off after I'd whipped him awhile, but I never had to touch the other ones.

QUESTION: Did you ever have to get undressed yourself?

SALLY: No, not that night, and hardly ever any other night either. Even then, it was usually just a matter of pulling my top down for a "breast massage." Thing is, doing S & M, you don't *have* to do *shit;* the customers come in there with their particular little wants and preferences, but mostly they just involve the same old thing, whipping and yelling at them. And anything else, if you don't feel like it, you just say, "Hell no, motherfucker" and hit 'em another lick. That's what they come to pay for, and it's up to you to decide how you're gonna dish it out; which they love anyway—they *want* you to take command of them, to totally control the situation and tell them what they can do and what they can't do.

QUESTION: What is a "breast massage"?

SALLY: Oh, that just means rubbing your tits around on their body and maybe kind of slapping them in the face with them, you know? Some of the straighter customers might want to come on your tits and that'd be an extra charge.

QUESTION: Did you wear the same black leotard outfit every night?

SALLY: Most of the time; then sometimes there'd be a fetishist who'd want you in some kind of special costume.

He might bring it along himself, or, if not, there was a stock of things around—mainly oriented around the garter-belt-and-stocking theme—that seemed to get a lot of people off. The fetishists would want you to order them to lick or touch the clothes; you might have them do that while you were wearing them, or you'd take them off and throw them to them, or maybe you'd stay dressed and just have them munch on a spare garter belt that was laying around. I had two or three who liked to be tied up with stockings or have them wadded up and stuffed in their mouths as a gag. Some of them would kiss and hug those clothes like they were holding a girl, while I whipped them or jerked them off. One guy would lie there with his eyes closed and I'd work him over with a whip in one hand and a stocking in the other; he'd never know from one minute to the next whether he was about to get caressed or hit, but he loved them both, and he loved not knowing what was coming. Another guy liked me to put a stocking over his penis to masturbate him with, and another one wanted me to pretend to smother him to death with a pair of lacy panties.

QUESTION: Did you have any transvestites?

SALLY: Yeah, quite a few; most of the clothes we kept in stock were for them. They'd get all done up and then want to be talked to as if they were women. We'd talk about the things they liked to wear, and how nice the smooth nylon felt against their skin, or about the men they supposedly went to bed with, or they'd like to be accused of being "unfaithful wives." Most of the TV's were into a sort of caricature of female sexiness and imaginary promiscuity. Most of them weren't into anything sexually except pulling off their act; they seldom wanted to be jerked off or beaten or anything. Except for this one guy, who'd always bring his own costume; he always got dressed up like a nun, and after we'd "prayed" for a while, I'd beat him with a whip.

QUESTION: Were most of the transvestites feminine in appearance to begin with?

SALLY: No, not all of them, or even most of them; some of them just looked totally incongruous in their clothes and makeup, although a few of them were small-boned and smooth-skinned, and they looked pretty realistic as women. And a lot of them did a pretty grotesque imitation of female mannerisms and speech. The main giveaway was usually their jawbones; even if a guy has small features and almost no beard at all, he's bound to have a thicker jaw than a woman of the same size, and he usually has smaller eyes, too. But you had to act like they were the loveliest young things on earth, regular Miss Americas, even if they were fifty years old and six feet tall. Also, most of the older, "secret" TV's couldn't get away with shaving their legs or arms at home, and it was a pretty hideous sight to see them in a sleeveless dress and sheer stockings.

The younger ones, the ones who were really committed to it, would sometimes come in to the studio around eight o'clock on Friday or Saturday night just to get ready to go out for the evening. They'd spend half an hour or an hour getting their wigs and their lipstick straight and soliciting advice and compliments from you, and then they'd sashay out on the street like that for a night on the town. God knows where they went or who with.

QUESTION: What would you charge them for that?

SALLY: The same as for just about anything else—fifty dollars. Pretty expensive maid service, hmmh?

Oh, there was this one guy who was a frustrated entertainer; he'd bring a portable cassette recorder with some Bette Midler or Judy Garland tapes with him, and once he got dressed up you'd have to sit there for the rest of the session and applaud while he danced around and did these dreadful pantomime numbers to the songs. He was in his late forties, very fat, and always with a heavy beard-stubble that he said he just couldn't get rid of. He was without a doubt *the* worst drag act that has ever existed, but he really believed that someday he was going to make it "on the stage." Once in a while he'd even sing alone with the tapes himself, in this cracking, whiskied falsetto; and when he was done his eyes would light up and he'd grin a foot wide, taking bow after bow after bow while the girl he was paying sat there being sick to her stomach but clapping until he got ready to do his next number. Sad, sad case.

I had another guy who'd just discovered he was a TV and wanted me to give him lessons in being a woman; he'd sit there patiently, making mental notes while I demonstrated the "right" way to hold a cigarette or whatever, and then he'd try it himself, with me watching and making comments on his progress. He was a pretty nice guy, actually, very polite and well mannered, but he was worried to death about this transvestite hang-up of his and what his wife might think if she ever found out. They were a relatively young couple, in their early thirties, and from what he said it seemed as if she was fairly intelligent and understanding; so I finally told him that I thought he ought to go ahead and tell her, explain to her that the dressing-up was all that was involved, that he wasn't a homosexual or anything. He was scared shitless, but he eventually did confide in her; and apparently she reacted a lot better than he'd expected. He stopped coming into the studio, and I guess he started doing it at home, which I thought was good; not many wives would be able to go that far. At least, I *hope* that's what happened; I never saw him again.

QUESTION: Did you have many customers who asked you to help them out with their problems in some way?

SALLY: No; very few. Very few. Most of the people I saw were pretty far gone as it was, you know, and I don't think they could've changed their sexual orientation even if they'd wanted to. But I did try to ease some of their fears' and concerns about it, if they seemed to have any. Some of the people who were just experimenting to see if that was *really* what they wanted would ask for my advice about it, and I'd usually just say that I thought it was a good thing they were open enough with themselves to be willing to try something different. I thought it was a good idea that they went through with it and had a pretty thorough session, so they'd be able to make an honest judgment later.

I couldn't come on too understanding and helpful; that was the opposite of the role I had to play with most of these guys, particularly the masochists. If I'd acted all sympathetic and kind with them, they'd've had a lousy time and I'd've gotten fired. Even if that's what some of them may have actually *needed,* they were there for what they *wanted;* and those can be two totally different things with a lot of people, you know, not just those that are kind of sick about it.

I must admit, that caused me a few bad times with my conscience; with some customer that I really felt sorry for, some poor, meek, repressed little man who'd obviously gotten a dirty deal out of life, it was sometimes kind of hard to yell dirty names at him and beat him with a whip. Particularly when he'd start "begging for mercy," which was something a lot of them did just to make the thrill that much more; they didn't expect you to really stop, but to just go on hitting them even harder.

QUESTION: What if somebody had come there just to experiment with S & M, found out he didn't like it, and *did* want you to stop? How could you tell the difference?

SALLY: That didn't happen too often, but when it did it was always obvious. They'd switch back to a more realistic, a more commanding tone of voice, reverse the roles that had been established, and *tell* you to stop. The true masochists, the ones that wanted you to continue, begged you or pleaded with you to stop; it wasn't a realistic or believable request at all—you could tell that from their attitude, you know? Nobody was ever in any danger of getting hurt any more than he wanted to be.

But I still feel a little guilty about it once in a while; it just hadn't been part of my upbringing or character to hit people in the first place, let alone to keep on hitting them when they were tied up and moaning and saying, "Oh, please, please, no. . . ." I had to do some pretty heavy dissociation sometimes. Even more so than a regular prostitute just having intercourse with a customer, I believe.

Of course, I've also got to admit that I sometimes—often, even—*enjoyed* what I was doing. There's a little bit of the sadist in everybody, you know, and when you're in a situation of absolute power like that, when you're being worshiped and adored for your supposed strength and superiority over someone, and when they're *literally* kissing your feet and obeying your every command, no matter how insane it might be . . . it's hard to not get off on that, at least a little bit, you know? Sometimes it would be kind of a strain to leave the place and readjust to normal social dealings. I'd find myself unconsciously taking command or assuming that I ought to have command; and if I was on a date, say, I'd sometimes feel a sudden urge to slap or kick the guy I was with if he wasn't pleasing me. You learn to repress those urges pretty fast, though [*laughs*].

I guess that kind of reaction, that enjoyment of the dominant role, is much more intense once it's released in a woman because we've had so little opportunity to be that way, you know? I was never any heavy women's libber, but I did kind of dig the fact that I could turn the tables around completely, even in a grossly exaggerated way, and it got a lot of my frustrations out. The same holds true for me being black; I was never super hung-up about that either, but all sorts of tiny angers and unexpressed emotions just naturally build up over the course of your life; you never really know *how* many until you have a chance to let them all out. Almost all of my customers were middle-aged white businessmen, and a lot of them specifically chose me because I was black; they'd even ask me to insult them racially—they'd want me to call them "no-good honkie cowards" and so forth. I'd be a liar if I tried to pretend I didn't appreciate that opportunity once in a while. I don't know how an ordinary black prostitute feels about her work, but I certainly never felt as if I was betraying my race by letting white men "use" me; nobody used me, they just paid me good bread for the privilege of lettin' me beat the shit out of them.

QUESTION: Did you ever have any "slave" customers?

SALLY: Oh, yeah, there was this one guy in particular that I took on as a regular slave, even when I wasn't at work at the studio. After I'd moved into an apartment in the city, he used to come over two or three times a week and keep the place clean for me, and cook dinner, and scrub the floors,

and defrost the refrigerator.... If I'd been able to plant
cotton in a window box, I'd've had him picking that [*laughs*].
It was a weird trip, you know? I mean, fitting in with this
whole racial thing, it was like *the* turnaround of the traditional
situation or the thing that black people are most sensitive
to any mention of. I used to just sit back in my living room
sipping wine and laughing, watching this gray-haired white
man in a suit scramble around my apartment, sweeping up
and washing my clothes, hopping to every time I yelled at
him.... Obviously, I'd never tell my family about any of
what I've been up to, but, oh Lord, I wish they could've
seen *that!*

QUESTION: Were the other black girls at the studio equally
popular with the customers?

SALLY: Now, I don't know about *equally*.... Ruby had
herself a pretty heavy reputation, you understand [*laughs*].
No, seriously, they were; an awful lot of masochists seem
to prefer a black girl. All the ads for the place had pictures
of black girls in them, and, remember, it was *owned* by a
black woman.

I think the reason for that is basically two things: First
off, blacks just give a good impression of strength and maybe
with a little imagined hint of "secret evil" or whatever; and
second, it's related to the whole basic cause of masochism
anyway, which is guilt. I think all these guys, every one of
them, got into his trip out of feeling guilty over sex; maybe
there were other things to go along with that, childhood
associations and so forth, but there was *always* some guilt,
some repression, to one degree or another. They came to
attach that guilt as an inseparable part of their sexual feelings;
they'd been bothered by it so long, the only way they could
deal with it was to start enjoying it. And if there was any
other aspect of guilt they could throw in there, too, then
all the better; so an awful lot of these middle-class white
men leaped right onto the idea of racial guilt feelings, and
they'd always pick a black girl to have a session with. Two
guilts for the price of one. Whip out their sex, whip out
their prejudice

Ruby herself was *married* to a masochist, a shrimpy little white guy; she'd been so wonderfully mean to him over the years, he suggested she open this place up and she did. He used to come around to help clean up the studio, and the first couple of times I saw him I thought he was just another customer; but he was the *boss* boss's husband. He was the *ultimate* customer [*laughs*]. You really should've seen them; they made quite a pair: She stood half a head taller than him and outweighed him forty or fifty pounds. They must've had a very, very happy marriage.

There was also an Oriental girl working there, and she was pretty well liked, too—especially by the soldiers just coming back from Nam. You wanta talk about *guilt*, man, just think *that* one over. From what they said, a hell of a lot of guys got into S & M over there; there was a mighty heavy "dominant massage" business going down in Saigon. Just the way to relax after a hard day's work at My Lai, right? You know those dudes was getting their heads fucked up over there, and that sounds like a damn logical direction for 'em to go.

You know what they call a dominant session, don't you? An "English." Next to homosexuality, it's the official perversion over there; and this country's looking to go the same route. It's a disease of dying empires, the last sexual resort of a worn-out, impotent society; all that vanishing power just starts to turn inward, and that "big stick" they've been so proud of carrying starts to feeling good on their own backs. I don't know for sure, but ten-to-one the same thing happened in Rome and Egypt and a lot of other places, on a smaller scale. It's all just part of the cycle of sickness, and we're right in the middle of it now.

QUESTION: You think that masochism, or sexual perversion in general, is on the increase in the United States?

SALLY: In some ways it is, like, among older white middle-class men or ex-soldiers, there seems to be more masochism than there might have been before. But that's not true with the majority of the younger people, the black kids or the white kids who're relaxed enough to know where their heads are at. I think there's a lot more sexual experimenting going on in our age group today, and lots more people owning up to preferences they have that might've been considered sick a few years ago, like bisexuality. But as far as the "perversions" that come out of being repressed, they're practically disappearing. People are just more honest now about choosing from among the alternatives that are left; and a very small degree of S & M can be one of those choices, as long as it doesn't come out of feeling guilty over sex and isn't carried to some crazy extreme. I dig it myself, *both* sides of it.

QUESTION: You mentioned a few minutes ago that you moved into an apartment in Manhattan; did you eventually quit your nurse's job?

SALLY: Yeah, after about a month of working both jobs, it just got to be too much of a hassle to deal with. I wasn't getting any sleep, I was always driving back and forth to Long Island at weird hours, and I was making about eight times as much bread at the studio as I was at the clinic. I decided I might as well just work there for about six months and save as much as I could, and then get back into what I was more interested in as a career. So I quit and got myself a place in the Village.

QUESTION: What were some of your customer's more popular requests in a session?

SALLY: Most of these guys were pretty hung-up on anal things; they wanted to be fingered there or have something shoved up inside. One reason for that was probably just the image of abasement that it has for the normal male, like they were really being "violated" and forced to do something unnatural or unpleasant. But a lot of older men seem to be into that kind of thing anyway; they might have trouble getting it up or coming, and they need some direct pressure on the prostate gland before they can ejaculate. One of our favorite accessories around the place was this huge dildo, two or three inches across and over a foot long, that we nicknamed Big Eddie. He was a mean motherfucker and blacker than I am [*laughs*].

We also gave a lot of enemas; I was used to that from being a nurse, and I'd often noticed then that some patients actually seemed to look forward to their enemas. I can't really see it myself, but I guess it's understandable: all that warm fluid inside you, and the tension that's built up as you get fuller and fuller, and then suddenly release it all. And again, for a man, there's the prostate-pressure thing. I've always just preferred to kind of ignore my intestines until they start getting demanding on their own, but other people apparently enjoy some of the sensations they get in that area.

I guess one of the main sources for the enema hang-ups is a childhood association thing; maybe their mothers used to do it to them all the time, or maybe they were getting an enema the first time they ever got an erection, or maybe they used to get them from some cute nurse or baby-sitter or something. Whatever the reason, there was more of a call for them than you might expect.

Also, different versions of the "slave" thing were very common; just about all of the customers wanted to be ordered around during the session. The most extreme cases of that, like the guy that would come clean up my apartment, don't care what you tell them to do; it's just the fact of being commanded that gets them off. The others want you to dictate certain sexual things for them to do, which they've somehow gotten across in advance that they want to do anyway—like analingus, say. That was the high point of a lot of sessions after I'd whipped them, but they'd always want me to *order* them to lick my ass. I'd get down on my hands and knees with them in the same position behind me, and I'd shout and yell at them that if they didn't do it, and do it right, I'd whip them again. Of course, they'd want that order repeated several times, and they'd also want a few more slaps of the whip, so every once in a while they'd kind of stop doing it and look over at me coyly, like a little kid that knows he's done something bad; then I'd say, "You sorry son-of-a-bitch, I *told* you not to stop!" and I'd crack them across the back with the whip a couple of times till they started in again. Again, I think it was just the general image of abasement and the feeling of being ordered to do something humiliating; I doubt if any of them really dug the taste.

QUESTION: Did you ever have a customer who wanted you to urinate on him?

SALLY: I had several who were freaks for urine; pissing on their head, in their mouths, giving them little bottles of it to take home . . . .

Some of the customers would choose the girl they wanted for a session by going around out front and asking everybody who had to go to the bathroom the most. If you had a regular coming in at a certain time, you might drink a couple of beers just before he came, so you'd be good and ready for him. One of my customers liked to have a shampoo with my urine; he'd come in with a big empty cup and a tube of Head and Shoulders, and as soon as I'd filled the cup we'd go in the bathroom where he'd lean over the sink and wash his own hair with it. I'd sit there and talk to him while he worked up a lather, and that was all I had to do. It seemed to get his hair pretty clean, too.

That's one thing about these piss-freaks; it sounds totally disgusting and filthy, but urine isn't dirty at all—it's almost as clean, in terms of bacteria, as distilled water. In battlefield hospital tents, when they can't always be sure of sterile conditions, the medics often use urine to wash their hands and instruments before surgery; and American Indians used to apply urine-soaked rags to open wounds. The uric acid kills practically every kind of bacteria there is.

QUESTION: Did many of the customers want you to verbally insult them?

SALLY: Yeah, just about every one of them; the masochists are usually into a very heavy verbal thing; you have to keep up a running stream of patter while you work them over. Calling them faggots, insulting their masculinity or their appearance, making fun of the fact that they want to get beaten, telling them they're no good at all to anybody in any way . . . you really have to put them down.

They also want you to tell them how much you enjoy hitting them or whatever, to talk about how good the whip feels in your hand as you bring it down across their backs. Sometimes they'd have specific phrases they wanted you to use, that they'd tell you about in advance. I had this one guy, a fairly young guy, who wanted me to kick him in the genitals and each time say, "Oh, it feels good to mash those balls with my toes." I'd kick him pretty hard, too; sometimes I wondered how these people could physically tolerate the things they had me do to them.

QUESTION: When they asked you to do or say particular things, were they pretty open about making those requests?

SALLY: They were generally kind of nervous and ashamed about it at first, but I could gradually get it out of them by playing little guessing games, you know; and then there were a few who came on like movie directors, just immediately and without hesitation, saying, "All right, first I'd like two dozen strokes across my upper thighs with the second whip from the right, and then I'd like you to bend my penis backwards with both hands while you say so-and-so, and *then* . . ." [*laughs*].

A lot of the guys wanted me to send them through fantasy trips, too, either telling them stories or acting something out.

QUESTION: What kinds of fantasies?

SALLY: Well, childhood things were pretty common; like, sometimes they'd want to pretend I was their mother or their nursemaid, and they'd confess to me about masturbating or something, which would make me "angry" so I'd whip them. One guy actually played like he was a baby; he'd lean over my knees and cry while I spanked him, talking baby talk and calling me "mommy." Most of the fetishists were into a regression thing, from having seen their mothers or sisters wearing spiked heels and stockings with garters. One guy used to have me put those things on with a calf-length dress, and he'd crawl around on the floor and occasionally peer up my dress; at that point I was supposed to grind my heel in his face.

Somebody else managed to find out that I was a nurse, and it drove him wild. This was apparently his major fantasy image, and he said he'd give me a hundred dollars if I'd do exactly what he asked. So the day after that he came back in and I'd brought my uniform and all sorts of paraphernalia; I gave him an "examination," and then I hauled out a hypodermic I'd ripped off from the clinic and gave him about fifteen of the most painful injections I could do. I must've injected a gallon of water in that guy, mainly his buttocks, before he was satisfied.

Then there was my foot-fetishist . . . this guy seemed to think the entire human body was an appendage of the feet. There were a couple of customers who were into feet, but nothing like him. He always wore three pair of socks and special soft-leather shoes, and he carried around this briefcase full of foot lotions and foot pads and extra socks and manicure equipment and slippers . . . he'd have me sit on the edge of the table while he gave me a long foot treatment, bathing them and clipping my toenails and rubbing them with oils, and then kissing and caressing them like they were my face. He'd jerk off while he did that, and then he'd pack away his little case of foot goodies till the next time. After three or four times, I got curious about how he'd gotten into that, and I started rapping to him more about his life. It turned out that he was a church organist; he'd played the organ since he was about four years old. His parents had been very religious and restrictive, and the only real outlet he'd had in his life was his music; so he'd come to associate the gentle pressure of his feet on the organ pedals with everything that he found pleasurable, and he considered the feet the most delicate and sensuous parts of the body.

Another type of fetishists were the rubber people; they'd come in wearing tight rubber underwear, and there was one guy with a whole rubber suit that completely covered his body. It had gloves and feet in it, and even a mask that came all the way down over his head, with just two tiny holes at the nostrils to breathe through. He'd bring this thing in, all folded up, and he'd set it to one side at the beginning of the session; then he'd take off his clothes and I'd start whipping and humiliating him. After a little while he'd reach for the rubber suit and start slowly pulling it on and I'd continue to whip whatever parts of his body were left exposed. But as an area was covered by the rubber, I'd leave it alone. Then when he had the whole suit and the mask on, he'd curl himself up into a ball on the floor and I'd stop hitting him or yelling at him; I'd just sit down beside him and rock him back and forth very slowly. Not rocking him like a mother would a baby, nothing affectionate or personal; he just wanted me to push him gently with the heel of my hand, so he'd sway back and forth, and he'd hum to himself while I did that. After about ten minutes of that, he'd change back into his street clothes, and he'd pay me and leave. Apparently the rubber getup was some sort of security thing to him: a security from being hurt and a security from admitting to himself that he *liked* to be hurt, you know? It was very tight and confining and must have made him feel like he was thoroughly held-together, with all the bad things in the world shut out; I can see it being a very womblike sensation, except for the texture of the rubber. I'd probably enjoy it myself, except for that.

QUESTION: Did any of the masochists ever get into having intercourse with you?

SALLY: I never had one that did. I spent over six months as a prostitute, and I never screwed anybody once. There were two or three guys who wanted blow-jobs as part of the session and several who wanted to be jerked off, but nobody ever asked to screw. I think most of them have gone beyond that; they just wouldn't be able to enjoy ordinary sex at all or even be able to accomplish it in most cases. They need a great deal more stimulation than intercourse could offer, and they'd probably go crazy with guilt if they just screwed somebody anyway.

That need for more and more stimulation is an important part of masochism, I think; they've been so totally repressed sexually that they've managed to shut off their responses to everything most people would think of as pleasurable. The only sensations that can still get through their brains are painful ones. They can deny the existence of pleasure, and they can suppress their responses to it, but pain is something they *can't* ignore. It's something that's inflicted on them from the outside, you know? With normal sex, you have a choice as to whether or not you're going to enjoy yourself and get aroused, but if somebody's domineering you in a sexual situation, you can at least make yourself believe that the decision is no longer in your hands. You can overcome the guilt by thinking the excitement is being *forced* on you, and simultaneously you're being punished for it, too; so everything's cool—it's possible to more or less relax and enjoy the orgasm.

The guilt they feel over any sexual excitement is just too strong to be handled, but it's impossible for them to destroy the desire; so they start lusting after *punishment* for that desire, and the two contradictory desires just merge into each other until they can't tell one from the other. And if they start feeling guilty about enjoying the pain, then they cry out to be hit even harder, so they can justify it to themselves by thinking they got whipped to a point that was a little beyond what they might consider pleasurable, and therefore they really got punished for their "evil" desires. It sounds like a neat balance, but the problem is that they do want to be hit a little harder each time, to "make it all right"; and if they aren't able to even off at some point, then that can just escalate to some pretty frightening levels.

Most of the customers were just into being dominated and maybe whipped until they'd get light red marks on their legs or backs; but some of them wanted to have some incredibly painful, and even dangerous, things done to them. One of the items we kept in stock at the studio was a tiny leather strap, like a miniature belt a couple of inches long, with sharp metal studs imbedded in it on one side. There were customers who wanted this thing strapped tightly around their penis while it was still flaccid, so that as they got an erection the metal studs would bite into the flesh; but the more it hurt, the bigger their erection got. I've seen guys leave there bleeding from that thing but happy. There were also various steel clamps and tongs to attach to their genitals, and tiny vises to crush their testicles. A few of them would ask to be burned with cigarettes and matches, and one man brought in one of those little hand-crank electrical generators, with electrodes to wire up his testicles. Somebody else had a jewel box full of plastic tubes that he wanted inserted in his urethra . . . and there was one man who had gradually *drilled a hole*, like piercing an ear, through the head of his penis, from top to bottom, right in the center. He wanted pieces of coarse thread to be strung through it and tied off as tightly as possible all around the hole. If I hadn't been a nurse, I think some of this shit would have been enough to make me faint, just watching it. We, and I in particular, wouldn't do anything that looked like it might really cause the customers any permanent harm: cigarettes and matches were out, and so was the guy with the electrical generator. But I'm sure they managed to find somebody, somewhere, who'd do what they asked . . . and if not, they'd go home and do it themselves. I wouldn't be surprised if some of those guys ended up in the hospital. If they kept that kind of crap up, it wouldn't be too long before they wouldn't have any sex organs to feel guilty about; and maybe that's what they secretly wanted to happen anyway.

QUESTION: Did you ever have any customers who wanted to perform sadistic acts themselves, on you?

SALLY: Not really; I think they knew better than to ask, even if they wanted to. There were a couple, though, who . . . well, there was one guy who brought in a Polaroid camera, and he wrapped some rope around me like I was tied up, and then he squirted some ketchup on me, and he took a few pictures of me like that. I don't know where his head was at; it was probably just for some practical joke, to freak his friends out with the pictures. But then again maybe that was his real fantasy . . . whatever, I'd just as soon not run into him again.

A lot of people would show up with their own special props; there was this other guy who obviously *was* into a sadistic trip, but trying to control it: and what he'd do was bring in one of these life-size inflatable dolls that looked like a woman. He'd prop the doll up against the wall, and he and

I would stand around and talk to it; I was supposed to pretend it was a friend of mine, and the three of us would have a whole conversation. Finally he and I would get "mad" at the doll, and then we'd both start cursing at it and end up whipping it [laughs]. One night we hooked "Judy" up to the ceiling-suspension equipment in the big room, and he was beating the shit out of it with one of the big leather whips; then all of a sudden he hit it too hard and the damn thing popped! There was this whoosh of air, and it just started collapsing, still strung up in these straps with its arms and legs drooping down and its face going flat. I've never had that much trouble not laughing in my life, but I didn't know what the hell he might do if I cracked up; he came back in the next week, and he'd gotten her all patched up. We never used the big whip on her after that; she was a frail creature [laughs].

QUESTION: Aside from their sexual hang-ups, what sort of people were these to deal with?

SALLY: There were three basic types: the ones who were very meek and withdrawn and acted humble toward you at all times; the ones who felt disgusted with themselves because of their need to be submissive, so they'd act very hostile and nasty to you, bitching about money or something before and after the session; and then the ones who were just polite, normal-seeming individuals, people you'd never dream might be hiding something like that in themselves. They were in the majority: lawyers and salesmen and advertising executives with a wife and kids in the suburbs. It was strange to watch them go through the transition from their everyday selves into the head they had to get into for the session: their faces, their voices, everything about them would change. Real Dr. Jekyll and Mr. Hyde, only in reverse.

QUESTION: Do you think it's healthy for them to be expressing these desires?

SALLY: I don't think it's healthy for the desires to be there, not to the extent that some of these guys take it; like I said, it's a matter of their having been repressed and made to feel guilty over their own sexuality, and I don't think sex is something for people to feel guilty over. But as long as they have come to feel this way, and this is the only way they can achieve sexual satisfaction, then I think they should be free to do that, if they don't inflict their trip on anybody else and nobody gets hurt. It's stupid to say that they should suppress their wants even more; that's how they got to be so fucked up in the first place! It's always better to express something, maybe get it out of your system, than to lock it up inside and torture yourself and everybody around you with the results of your frustrations.

QUESTION: Do you think that sadomasochistic prostitution is a good social outlet itself?

SALLY: Yes, I do; these people have got to find partners somewhere, and until all their wives or girlfriends are able to understand where they're at and deal with it, they should definitely be able to find somebody who won't be shocked by what they want. I never hurt anybody, and I don't think any of my customers would've been better off if they'd been unable to come see me; they'd just be walking around the streets that much sicker.

QUESTION: Do you think prostitution, including S & M prostitution, should be legalized?

SALLY: Do you think grass is green?

QUESTION: Are you still working as a prostitute?

SALLY: No, I worked for about six-and-a-half months and saved up several thousand dollars, just like I'd planned; and it looks like the law's gonna be cracking down soon, and I don't want any part of that. I'm gonna take a few weeks off, go out and see my family, and then take a vacation in South America. After that I'll probably move to some smaller town in the Midwest or New England—I'm sick of New York —and go back to work as a nurse. I might even decide to try med school now; at least I've found a good way to earn the tuition [laughs].

7. *Cassandra*

CASSANDRA is an unusual and very pleasant person to meet. She is stunningly attractive, tall and slim, with waist-length blond hair and a perfectly proportioned body. Her facial features are almost flawless, and she would resemble a Vargas Girl in animation were it not for the obvious intelligence in her eyes.

Cassandra is a highly independent person, a magnetic individual whose awareness and unpretentious self-confidence alone would suffice to give her an extraordinarily powerful advantage in almost any situation.

Despite all this, Cassandra is a remarkably unconceited person, without a trace of the bitchiness or manipulative behavior that one might expect from her appearance. Her competitive nature seems almost entirely self-directed, leading her to surpass her own goals and achievements, rather than to enter into mutually destructive confrontation with others. She is relaxed and easy-going, but with an appealing streak of periodic shyness.

Although she is one of the youngest subjects in this book, Cassandra seemed to exhibit more maturity and genuine, not falsely egocentric, sophistication than most. As you will see, she is best left to speak for herself.

* * *

QUESTION: What was your childhood like?

CASSANDRA: Well, I was born and brought up in a small town near Boston; my parents were typical middle class, and I got along fine with them. I also have an older brother and a younger sister, and there weren't any real problems there either.

I never got hung up on any particular role as a kid; I was into playing with dolls *and* climbing trees. As a matter of fact, I used to take the dolls up into the trees with me, and I even built them their own little treehouse. They hunted squirrels.

I guess my childhood was just pretty normal basically; I

got along all right with the other kids, and I didn't resent being born a girl or anything like that. As a matter of fact, I was glad I was a girl because the boys all seemed to have more shit laid on their heads than I did. At least I had more options as a girl; I could wear dresses or I could wear pants and T-shirts, and I could do my doll number or I could go build a fort with the boys; but the boys *had* to wear pants, and they *had* to build forts.

Then when I hit puberty, though, things started to change a lot. The whole thing didn't come as any big shock to me or anything because my family was pretty good about sex education and there were some good books around the house, so I had a pretty good idea of what to expect before it ever happened; but it did cause me some hassles in other ways. I don't mean to sound like I'm conceited or something, but I was kind of noticeable for my appearance, you know? I was always pretty as a child, too, but it didn't make that much difference until I was a teen-ager, and I never really knew just how much of a drag it could turn out to be. I only realized that when my breasts started to grow; because even though getting your period is supposedly this big psychological heavy, at least it's a private kind of thing . . . whereas tits are *public*, they're just sticking right out there, and they *hurt* all the time. It's something people can notice and comment about, and they do; like calling you "Hey, Little Ones" and shit like that. Mine weren't particularly large or small, but they were definitely there, and I just wasn't allowed to forget it, you know?

Then just being good-looking or whatever in general helps you to lose a lot of friends very fast, which is a bummer. The boys all resent you if you don't act giggly and flirt with every one of them, and the chicks hate you no matter what you do. Even if you're just quiet and keep to yourself most of the time, they figure you're trying to be mysterious or something. I really lost several good friends, and that upset me a lot because I honestly couldn't understand why they hated me all of a sudden. And I really hadn't done anything that should've pissed anybody off—it wasn't like I was running after people's boyfriends or anything; I was just trying to be a pleasant person with everybody, but they didn't take it that way. Also, all the older people, women especially, can't stand you; they figure you're automatically some kind of little slut. So all of a sudden, at the age of fourteen, I'm supposed to be personally responsible for everybody else's fears and regrets and hang-ups.

The whole thing made me become very introverted; I dressed very plainly, and I didn't date much at all, and I did my best not to offend anybody, but of course there was no way I could do that because my very *existence* was offensive to so many people. So I learned in high school that everybody should relax and be themselves, as long as they're not too attractive and not too intelligent.

QUESTION: Did you start dating early?

CASSANDRA: Well, that's really hard to say because I just wasn't into the whole straight "dating" pattern; I preferred to just be friends with guys, mostly. Although, of course, I would get horny, and I also had a couple of "serious" relationships.

Things got better when I went to college at B.U. [Boston University]; there were a lot more trips to get into and a lot more people I could get along with. When I was a freshman, I did the whole guilt-expiation number and I joined SDS; but that didn't last too long because they were just into too heavy a reverse elitist trip, and that wasn't at all what I needed. So then I met some people in the film and journalism departments, and they were all good heads in the best senses of the word; we were all getting into a lot of interesting shit, like Soleri's whole-system architecture, and Lilly's things with dolphins, and I got into editing a couple of films . . . and also, these people were generally a little looser and less uptight around me than the other people I'd dealt with before. They weren't into such heavy jealousy numbers, they were all very relaxed about their sexuality, and it was just a very nice, very free-flowing mixture of friendships and other things, among a group of maybe a dozen people.

The summer after my sophomore year, five or six of us

went to Europe together. We spent a couple of months there, mainly in Yugoslavia and Italy, camping out along the Adriatic and things; then we went to London and I decided to hang around there for a while instead of going back to school with everybody else, so I found a flat that I was sharing with a bunch of British and American freaks that I ran into. I was having a fantastic time until the bread started to run out, and I didn't want to leave London yet, so I had to start looking for some jobs that I could get without a work permit.

That kind of limitation can lead you into some very weird levels of society, basically like the nightclub sort of scene. I did a couple of cocktail waitress gigs, but the money wasn't that fantastic, so I ended up going to one of the strip joints in Soho one night, and I got drunk enough to "audition" then and there.

Working there was really weird, really a cathartic kind of trip; I was used to being naked in front of a lot of other people because we'd been to several of the nude beaches in Yugoslavia and so on, but this was totally different, and it was also totally different than any way my personality had ever been before. Like I said, I had really freaked out about being attractive, so I'd been pretty shy and introverted, and I usually just wore like jeans and a sweater or something like that; so it was very strange to just turn that a hundred and eighty degrees around, and literally put myself up in a spotlight and be as enticing and as erotic as possible. It was just like a negation of all the crap I went through in high school; it was like giving the finger to all those people who had made me feel guilty about expressing myself sexually.

I did some interesting things there, too; after I'd been there a few days I started really getting into ways that the whole thing could be improved, and I developed a very simple but very sexy act; I junked the whole floor-length sequined gown kind of shit and just danced in some nice "trendy" regular clothes, like crushed-velvet bells and appliquéd tops, that kind of thing. I think it was a lot sexier because it was more realistic, you know?

Then after a few days the manager asked me to help

restructure some of the other girls' numbers, so I jazzed things up a little with some more rock music and a little gutsier, but subtler, kind of dancing, and I changed the costumes around and played with the lighting possibilities; it was really kind of interesting. I also had one act with two girls removing *each other's* clothes, and that was interesting.

QUESTION: Were any of these other girls involved in prostitution on the side?

CASSANDRA: Yeah, sure, a couple of them would take tricks from among the customers, and a couple of others were working out of flats in Soho; you know, they have these places with little nameplates on the front door that say things like MICHELLE: FRENCH LESSONS, SECOND FLOOR or LARGE CHEST FOR SALE: SEE AGNES, 5-A. That was the first time I'd ever been that closely exposed to the business, and it didn't occur to me to do it because it just didn't really seem like a logical or feasible thing to do at the time.

Then I also got involved with this whole black-magic group, a Satanist cult in London; that was fascinating. They really went through a whole heavy ceremony number, with black robes and lighted tapers and women dressed up like nuns pissing in chalices . . . the whole bit. England is very big on that kind of thing. It was partially just an excuse for an orgy, but a lot of the people were really into the whole concept as a sort of religion. It's like a unique way of celebrating nature, and they're into merging the pleasure and the pain of existence, which means they also get into some mild S & M stuff, which I can dig. In the right setting, and with the right people, that can really be a turn-on. Nobody actually gets hurt, it's just a matter of creating sensations that border on pain, and that element of suggestion can be very titillating. It's helped me understand my masochistic customers a lot better; I'm not hung up on it like some of them are. I just like a little slapping or light whipping as part of the foreplay, but I can understand where their heads are at.

Anyway, I stayed in London for about four months, and then I came back to New York; I didn't really feel like going back to school yet, but I have kept in touch with all my friends there. So I came here and hung around, got another job

working on a documentary for Channel 13; but even though
I'm really into film, and there's a lot of shit that I want
to do with it, I'm just not that committed that I want to
put up with starving for six or eight years before I can get
it together the way I'd like to. I'm not greedy or materialistic
or anything, but money does mean freedom and options,
you know? So I started looking around for some fast ways
to get a lot of bread together.

I tried getting into modeling for a while, but that just
became a total bummer; there's even more bullshit in that
business than anything else. All the stereotypes are
true—lecherous photographers, lecherous casting directors,
lecherous vice-presidents. . . . It's still like the thirties or something, really. And they really seem to think they're being
very cool or very original; it's amazing. I was with an excellent
agency, and I was getting some very good jobs, and I was
going to all the right parties, and I was starting to get film
offers; serious offers, in good movies, not just bullshit lines;
but even at those levels, it's such a bullshit, ass-kissing business.
I really considered going along with some of the crap, going
ahead and laying some of these idiots; because I'd gotten
into it to make money, and I had pretty quickly worked
my way up to the places where the real money was. . . . But,
in order to do that, I really would have had to *commit* myself
to the whole trip; I would've had to define myself in that
mold and play it to the hilt, you know? Give in, sexually
and every other way, to all these egotistical fools who thought
they were doing me such fantastic favors. I was having enough
difficulty just dealing with the other chicks who were around;
they actually honestly *cared* about what they were doing. They
were *proud* of the parts they'd gotten, or that they might
get, or that they might get auditioned for. . . . They were
even proud of the producers they'd screwed—they'd brag
about it. At this same time I was also attending a modern
dance workshop here in the city, and these starlet chicks
reminded me a lot of more attractive, but even dumber,
versions of some of the people I met there. I was doing
that basically just to keep in shape and because I dig movement and rhythm; but these chicks at the workshop were

incredible: They could all kick so-and-so many feet and inches, and they were great at following directions to put their feet right *there*, and they knew exactly who was the most *avant* of the *avant-garde* at the Joffrey this week, and they were *terribly* good at jumping up and down and waving their arms in purple spacesuits to symbolize the Decline of the West . . . but not one of them could *dance* worth shit. They were too busy being "dancers." They were just unbelievably fucking serious about this one, tiny, limited little trip; and these starlet chicks were exactly the same way. They were Actresses, they were Sex Goddesses, they were Serious Artists, they were Striving to Express Themselves, all in capital neon letters. In fact, they were just whores, and they were dishonest, hypocritical ones at that.

It's an obvious point, and not very original, but the whole modeling-acting bit really *is*, to an incredible extent, just a nicey-nice, glossed-over form of prostitution. I knew that in advance, of course, but I really never knew just how heavy it actually gets, and it hasn't changed in years. It's just an amazing degree of exploitation, everywhere you turn; and it isn't just the women that are being exploited either; even from the male point of view, this whole pretty-pretty advertising thing is just a creepy-crawly, sexually repressed and reppressive kind of voyeurism. It's really insulting to men because they're being treated like children; they're supposed to be begging and whimpering for all these half-licks of the lollipops . . . and it really seems to me that they'd resent having that kind of self-image imposed on them.

So I ended up having a big confrontation with my agency; I told them I didn't want to be Cybill Shepherd; I just wanted to pay my bills and save up enough money to leave the city in comfort, and if they'd just keep me supplied with minor, no-hassle jobs that would be fine with me. They got really pissed about that; they just couldn't believe that I was capable of turning any of this crap down, and they were really after the biggest ten-percent pound of flesh they could get. They tried reasoning with me, sympathizing with me, badgering me, threatening me, ridiculing me . . . but none of it worked, and I just insisted on staying at the level I'd established for myself that could be easily handled and relatively profitable.

That didn't work out either though; there were fewer and fewer no-hassle jobs available, and the agency started giving those to other girls before me out of spite. So pretty soon it was obvious that I was either going to have to go along with their version of my "career" or else I was going to have to look for some other job, at least part-time, where I could make some *honest* bread. It didn't make that much difference to me what it was, as long as it was mildly interesting and there was good money involved; I still wasn't ready to either go back to school or to start off on some serious career thing, I just wanted some time to myself, with some financial security behind me.

Several of the girls that I knew were working nights or weekends as cocktail waitresses in various East Side bars, and I considered doing that; but I knew from my experience in London that the tips weren't really all *that* good, and you had to work like hell to get them.

I also didn't want to start playing Ruby Keeler at the end of some Broadway chorus line, and I wasn't about to bump and grind down the runway at some New York "burlesque house." There was just too much time and hassle, and not nearly enough money, involved in dance of any sort over here.

Then I noticed this ad in *Backstage*, looking for girls to work at a place called "Caesar's Retreat." I'd heard of Caesar's before—I'd seen a couple of copies of *Screw*, and I knew about the existence of massage parlors—I'd heard that they were fronts for prostitution in one form or another. I found the idea kind of intriguing, but I didn't really give it any serious thought at first.

But during the next week I had a couple of particularly raunchy experiences with grabby producers, and it annoyed me more than ever to think that I *had* to put up with at least some of their crap, no matter how strongly I felt against it, if I wanted any work at all. And even then, I was getting nothing in return except the vague promise that *if* I wasn't too rude I *might* be hired, at rip-off wages, to peddle their lousy dresses or toothpaste or brassieres for them.

Like I said, I'd thought about the analogies between modeling and prostitution a lot before, and I had tried, not too successfully, to start raps about that with some of the other girls that I'd met at the agency or on casting calls. I think they thought I was one of Gloria Steinem's secret agents or something [*laughs*]. But it really did strike me that that teasing, hypocritical sale of my pretty little *image* was a more revolting form of prostitution than the real thing. So I decided to go ahead and check out Caesar's.

The whole place is decked out to be some sort of Roman orgy spa, with acres of red and gold furnishings, plaster statues, and bunches of rubber grapes hanging here and there; and all of the girls are supposed to represent, as their ads put it, "toga-clad goddesses" who "pamper you breathless." As you walk in, there's a lounge where the customers can sit and wait for their session; they can watch television there, or they can have some champagne at the bar and rap to the girls who aren't busy at the moment. There are only nine session rooms and at least fifteen girls on a shift, so there are usually plenty of goddesses to spare; and if you don't have a specific reason to be in the back, you have to stay out in the lounge to show off your wares so the incoming customers can make a selection. I was usually in session and didn't have to spend a lot of time just being ogled by prospective johns; I didn't mind the actual work, but it can get really annoying when you're trying to read or just relax with a cigarette, and you have to put up with all these guys staring at your tits and trying to strike up a lively conversation. That may be what you're there for, but it gets difficult to abstract yourself enough to play toga girl *all* the time, without a break. It's hard to get away from the situation at Caesar's though; it's a very pressure-cooker sort of place, you know? I hear that other studios are less busy, and the girls have more time with nothing to do when there aren't any customers around or not as many anyway. But at Caesar's it sometimes got so ridiculous that when I absolutely had to escape, I'd go hide in the bathroom for a while.

Anyway, next to the lounge there's the reception area,

also fully mirrored and carpeted, plus with a running fountain full of plastic flowers; when the customer first comes in, he sits there in a big red-cushioned chair and looks over the menu of available programs. He has a choice of one girl for half an hour, one girl for an hour, two girls for a half hour or hour, a bath if he wants one; and if he's willing to blow a hundred dollars he can have *three* girls for an hour and a half on a king-size water bed. All these options are called programs, and they have names like "Gladiator's Dream" or "Marc Anthony's Delight," inscribed on this wooden scroll-looking thing chained to the desk. On the desk itself there's a large box with a map of all the rooms and lights to show which ones are in use. A green light means the room is in use, and a red one—ho-ho-ho—means the massage has begun, so they can make sure the girl sticks to the scheduled time, more or less.

After the manager collects the money from the customer, he pushes it through a slot in the wall that leads directly to the safe. As far as I know, there's never been even an attempted robbery there; but some of the other massage parlors are a little less careful with their money, and a couple of them have been held up once or twice.

When the customer's chosen a program and a girl, the manager calls the girl over the intercom and she comes in to show the guy to his room. The door to the back is always locked from the inside; the only way to get through from the front is when the manager presses a button under the desk. They're very security-conscious, which I always appreciated.

All of the nine session rooms in the back are completely private, and you can lock them from the inside; the number of the room is in Roman numerals, of course, on the door. All of these rooms are connected by one long hallway, also carpeted and full of plaster statues. Besides the session rooms there's also a shower area, a sauna, and the men's and women's bathrooms. The women's room obviously had to have a nameplate that said "Cleopatra's," and at least once a week they'd have to scrape off somebody's brilliantly original addition of the word "Asp."

Six of the session rooms are just equipped with a massage table, two have the table plus a sunken bath where the guy can be bathed and have a bottle of champagne—domestic, bad year—poured over his head . . . and finally there's the water-bed room, "Circus Maximus": red drapes and carpet, steps leading up to a raised water bed, a huge gold filigreed mirror behind the bed and a chandelier with variable brightness control over it. All of the rooms also have all the necessary lotions and what-not, plus a little burner for heating the oil, which was often mistakenly used as an ashtray by the customers—very messy. So the people really did quite a number in putting the place together, and it's all kept clean and tidy to the nth degree.

QUESTION: What happens to the customer once he's in the room?

CASSANDRA: Well, when you're called for a session you "proceed quickly," as the saying goes, to the desk, where you're introduced to the customer and given a printed sheet that tells you the guy's name, where he heard about Caesar's, whether or not he's a member—there's a five-dollar membership fee the first visit—the type of program he's supposed to get, and which room to use.

Once the two of you are in the room, you tell him to undress completely and to put anything of value in this metal drawer, the key to which he keeps with him, wherever he can find to stick it. Then you ask him if he wants a sauna or a shower or something to drink; if he does, you hand him a towel and lead him to the sauna. While he's in there working up a sweat, you go out to the lounge and daintily fetch his drink on a tray to the session room, so it'll be there when he returns. Then you check to make sure he hasn't completely evaporated in the sauna and hurry him along a little with some comment like "Hot enough yet?"

After his sauna you lead him to the showers, where you wait for him and then dry him off. By now fifteen minutes have gone by and you haven't even begun the allotted time for the massage.

Once you've got him back in the room you close and lock the door, then flip a switch to turn on the red light at the desk. And still, before you can get down to business, you're supposed to give the guy a goddamned facial and at least massage the front part of his body. You often even end up giving him a total real massage, in addition to whatever "extras" he wants.

What I'd usually do is give him a quick facial, during which I'd politely ask him all sorts of questions to determine how much money he's able to spend: like "Have you been to this or any other studios before?" which might indicate his experience in having to shell out bread for "special services" in case he's lied about his membership or hasn't been there before. And, obviously, getting him to rap about what kind of business he's in can tell me what kind of money he might have with him. At the same time I'd be looking over his body and deciding just what I might and might not be willing to do for him, "sizing up the job," just like with any other service.

Then I'd start to massage his legs to get him a bit excited, and usually by the time I'd gotten around to rubbing his chest he'd have a full erection and I could smile and ask if there was anything "else" he'd like me to do. The price negotiations revolve around twenty to twenty-five dollars for a hand-job, thirty to thirty-five for a blow-job, and seventy and up to screw. This is, of course, after the guy has already paid between twenty and a hundred dollars just to get in the place; and if he's having more than one girl, he still has to pay the same amount to each one of them for whatever's done. That means a minimum total of forty dollars for a quick hand-job, up to around three hundred dollars for a ninety-minute orgy on the water bed. They specialize in catering to the out-of-towner, or the guy who can't really admit to himself that he's just going someplace to get a blow-job, by putting on a heavy show of "luxury"; and it's really funny to watch the customers relate to each other in the lounge or the sauna. They come on with this big display of boy-scout camaraderie, as if they're all just there for a little back rub . . . and, well, all the plaster statues and the rubber grapes and the red velveteen *prove* that, don't they? Surely nobody comes there just to get his cock sucked . . . why, it's a *fancy* place, not one of those sleaz-o massage parlors. They really do act like that. Most of the guys act like they're at the Playboy Club, and occasionally they run off to hide someplace with a Bunny, but they're scared they'll get thrown out if anybody finds out what they did.

For a girl working there, that's all well and good; it does cut down some on the direct physical or verbal hassles you might otherwise run into in the lounge, but it also ends up wasting a lot of your time, in some silly ways. The guy may sit around for an hour working up his courage to pick you for a session, which didn't make any difference to me, but then when you finally do get him back to where the business transpires, he wants the full routine: sauna, two showers, facial and body massage . . . like, they really have to ease their consciences by continuing to insist, even to themselves, that they're in some straight health spa instead of a whorehouse. With some people, getting to the point of negotiations for prices is more like pulling teeth—they're feeling so guilty or scared.

The guilt and fear trip also leads to another real time-waster: alcohol. First of all, you have to keep running around bringing them drinks; and then, a few of them drink so much wine, besides the two or three drinks they probably had to see them safely through the front door, that they're damned near useless sexually. Drunks make bad customers, even if they're quiet drunks; a five-minute blow-job may take twenty and leave you with a case of lockjaw for the next hour.

So, all things considered, you end up spending forty minutes on a guy, whereas in other studios you might only be dealing with them for fifteen or twenty minutes. And if you have an hour session, forget it! Of course, even though the management keeps a watch on your time, you soon learn about ways to cheat a little; like, in an hour session you include their sauna time if you can; otherwise, it just gets to be ridiculous, and you never have a chance to take a break.

QUESTION: How well were you able to relate to the girls at Caesar's?

CASSANDRA: Very well, under the circumstances. There was

so much activity and so many pressures that there was always a high level of tension; but in spite of a few problems that came up, everybody managed to get along fairly well.

It's too much to expect that that number of different types of girls would get along *extremely* well anyway; they represented quite a range, and it was natural for something of a hierarchy to develop around who'd been there the longest or who got the most sessions. When I came, it was apparent that I'd be getting my share of the customers, and I was very quickly made aware of who had "seniority."

A couple of the girls kind of went beyond the bounds of that unspoken seniority rule, and they started acting like little Gestapo agents for the management. They seemed to think that passing on information to the manager about who was smoking grass or who was taking customers from the place would provide them with some kind of job security, and also maybe get a more attractive girl, or one who hustled harder, fired and out of the way. At least three or four of the girls also screwed the manager, for the same reasons; but I could never see that either snitching or screwing did any girl any good. They still had to put up with the same shit, and they were still just as likely to get fired as anybody else, basically; the only thing they accomplished was to turn the other girls against them.

So this and other problems did set up a few hostilities here and there, and as a result the girls would set up various "zero-sum game" situations for each other, to seek revenge. I was never interested in getting caught up in any of the crossfire, so I usually managed to play a kind of "mediator" role in most of the arguments.

QUESTION: What did the range of personality types include?

CASSANDRA: Christ—everything! Even at Caesar's, which has this whole mystique around it as being the best place with the best girls with the best bread, there were a couple of street-hooker types supporting pimps; then there were one or two girls who had either just gotten out of prison or were running from the police—that kind of thing. Nice girls with big problems. Then there was a huge contingent of the "girl-next-door" group: some of them were married with children at home in the suburbs, some of them were living at the Chelsea after having just come to New York from being cheerleaders and homecoming queens in Ohio, some of them were students, some of them were from Israel or England or Sweden or France, with accents and attitudes to match . . . everything.

I got to know one pimp fairly well through a friend at Caesar's; that whole pimp thing seems to be changing a lot; dying out really. At least, the image of it that I always had. You know, the heavy black dude who keeps his stable of "ho's" whipped into line while he cruises around in his El Dorado snorting kilos of coke or snatching up new "talent" from the Port Authority Bus Terminal; I'm sure that kind of thing still exists, but it's a lot less common now than it apparently used to be . . . it's very unusual among the girls in the massage parlors. Whatever needs there might have been for having a pimp, like connections or protection, have been pretty much eliminated. A massage parlor, particularly a well-operated one like Caesar's, is a very safe place for a girl to work, and she doesn't need somebody "steering" customers her way: Everybody who comes into the place is a john. The hard-core pimps are actually very down on the idea of their girls working in a massage parlor; they'd rather have them out on the streets because, besides taking over most of the pimp's supposed functions, a massage parlor puts the girls in communication with a lot of *other* girls. Chances are those other girls are in a much more independent situation and can easily convince a pimp's girl that she doesn't need the bastard at all, that there's no reason for her to let herself be exploited in that way: She can keep *all* of that fifty thousand a year. Pimps are becoming very unfashionable; the massage parlors are putting them out of business and they don't dig that.

A lot of girls may live with a guy that most people would think of as a pimp, but who's really just a gigolo of the girl's own choosing. He's still living off her, true but the situation of control is reversed. She's the only girl he's with, and she handles the money, sometimes even to the point of doling out necessary expenses to him and keeping the rest in her own hiding place or bank account.

So, anyway, with that many different types of girls at Caesar's, I'm sure you can imagine that the communications that went down weren't always just polite chitchat. Sometimes I'd find myself trying to clear up an incredible variety of intercultural misunderstandings; sometimes they'd simply never be able to understand the frames of reference that the others were coming from, just never understand at all. The best you could hope for in those situations was a long, silent stalemate.

Caesar's was like a mini-society oriented mainly around sex; when you walked through those doors into work, you left New York, you left America . . . sometimes it got so weird that you couldn't even be sure you were on the right planet!

Everything happened in little set-scenes, all happening simultaneously and rapidly changing, like some strange but well-edited movie. Except for escaping to the bathroom, there was no place you could go where some weird or intense situation wasn't happening or might not develop in the next ten seconds. Fast, fast switches from lecherous customers to girls freaking out that they've got a cop, from the manager getting righteously pissed because you've spilled wine on your toga to some weirdo customer with a whole new type of fantasy you've got to fulfill for your seventy bucks, from girls flipping out on THC or coke to *you* flipping out on THC or coke, from customers arguing over prices to girls in a hate-everybody mood because they haven't had any sessions yet, from . . . from just about anything to just about anything else. And *fast*. There are so many different approaches needed for different kinds of people and situations, in such short spaces of time, that for sheer survival you really have to develop a real ability at rapid-fire psychology.

QUESTION: What were your customers like?

CASSANDRA: Children, every one of them; little boys with their fists full of pennies, wishing they could buy up the whole candy store. Seriously, all the girls basically viewed the customers in one or both of two ways: as "bodies" to be worked on—like, "Hey, whose body is that still waiting in the fucking sauna?"—or as silly kids, sometimes obnoxiously so. I think the masculine personality and the male ego are generally very childish structures anyway. Sometimes that's a drag, and sometimes it can be fun; but in a massage parlor, you really get confronted with the straightest and the worst extrapolations of that childishness. Grown men playing all these cutesy-pouty little guessing games or doing things like pissing on the rocks in the sauna; you wouldn't believe the smell. Dumb, bratty nine-year-olds, playing "advertising executive" or "sales manager." Amazing.

QUESTION: What were some of the specific types of customers you encountered?

CASSANDRA: Well, there's always the Young Romantic who ends up falling hopelessly in love with the golden-haired, golden-hearted girl of his wet dreams; those are a bitch to deal with. Sometimes they'll even wait outside after closing and try to follow you home or send you roses and love letters at work. Or the Lancelots who want to "rescue" you to their castle in Queens, and when you finally force the conversation back to business, it turns out they only have twenty dollars on them and figure you'll just fuck them for their beautiful bodies. And Mr. Milquetoast who teaches the fifth grade in Staten Island and comes in covered with goose bumps. Once I had a four-foot elf from Vienna who'd stand on the chair in the session room and have me dig my nails in him for thirty dollars—forty if he could come on my tits. Most of the customers are just faceless, middle-aged executive types: a quick blow-job and they're out. But there are some more exotic specimens now and then.

I've had several rabbinical students in full regalia; they always keep their yarmulke on for the whole session. I guess they use Elmer's glue or something. They never have any money, and they usually want to tip you with some piece of cheap jewelry from their uncle's shop. Foreign customers are almost always cheap, too; they seem to think *everything* in the States has been devalued. The Japanese are an exception, though; You really have to be able to tell them from the Chinese because you can usually soak the Japanese for some heavy bread: name any price, any price at all, and they just leap up and hand you the money with a little bow. They're very pleasant to deal with anyway—always extremely clean and efficient, very polite and intent on what they're doing. Never offensive.

This elderly Japanese man came in once with his five sons; he'd actually brought them in there to lose their virginity, like some old novel. It was really funny, seeing them all lined up together on the couch. I got the youngest one, and he was absolutely fascinated with every aspect of sex. Since he'd given me seventy-five dollars of his father's money, I laid a "birds & bees" rap on him that Masters and Johnson would've been proud of.

Then there was Malcolm—God! Malcolm has been known to take a girl for *five hours*, sometimes even seven or eight. When I had him I could pull it all off in two, but even that was more than enough to mess up your head. He became a regular of mine on Sundays, and he'd always give me a hundred and fifty, which was a piss-off because that was the average amount you might make in four half-hour sessions, and you never knew whether you'd have twice that many or none at all if you didn't go ahead and take Malcolm; so I always did, even though he got to be a heavy drag very soon.

Malcolm looked like Fred Astaire with bad teeth. He had this puny little pale pink body, and he always wore these bright blue socks which he never took off because his corn pads would fall off. He was also afraid of picking up some kind of germs from the floor, and he claimed that the foam rubber on the massage table gave him itchy scaly spots on his elbows. I tried to explain about psoriasis, but he was too convinced of his rubber allergy. He also wouldn't let *me* stand on the floor without my shoes on, and he used to lecture me about the dangers of V.D., pointing to his penis and saying, "If anything yellow comes out of one of those, do . . . on't you *touch* it!"

The poor guy lived all alone in some room and got henpecked by his landlady about eating better. He was a panty fetishist; he paid twenty-five dollars for mine one day. Then the next time he came in he brought me a new pair of oversized red ones with this gross cake-decoration kind of lace trim. They still had the tag on them, he pointed out, because he wanted to prove to me that they were new, not just some pair out of his collection of other girls' dirty underwear that he kept in a glass case at home.

One time he came in all bandaged up because he'd been mugged; he said he'd had to spend six hundred dollars getting new teeth; I never quite understood whether the mugger had stolen the other set or what. I also never found out what he did, except that he had had some sort of nomadic life, supposedly as a sailor, and now he made weekly trips to get his money from some "guy uptown." He never wanted to talk about that and I didn't ask; but he always had plenty to spend at Caesar's, even though he always looked like he was flat broke.

At one point he started corresponding with some chick in Pennsylvania who'd send him photographs—he showed them all to me; they were mostly spread shots of this busty redhead in a Holiday Inn room. Apparently he sent her quite a bit of money and finally, with my help, he got up the courage to ask her to come to New York so he could meet her. Sure, Malcolm.

He'd also usually come in bearing all kinds of gifts and gadgets: a carton of cigarettes, a box of Wash 'n' Dri's . . . one day he brought something called Joy Gel. It came in flavors, and he had me spread raspberry on one tit and peach on the other one. He sent away for things like "stimulating creams" to help him get it up, and somewhere he found a little black clamp that goes around the base of the cock and helps to force an erection—kind of like squeezing on the end of a balloon. Of course, he wanted me to French him while he wore it.

Malcolm had a hard time coming though; he'd usually have me sit on a stool and blow him off while he stood up and leaned against a wall. I guess he thought his bodily fluids might move faster in that position than they would lying down. The man was even getting weekly hormone shots from his doctor, and he told his doctor all about me and the "problems" we had. The doctor told him to take hot baths when he got excited during the week, so he could save it all for "Miss Cassandra" on Sunday.

It was always strange to think that these guys thought about you during the week and that, when they came in, it was a special occasion for them to see you, no matter how you looked or felt. And whether you were stoned, drunk, exhausted, or just normally flipping out, you'd have to pick up with these situations wherever they had left off the week before; remember all their special little requirements or preferences, know what to ask and not ask in their personal lives . . . it could be fairly interesting the first couple of times, but your enthusiasm begins to drain pretty quickly. I did a lot of coke when I was expecting a regular like Malcolm.

QUESTION: Have you ever had a customer that you suspected of being a policeman?

CASSANDRA: Oh, sure; I've never been busted, but you do get an obvious cop every now and then, trying to trap you. They're usually pretty easy to spot, mostly through mannerisms and attitudes that they just can't cover up: they always act like they're there on business, no matter how cool they may think they look. They never get an erection, and they ask all these questions about how much money you make and so on. It seems to be very difficult for a cop to pretend he's human.

If I suspected somebody but I wasn't positive, I'd always get them into a relatively involved rap about their "business." When an "advertising man" couldn't tell you in half a second exactly what his agency's billing is or when a "photographer" couldn't explain solarization in twenty-five words or less . . . then they'd get a very nice backrub and "No, I don't know of *any* girls here who do *that* sort of thing."

Some of the other girls seemed to think that every third customer they had was a cop, though; one of the most common sounds in the hallway or the bathroom was some girl whispering, "Did you see that guy? Do you think he's a cop?" I think they enjoyed that actually; it added a little drama to their day, and it let them get a little tingle out of being a "Wanted Woman." Crime, suspense, intrigue . . . the same reasons a lot of people *really* have for doing dope: It makes them feel like somebody important, an *outlaw*, for a little while. But it also cost those girls a lot of tips, and a lot of poor little horny lawyers and accountants left there wondering what was so fucking great about Caesar's Retreat: They might as well go to the "Y."

I don't know why anybody needed any extra excitement around there though; it was hectic enough to begin with. Sometimes, after eight and a half hours of difficult sessions, one right after the other, you'd acquire this glazed, manic appearance and start feeling incredibly harsh and aggressive. Then, at two thirty-five in the morning, with twenty-five minutes to go, in steps some mousy, friendly little guy and you could just about throw him down on the massage table and start throttling him [*laughs*]. I really do feel sorry for some of the guys who come in at the wrong time or pick the wrong girl at that moment; they come in there to get away from their wives' bitchiness, expecting to spend half an hour doing all the sexy things they've ever dreamed about doing with a girl. Instead, they may get some very rough and humiliating treatment with some girls; maybe she's just pushing to get it all over and done with fast, or she cheats him on his time, or she holds out for just five dollars more than he's got with him ... or maybe she just won't do what he wanted done at any price. Every girl there runs her own business as she sees fit; some of them refuse to even give a blow-job, others won't screw, and almost nobody would agree to a "Greek"—me included.

Even if the price is right and the girl is willing to screw, it can be done in a very perfunctory way if the guy is somebody you wouldn't want to have much physical contact with. Some girls give a pretty clinical kind of blow-job, too; they don't want to take the come in their mouths and they lay towels all around the guy's cock to catch it when he shoots; and they refuse to let the guy tough them at all—they get very snappy if he even lays a finger on them while they're doing their mechanical-milking-machine number.

QUESTION: Is fellatio the most popular demand?

CASSANDRA: "Request" is the word; a guy's sure to be put down if he's too demanding. If somebody's too obnoxious, I either won't do what he'd like or I'll do it so poorly that he won't ask for me again.

Anyway, yes, blow-jobs are very popular—a lot more than straight screwing. Mainly, I think, because there are still a lot of wives who refuse to do it. Also, there are a lot of men who feel less guilty if they're just having the girl give them a French, and they're not having any reciprocal sex with them. The very fact of coming to a massage parlor is seen by a lot of men as a way of justifying their extramarital sex trips. They *are* paying for it, and they *aren't* committing themselves to a relationship, and men *do* need more sex with women, right? All the bullshit lines. Whereas the truth is that they want a short, noninvolving but *total* fantasy trip with a whole range of women of their choice, while their wives have to sit home and pretend they never get horny. The men just want to have their cunt and eat it, too.

QUESTION: What sort of unusual sexual requests have you had?

CASSANDRA: I haven't had all that many really; I don't look like the kind of person who would enjoy a discipline session or who would want to piss in somebody's mouth, so the customers would tend to select one of the other girls for those things.

I have had my weirdos, though; a few guys have wanted me to blow them off and then spit the come into their mouths, for example. Then there are the pussy-eaters and the pussy-gazers; several times I've made twenty-five or thirty dollars by just lying there with my legs spread while some idiot peered and probed at my cunt and jerked himself off. Once I even fell asleep in a session like that.

Oh, yeah, that reminds me of this other guy who was into something of a necrophiliac trip; he wanted me to play dead while he screwed me. First he'd have me lie limp on the floor, and he'd pick me up and throw me over his shoulders and parade around the massage table for a while. When he got tired of that, he'd plop me down and kind of nudge at me, twisting my arms and legs and letting them drop over the edges of the table before he screwed me.

And I have had a few S & M sessions, like the guy who brought his wife, took a "bacchanal" with me on the water bed for an hour and a half, and wanted me to teach her how to discipline. She ended up more excited than anybody else, and after about forty-five minutes she was getting pretty good with a whip. Finally I just let her take over and I sat in the corner getting drunk off the champagne that came with his session. The poor guy had shelled out two hundred and fifty dollars for this, a hundred and fifty of which was mine.

One kind of strange scene I had was with a needle freak; one of these guys who's broken his junk habit, but he still gets high just plugging the hypodermic into himself and drawing the blood in and out of his veins. He wanted to do this while I blew him off. And then there was the feces fetishist who still couldn't really admit his hang-up to himself yet, let alone to some strange girl; so he sublimated by having me cram three Hershey bars in my mouth and then spit the wet, mushy chocolate out and spread it all over his chest while he jerked off.

I also had somebody that I found particularly interesting; he'd been brought up a strict Catholic and he was into a "mocking religion" trip sexually. He'd have me play the Virgin Mary, and he'd get down on his knees and worship me, calling my cunt the tabernacle. Seriously. He also wanted me to twist and mash and bend his penis and order him to lick my anus. The finale was to "baptize" him; first I'd piss in a little plastic vial that he brought so he could take some home with him, and then I'd let go all over his body; he'd come at that point, without me touching him. The guy would have been a prime candidate for Satanism, but I never told him I'd been into it.

I also had a regular who was a double amputee, no legs; I'd kind of ride his stumps, horsey fashion. He and I became very good friends though, and I really got to like him; he always got treated extremely well when he came in.

That brings up one point I'd like to make; I may have had some freaks with weird desires, but the *real* frustration and desperation comes from the ordinary guys with the wife and three kids in Queens. The so-called perverts are often a lot healthier mentally because they've discovered some way of thrusting a lot of their tension into fantasy-fulfillment.

Most people think they act insane twenty-four hours a day, but unless you're talking about real psychopathic individuals, that's not at all true. The majority of the "perverted" people I've had have been more reasonably together and happy than most of my other customers. It isn't as if they come in all withered and whimpering or with drooling fangs. They're quite normal-looking people who know what they want, get it, and leave feeling much more relieved than some other guy who comes in all pent-up with frustration from his marriage and expects the thrill of his life, after which all his fears and problems will go away

A massage parlor is a very interesting place to observe the results of some of this society's fucked-up attitudes and expectations. All these middle-aged men—and I've seen some guys who were middle-aged at twenty-six—have grown up anticipating a life full of good feelings and satisfactions as their reward for working hard and being responsible husbands; then, when that falls flat, they figure they can Make It All Worthwhile by indulging in as much sex as they can handle or afford. But it's just not that easy.

Right now, I sometimes see the whole planet as a huge S & M massage parlor; we're *all* perverts, only some of us live out those sick fantasies all the way. You don't think Nixon *enjoyed* dropping that shitload of bombs? You don't think some of those dudes in Vietnam started to *dig* killing and mutilating people?

QUESTION: Did you have many customers who had been in Vietnam?

CASSANDRA: Yeah, several of them; and it's really messed up their minds, all the way down to the sexual level. A lot of them have become masochistic, obviously as a direct guilt reaction to what they were doing over there; I think that shows something very important about the extent and the depth to which these guys have been affected, and the difficulties they're going to face in readjusting.

I've tried to help some of them through the early periods of that, through some involved raps and some careful demonstrations of the balance in mild S & M: not whipping and beating, but the back-and-forth, taking-turns "struggle" aspect of the situation. Playful conflict, flirtatious slaps—that sort of thing can be very erotic and therapeutic . . . a mutual expression of the passive-active duality, with smooth and regular shifting of the roles. I taught them not to be afraid to experiment, even if the desire for that experimentation came out of a deep-seated problem; you can get an incredible amount of anxiety and general shit out of your system by sexual experimentation in the right sort of way.

QUESTION: Did you often get into really communicating with and trying to help people with other sorts of problems?

CASSANDRA: When I thought I could or when it seemed worthwhile, yes; and I also got a lot of emotional satisfaction myself from communicating and empathizing with so many different people in such a gut-level way. I tried to approach every person with that in mind, even though I was sometimes too stoned or too tired or too fed up, and maybe eighty percent of the time I was dealing with some characterless asshole that I'd have to abstract myself from and depersonalize . . . but I did have a lot of mini-relationships, sometimes very heavy ones in different ways.

A lot of people come in and you immediately think, "Oh, blah, what a drag this is going to be," and then they end up being entirely different than you had assumed or they strike a particular chord in you that opens up an avenue of communication with them.

The massage parlor situation does tend to intensify a lot of different areas of human contact aside from the sex thing, though. That sudden, total physical intimacy just naturally leads to a magnification of other aspects of your feelings. Most girls consciously fight that by totally depersonalizing every situation as much as possible, and you have to do a lot of that to keep your sanity; but I found that I had to try and basically understand every customer's head in order to have a successful session. Even if all you're interested in is the amount of bread you're going to get, you can't treat the guy as if he has no emotions at all. You may despise him for being unbelievably chauvinistic and obnoxious, but unless he's just absolutely impossible to deal with, it's much easier and more profitable to give some thought to where his head is at so he'll calm down and let you take control. I have no interest in riling some guy's ego to the point where I don't get any money and the session takes ten or fifteen minutes longer than it should because you're arguing with him; instead, I'd rather handle the situation logically and efficiently and get the guy out of there quickly.

That's not to say that I'd pander to anybody's egocentricity. It's very possible to handle the scene well, and not provoke any hassles, but to very clearly let the guy know just what you think of him.

But if a guy is nice, even if he doesn't have any special attributes or anything in particular to say, then I'm likely to give him a nice time—still in relation to the amount of bread I'm getting usually, although I've had plenty of hand-job sessions where the guy walked out feeling pretty high because I was concerned about his feelings and did what I could to make him happy in the circumstances. To so many of these people, coming to the massage parlor is a onetime experience that they'll remember for years, and I enjoy making it memorable for them.

Like one night at two A.M. when I was getting a little groggy, there suddenly appeared a whole group of young guys in the lounge. They were just a bunch of kids really, and they were all part of a bachelor party; naturally, it's just my luck that I get the groom. So into the room I go, and there sits this little forlorn, confused, uptight guy on the eve of changing his entire life, and probably not for the better. I couldn't just whack him off and shove him out in five minutes; this is a whole ego trip for him, an important tribal rite. He needs to have something nice to remember and a not-too-inflated story to tell his friends. Now, if he'd been an obnoxious pig about the whole thing, I probably would've just jerked him off fast and gone out and told his friends to warn the bride not to expect much; but he was a shy, nervous kid, so I did a pleasant number on his head. A little sweet talk, some playful titillation, dimming the lights and bringing in a candle, some wine, and a nice blow-job. I made him feel good and appreciated, and I was really supportive about the life he was setting out on. By the time he left he was really feeling thrilled, and I could go home feeling that I'd done something nice.

Then there was Marty, the construction worker, who never wanted sex but would give me twenty dollars just to sit there and talk awhile, with both of us fully dressed. I can see some people getting pissed at me for being so mercenary as to charge twenty dollars just to sit around and rap to somebody for half an hour; but this was my job, this was what he wanted most, and I was there to earn a living by pleasing people. So it wasn't like I was saying, "Hey, Marty, I won't talk to you for less than twenty dollars," but instead, "Hey, Marty, I really dig talking to you, but as long as we're here I have to remind you that this is my place of work."

QUESTION: Did you attempt to deal much with more specifically sexual problems that people might have, like impotence or premature ejaculation?

CASSANDRA: For whatever reason, I generally found myself handling more premature ejaculation problems than impotence. This is all aside, of course, from the guys who are just so excited that they shoot almost immediately or the ones who are a little nervous and can't get it up for a few minutes. But you do run into people with very real problems along those lines; and they're always just head problems.

In dealing with premature ejaculation, the thing to do is to start very slowly, and then as soon as it starts to throb, you pinch the head of the penis till the orgasm is suppressed —standard sex-manual technique. The problem is just that the guy doesn't have much control over his functions because he's seldom been in relaxed sexual situations, and he needs to be literally trained to overcome his anxiety.

The same thing is true for impotence, of course; in that case I found that extreme kindness, helping them to relax, gentle, rhythmic arousal, and squeezing at the *base* of the cock was usually enough. Very rarely did anybody not ejaculate in a session, and those few times it was generally because the guy had had too much to drink.

Both of these problems seem to be related mainly to certain bad associations with sex that the person might have: doubts about his ability to perform, a feeling of being *pressured* to perform, anxieties over lack of experience, guilt feelings from a repressive background, and so on. The guy comes in *expecting* to have difficulty, and because of that expectation, he does have trouble; then he's got a whole new lousy experience to add to his previous associations. He can't help himself out of this syndrome—he needs assistance.

QUESTION: Do you think a massage parlor is a good place for someone with a sexual problem to go?

CASSANDRA: It can be, particularly if he doesn't have anybody who loves him enough to take the time to work him through his problem. Of course, he'd better have enough bread on him to provide somebody with the incentive to help him out; and I suppose most girls don't really give a shit anyway. But if he gets a girl who knows what she's doing, and who can understand his problem, it can be a very good experience.

Of course, I was sometimes almost stupidly altruistic; if the guy had been a gentleman with me, I'd give him his money back if he wasn't able to come or allow him to come twice if he shot immediately the first time. That sort of business practice ended up bringing me a lot of steady, well-paying customers, though. Naturally, if I've done a whole number on him and it's been his own fault that he had some kind of trouble, I deserve the bread and I take it; but otherwise I like to play fair. Anybody who's polite and cooperative is going to get his money's worth; but if he's aggressive or demanding, he's guaranteed to have a lousy time.

I did manage to help a number of people with problems by seeing them once a week and each time progressing to a new stage of overcoming the difficulty. Several of them became almost obsessed with coming to see me because I was the only person they'd found who had been able to help them at all. It may not have been cheap, but it was less expensive and more worthwhile for them than spending the time rapping to a shrink; and from my experience with psychiatrists, they're *real* hookers.

QUESTION: How did the job affect your personal life?

CASSANDRA: Jesus—totally. I tend to get completely

wrapped up in whatever I'm doing, anyway, and working at a massage parlor just automatically affects practically everything that you do. Working at night until three or four in the morning, then going out for champagne and eggs with your friends until five, getting to sleep around six or seven—you don't get a lot done during the daylight hours. Maybe you get up at three o'clock in the afternoon, have an orange, three cups of coffee, and half a pack of cigarettes, just read the headlines of the paper, put on your false eyelashes, then take a couple of multiple vitamins, a few thousand milligrams of Vitamin C because you're coming down with a cold, and a cap of speed and a snort of coke so the sunny street scene won't shock you too much.

The schedule is terrible on your health though. Some people thrive on living at night, and I can enjoy it for certain periods of time, but not for weeks on end. You never get enough sleep, you eat poorly, you don't get any exercise except bending over massage tables, you smoke too much, you do too many drugs and take too many nips from the flask of brandy in your locker . . . and as interesting as the job can be, there's still a severe lack of real mental stimulation.

It was amazing to see the extent to which "the life" tends to suck you in; even on your off hours, you find everything revolving more and more around the business and the people involved in it. A lot of girls get literally addicted to it; if they're into a heavy materialistic life-style, buying expensive clothes and taking weekends in Barbados, it's hard for them to give up such a simple way of making so much money so fast. Some of them never save anything at all; they just keep working and spending for months and months without even considering the possibility of going on to something else.

QUESTION: How did working at Caesar's affect your sex life?

CASSANDRA: What sex life? [*laughs.*] By the time I'd get off work, I couldn't bear to see another cock.

Seriously, though, working in a massage parlor can actually make you very horny because you're constantly seeing all these other people getting off, and you'd like some satisfaction yourself for a change. Even if a customer is attractive and nice, it's very difficult to really enjoy yourself in that kind of pressured situation and environment. I did still date and get laid occasionally while I was working, but I found myself becoming very choosy about the quality of the sex I'd have in private.

My bisexual encounters have also become a little more frequent, although I don't think that's directly related to the work I did; it's just a pleasant change now and then, and I don't feel at all hung up about it. A couple of times I've gone with a group of girls to· a place that has saunas and a dance floor and private rooms; they usually cater to male homosexuals, but there's a "ladies' night" once a week.

I also have a fairly regular boyfriend *and* a regular girlfriend; they know all about each other, but it does get funny sometimes, balancing them off and making the necessary alterations in my personality traits to deal with each of them. I'm very feminine when I'm with a guy, but with this girl I've tended to more or less take the masculine role—not in some heavy "bull-dyke" way . . . I think of myself as a sort of "soft butch" with her.

QUESTION: Did this girl also work at Caesar's? And, if so, how did your relationship affect the other girls?

CASSANDRA: Yes, she did and still does work there, but we never made our interest in each other that obvious. Most of the other girls were aware of it, but we weren't into pushing our trip on their heads, and they respected us for that. Of course, if she and I happened to get a double session together, then the guy really got a show; although we'd pretend disinterest at first and jack up the price for any lesbian activity he might want to see.

But, as far as the other girls went, I was never into inflicting anything on them one way or the other or setting up any sort of jealousy hassles. For the most part, everyone there remained fairly independent; they were just there to work for themselves, and they avoided confrontations as best they could, although, of course, they would often naturally happen, like I told you earlier. You've got fifteen girls of all different types, some wiped out, some alert; some speeding, some on downs; some in a good mood, some depressed. And in nine hours there can be a lot of mood change among everybody, so you never know from one minute to the next how someone may react to you; but it usually all works out, and the responsibility of helping to ease various situations is shifted around among whoever's present. I was really amazed that things tended to run as smoothly as they did.

QUESTION: You've mentioned that several times; just how confused and disorganized did things really get at Caesar's?

CASSANDRA: I guess I have sort of focused on that aspect, huh? I guess the sudden contrast of being free and idle again has made it stand out in my mind. I don't want to give the impression that there was just nothing but nightly anarchy there; but it did get pretty heavy, particularly around midnight on a Saturday, when all the rooms were filled and there were twenty or thirty other guys waiting in the lounge.

I remember one night in particular, when it seemed like everybody was getting a string of weirdly contrasting sessions. I'd had a couple of Englishes, a couple of heavy emotional scenes with two of my weirder regulars—some kid I'd seen once or twice before had half-seriously threatened to commit suicide then and there if I wouldn't marry him; somebody else had thrown up all over the floor and I'd had to clean it up and then blow the fucker off. . . . On and on like that, and all the other girls had been going through equally strange scenes. Meanwhile, we're also having an unusually large number of young freaks as customers, and everybody's been getting more and more stoned.

The air in the halls was enough to get you stoned, so I was madly spraying Lysol all over the place, and meanwhile I can hear all this giggling and moaning in every direction, and a couple of the rooms are having discipline sessions, and the slaps are going in syncopation, and some customer in the hall has cut his foot on a piece of broken glass. . . . It was just absolute chaos or close to it.

Sometimes when I was in a session I'd start wondering what was happening in all the other rooms, and I used to fantasize about taking the roof off the place, like a dollhouse, so you could look into all the rooms at once. It would've been fascinating because in every room there might be ten *entirely* different scenes happening during the course of an evening, all of them totally different from each other.

Most businesses flow pretty smoothly, more or less, because everybody's working basically on the same thing or toward the same basic goal: like, say, in an advertising agency, everybody's doing something different, but it all ends up in getting the account together or whatever. It's all the same trip, you know? But at Caesar's, it's more like every girl in every room is just operating her own private business, more like concession booths at a carnival or something; so instead of everything being basically kind of controlled by everybody being on the same general project, in a massage parlor nobody *really* knows what anybody else is doing, and it can get very confused.

That can end up affecting everybody, sometimes in some very negative ways. I've even seen customers break down in tears and run out of the session rooms half-dressed because somehow it was all just getting too heavy for them; they were having to face some realities they just weren't prepared to cope with, you know? And, of course, the girls get upset all the time, too, by all kinds of things; there's just a pretty heavy tension level operating there almost all the time because you're dealing with some gut-level things, and it's all so organized or anyway it's supposed to be; but it just can't stay that way. There could've been some very heavy chemical reactions 'here potentially, some real freak-out scenes all around. It never happened, and I don't know if it ever really might have gone that far; but there was sure more chance of something weird happening there than, say, having everybody in the menswear department at Macy's all of a sudden flipping out simultaneously.

The main control factor was the fact that all the scenes happened separately, in the separate rooms; so they didn't really have that much of a chance to affect each other. But if they had . . . do you know about "tickling the dragon's tail," in physics?

QUESTION: Go ahead and explain it.

CASSANDRA: Well, when the people who invented the atomic bomb had it all worked out, in theory, that it would work, they still had to determine exactly the right critical mass, just the precise amount of radioactive material that would lead to a chain reaction when it was suddenly crammed together. But there was no way they could really figure that out on paper, so they had to actually pile up all these little blocks of U-235 and plutonium until they could detect a chain reaction just starting; and they weren't really even positive that they could detect it in time to stop it. So if they stacked one block too many or if they were a little slow in pulling the last one back, then we would now have a very large and a *very* polluted lake in the middle of Tennessee. That little game was called "tickling the dragon's tail"; and at Caesar's, the dragon of all our psyches together got his tail tickled or maybe massaged every night.

Working there did tend to strengthen your ego pretty quickly, but it definitely wasn't the place for anybody who was squeamish or defensive to begin with. You just don't have a lot of time to mess around; you've really got to be able to deal with a lot of different types of people and situations very fast. It's a good ego exercise, and it is a good way to get rid of some of your defense mechanisms and to learn how to use the ones you hang onto to your best advantage.

When you see some of the shit that other people go through . . . Christ! I had this one customer, he was a thirty-eight-year-old virgin. He still lived with his mother, and the first time he came in all he wanted to do was sit down and talk to me and just slowly get used to the idea of being around a chick and touching her. He started coming in twice a week, and the sixth time he came in we finally got around to screwing. That first time, he got himself up on his knees in the closest thing he could manage to a fetal position, under the circumstances; and while we were fucking he just whimpered and gurgled like a baby, sucking on my breast and saying all these unintelligible, babyish things. After about six weeks I finally got him to relax and do things in a little more normal way, and then I had him take a session with another girl, sort of like a "final exam." She was a good friend of mine, and I knew she'd treat him well. After that he stopped coming in; and then, three days before I quit, he came back in, just beaming, and he told me that he'd moved out of his mother's house into his own place, and he'd even found a girlfriend that he was sleeping with, and everything was all right.

Now what *should* that guy have done? He could've just stayed a virgin and rotted there in the house with his mother, or he could've humiliated himself by trying to go through that whole baby routine with some uptight, egotistical chick he might've picked up at Friday's, or he could've gone to a psychiatrist and *talked* about his problems for four or five years; but as it was, he could bring all his problems right up front, and deal with them in the most direct way possible without getting hassled.

I really respect that guy for having the guts to deal with his paranoias, even by coming to a massage parlor. I think it was the best thing he could've done, and anybody who thinks it was dirty or wrong of him to do it is just full of shit, that's all.

The only thing that really bothers me about the way people might react to the fact of my working as a prostitute is the imbalance of their attitudes; like, they made such a big hero thing out of the P.O.W.'s, who were just nothing but these hot-shot macho dudes who got caught pouring napalm on babies; but *I'm* the one who's the nasty, horrible criminal, right?

QUESTION: Do you feel any guilt or shame about your work?

CASSANDRA: No, that's what I was just saying; I really even dug the whole debauchery and degeneracy trip; it was fun to play on it, like in a Belle de Jour kind of way. I'd take off my old jeans and my sweater, I'd throw on my makeup and my toga, and—boompts!—I'm a very sexy, very wicked lady. [In a perfect Mae West voice.] "Is that a gun in your pocket, honey, or are you just glad to see me?" [*laughs.*] I really dug trying on all these weird personalities that I'd never think of using in any other situation; I had several wigs in different colors and styles left over from the whole modeling trip, and I invented two or three different characters to go with each one of them, plus four or five different characters to play in my own hair. I was in the business of providing fantasies, and it was up to me to choose what kind and how much to provide, depending on the mood I was in and the person I was dealing with. Like, I'd never think of running around in public or with my friends as some dumb, cutesy-wootsy redhead; but at Caesar's I just didn't give a shit what anybody thought of me at all. I felt absolutely free to play with all the different aspects of femininity and not worry about making a fool of myself. I was conning people, sure; but they had fun, and I had a really interesting time doing it. It was much more fun than acting because it was all in a real situation, so the tension level was that much higher, and you had to be "on" for long stretches of time. I really enjoyed it; it was a great opportunity to get into a lot of other kinds of heads.

QUESTION: Do any of your friends from college know what you've been doing?

CASSANDRA: Most of them, yeah; I even gave a couple of them a guided tour of Caesar's one weekend. They were very hesitant about the whole thing at first, their reactions were very mixed; a couple of the girls were just outright, openly hostile when I first told them about it. They went through a whole dumb-shit, primary-level rap about "exploitation" and "oppression" and so forth. I was disappointed, and it really pissed me off because I thought they knew me better than that, and I thought they were a little hipper than that themselves; so I told them that, and then I laid a pretty heavy reality rap on *them*. It took some time, but they finally started to understand the whole trip and the ways in which I was approaching it. Now one of them's working weekends in a massage parlor in Boston. Live and learn, right?

QUESTION: Do you think prostitution should be legalized?

CASSANDRA: That's actually a very tricky question to answer. I don't think anybody ought to be arrested for prostitution, but I also don't think it should be "legalized." That would lead to all kinds of government crap, licensing and I.D. cards and controls and just all kinds of nasty shit. That could get very, very freaky, particularly with the government we've got now. They legalized it in Germany, and they even stamp PROSTITUTE in the girls' *passports*! Real Scarlet Letter trip, and I know it'd be the same way here, particularly if Nixon's still in power, or anybody like him. By the way, those bumper stickers that said, "Lick Dick," were very popular around Caesar's at the last election.

It's just like marijuana; I don't think prostitution should be legalized—it should be decriminalized. If they legalized either one of those things, the only people who'd make any money would be the tax people, and the licensing boards, and all that shit. Can't you just see a State Prostitution Authority or a Federal Marijuana Control Comission? There'd be some fat pockets there, let me tell you, and none of the individuals involved would get anything.

I think they should just stop arresting people for prostitution or for dope; then if any *real* crimes are committed along with them, like mugging or stealing or something, then they should just handle them the same way they would if they happened anyplace else. And I hate to say it, but I guess you'd have to include income tax evasion in those crimes; but if they let it be known that prostitutes or dealers could file a tax return and not be hassled, I bet they'd get more money than they think.

Another thing, if they legalized it, would be enforced V.D. tests, which is a stupid, obnoxious idea. Prostitutes have one of the lowest V.D. rates in the country because it's your *job* to take care of yourself down there, so you're ten times as careful and you know what to look for and how to protect yourself. If anything does go wrong, you get it taken care of as fast as possible because that's like having a broken cash register [*laughs*]. I've never had V.D. and I only knew of one girl at Caesar's who got it; she just took a week off from work until she was well. That would just be a shitty thing, it would be a very demeaning thing; it's bad enough just going to a male gynecologist on your own, but can you imagine what it would be like to go to the official prostitute doctor for the state? Jesus! I'm a firm believer in private women's clinics, with women doctors on the staff exclusively; just open enough of these and there'd be no problem in getting all the prostitutes to have regular checkups on their own.

Speaking of that V.D. test thing, did you know there's already a law on the books that any girl arrested for prostitution can be held without bail until a test can be taken, against her will, and the authorities get the results? I don't think they use it all that much, but it's really fucked up that it's still on the books. I'd really like to see the constitutionality of that tested. I'd also like to see some more publicity about the fact that they arrest maybe one john for every thousand or so prostitutes; the last I heard it took *two* people to commit that "crime."

Women have just always been socialized toward a whole prostitution frame of mind: dates buying you dinner, guys buying you presents, that whole image of "marrying well"... but any woman who openly accepts the idea, and her independence by carrying it to its logical conclusion, is despised and harassed and sent to jail for it. Every man in this country, or most of them, anyway, is a pimp, because of that whole image they've been laying on us all this time. And if they ever do legalize prostitution, then the first I.D. cards ought to be sent to Tricia and Julie and Pat and Jackie and all the other straight married women in the country.

QUESTION: What do you plan to do now since you said you're not working at Caesar's anymore?

CASSANDRA: Loaf and catch up on some reading. Then at the end of next month I'll be going back to London; I want to make some short films, and I've got enough money put away now to let me do all that, without any hassle.

QUESTION: Just how much money have you managed to save?

CASSANDRA: About twenty-six thousand dollars. I made fourteen thousand in two-and-a-half months at Caesar's, and I saved about ten thousand of that, and then I invested most of it in a couple of coke deals. It's been a good year.